THE GREAT DISRUPTION

ADRIAN WOOLDRIDGE is *The Economist*'s management editor and author of the Schumpeter column. He was previously based in Washington, DC, as the Washington bureau chief, where he also wrote the Lexington column, and served as *The Economist*'s West Coast correspondent, management correspondent and UK correspondent. His books include *The Company: A Short History of a Revolutionary Idea, God is Back* and *The Fourth Revolution: The Global Race to Reinvent the State.*

BRETT RYDER illustrates Adrian Wooldridge's Schumpeter column in *The Economist* each week. Some of these illustrations have been reproduced in this compilation. ryder.brett@googlemail.com

THE GREAT DISRUPTION

How business is coping with turbulent times

Adrian Wooldridge

PUBLICAFFAIRS
New York

Contents

Introduction: the age of Schumpeter

EVEN BY THE STANDARDS of the elite universities of the mid-20th century Joseph Schumpeter was something of a stick-in-the-mud. He failed to learn to drive, avoided aeroplanes as much as possible and, in his 18 years as a professor of economics at Harvard, only once took the underground that links Cambridge with Boston. He was so resistant to new-fangled devices such as carbon paper and photocopiers that he did not bother to make a copy of his masterwork, *Capitalism, Socialism and Democracy*, before posting it to his publisher. A book that dwells at length on the limits of the competence of government might have been lost forever if the US Post Office had been less reliable.

Yet Schumpeter was also one of the greatest apostles of disruptive innovation that the 20th century produced: a technophile technophobe and a progress-loving reactionary. Schumpeter was not the first social observer to notice that capitalism invariably brings disruption in its wake. Karl Marx and Frederick Engels talked about capitalism melting all that is solid into air. Thomas Carlyle argued that capitalism sacrifices humanity to the god of cash. But he expressed the insight as well as anyone – he said that capitalism is above all "a perennial gale of creative destruction" that blows through the world, overturning the old and clearing a path for the new. And he grasped that you cannot have the creation without the destruction.

Marx thought what he saw as the internal contradictions of capitalism would resolve themselves in a socialist utopia. John Maynard Keynes thought that they could be managed by a benevolent government. Schumpeter thought that all this turbulence had a hidden logic. Entrepreneurs are constantly generating innovations that give them temporary advantages over their competitors. And these innovations send gusts of disruption though the economy as their competitors try to adjust to the new business landscape and institutions scrabble to adjust to new realities. Entrepreneurs rather than the workers are history's great revolutionaries – the people who disequilibriate every equilibrium and summon the future into being through sheer force of will and imagination.

In 2009 *The Economist* decided to introduce a column on business on the model of its columns on Britain (Bagehot), America (Lexington) and Europe (Charlemagne). But what to call it? A lively debate ensued. There was some support for naming it after the newspaper's founder, James Wilson, who had the merit of being a successful businessman as well as a great benefactor (his marble statue stands in the lobby, silently reminding the staff of the virtues of free trade, liberty and self-reliance). Unfortunately, Wilson is an unromantic name that reminds Britons of Harold Wilson and Americans of Woodrow Wilson and doesn't get anybody's blood flowing. No sooner did the name Schumpeter come up than it was instantly adopted. If the post-war era was the age of Keynes, the modern era is the age of Schumpeter. Entrepreneurs have taken central stage. Change has speeded up. Disruption has become endemic. Over the past two decades there have been innumerable disruptions in almost every industry under the sun, disruptions that have not only forced incumbents to fight for their life but have frequently turned assets into liabilities and business models into prisons. So many disruptions, in fact, that they add up to one great disruption: a great disruption not of "traditional society" of the sort that Marx chronicled but of capitalism itself.

Consider a few statistics. Two-thirds of the companies on the *Fortune* 500 list for 1970 have disappeared from it (and some, like Pan Am, Arthur Andersen and Bear Sterns, have disappeared entirely). The average job tenure for the CEO of a *Fortune* 500 company has declined from ten years in 2000 to less than five years today; Leo Apotheker lasted less than a year as CEO of Hewlett-Packard. The average job tenure of American retail workers (who now outnumber manufacturing workers) is even shorter, at three years, and does not come with a golden parachute attached.[1] The rate at which US public companies in the top quartile of returns on assets changed leadership increased by 40% between 1965 and 2012. The chance of experiencing a reputational disaster in any given five-year period increased from 20% in 1994 to 84% today: think of News Corp or BP or Tiger Woods Incorporated. In 1937, at the height of the Great Depression, the average lifespan of a company in the Standard & Poor's 500 was 75 years. By 2011 it had fallen to just 18.

The 21st century has already produced two spectacular crises. In 2001–02 a cluster of leading companies, including Enron, World Com and Arthur Andersen, imploded. In 2007–08 Lehman Brothers exploded, producing the worst financial crisis in half a century, destroying trillions of dollars of wealth and forcing George W. Bush, a self-identified hard-headed free-marketer, to bail out two of America's big three carmakers. Schumpeter once said that the average firm stands on ground that is crumbling beneath its feet. The ground is more treacherous than ever.

Forces of creative disruption

What forces have unleashed this storm of creative disruption? Three stand out: information technology, particularly the internet, financial markets and globalisation. Each one of these is an earth-shaking force in its own right. Taken together they are producing unprecedented turmoil. Information technology is changing the world as dramatically as machine technology did in the Victorian age. Computing power is increasing at an exponential rate. McKinsey estimates that the amount of computing capacity being added to the global stock increased from 5 exaflops (exaflops are measures of computing power and might be translated roughly as "a hell of a lot") in 2008 to more than 20 exaflops in 2012 and to about 40 in 2014. Schumpeter once celebrated capitalism's ability to turn silk stockings from a rarity reserved for queens into an everyday luxury available to factory girls in a mere three centuries. Mobile phones went from being toys of the rich to tools of three-quarters of the earth's population in two decades.

The internet has accelerated what was already a high-speed revolution. The telephone took 70 years to reach half of American households. Electricity took 50 years. The internet took a decade: by 2010, there were more computers connected to the internet than people on the planet. The internet is also mutating at an astonishing speed; so astonishing that it sometimes feels like an alien invader that has implanted itself in our guts and is now taking over our lives. It has already evolved from an asocial into a social medium and from a desk-bound into a mobile one. Now it is embracing things as well as people. Tiny computers, embedded in objects, are closing the gap between the physical world and the cyber-world, extending the information economy ad infinitum.

The internet has rewritten the rules of the business world in a couple of decades, shifting the balance of power from incumbents to challengers and from the old economy to the new. Companies have already come from nowhere to reorganise entire industries – classified ads (Craigslist), long-distance calls (Skype), record stores (iTunes), research libraries (Google), local stores (eBay), taxi services (Uber) – and there is good reason to think that this trend will gather pace. Small companies can acquire a big company's computer power by plugging into the cloud; local companies can go global with the click of a mouse; obscure companies can go viral with the help of YouTube or Twitter. At the same time it has spawned mighty leviathans to organise its affairs and exploit its potential. Google, Amazon, Facebook and eBay all surpassed $1 billion in annual sales within roughly five years of being launched. Procter & Gamble, by contrast, took more than 20 years to reach $1 million in annual sales and more than 100 years to pass the $1 billion mark. In matters of size the new economy cuts both ways.

Capital is also at the heart of all this disruption, just as it was in Marx's day. The markets control vastly more money than ever before: the US Investment Company Institute calculates that the volume of money controlled by US mutual funds increased from $135 billion in 1980 to $15 trillion in 2013. Financial institutions not only put relentless pressure on companies to perform from quarter to quarter. They also subject them to regular earthquakes. In 2007–08 problems with arcane securities traded by often obscure financial institutions shook "real" companies to their foundations and threw millions of people out of work.

The digital revolution and the capital markets have both reinforced the third revolutionary force: globalisation. Between 1980 and 2007 global integration sped ahead at a faster pace than at any time since the late 19th century. The 2007–08 financial crisis slowed the pace of integration for a while, particularly in the financial sector, as banks tried to raise more reserves, but it is beginning to speed up again. The new economy is a born-global economy: companies such as Skype (founded in Estonia by a Swede and a Dane) can suddenly become internet giants. But globalisation is the ruling principle of the "old" economy, too. Every day tens of thousands of ships, flagged in Panama, registered in Malta, insured in London and staffed by sailors from every corner of the world, carry goods from one corner of the world to another.

These three great dynamos of change are spinning ever faster. Google is experimenting with super-high-speed networks that will operate more than 100 times faster than regular broadband.[2] Cisco claims that its latest router can deliver the equivalent of the entire printed collection of three US Libraries of Congress in just over a second. Growing wealth in Asia, the most dynamic corner of the global economy, is pouring trillions into the global financial system and introducing another source of both growth and instability. And global integration is resuming after pausing for breath in 2007–08: Pankaj Ghemawat, a professor at both IESE and Stern business schools and a leading student of globalisation, argues that global integration may be nearer the beginning than the end. Foreign direct investment (FDI) so far accounts for only 9% of all fixed investment, and cross-border internet traffic accounts for only about 20% of all internet traffic. Reid Hoffman, the co-founder and chairman of LinkedIn, warns that concepts such as globalisation and technology "may seem overhyped to you, but their long-term effects are actually underhyped".[3]

The world has lived with spells of dramatic disruption before: hence Marx's worry about all that is solid melting into air and Schumpeter's insistence that capitalism's gale of creative destruction is "perennial". The Industrial Revolution took an economy that moved at a snail's pace and forced it to move at the pace of a locomotive. Or perhaps even of a rocket: Walt Rostow, one of the leading economists of economic growth, employed the rocket-like metaphor of a "take-off" to describe what happens when society industrialises. The

Great Depression shook capitalism to its foundations, producing a depression in the US and propelling fascists to power in Germany, Italy and Spain. But as John Hagel, of Deloitte's Centre for the Edge, points out, these previous technological revolutions followed a set pattern: dramatic bursts of innovation in core technologies (such as steam or electricity) followed by a period of consolidation as entrepreneurs built infrastructure (often laboriously) and reorganised industries to harness the new technology.

This time it may be different: digital technology may produce sustained disruption rather than slowing down and stabilising. The most important law of the digital age is Moore's law, which states that the number of transistors that can fit onto a computer chip doubles every 18 months or two years. Moore's law has transformed the IT world; today, each smartphone (of which there are about 2 billion) provides 1,000 times more computational capacity at a millionth of the cost than the whole of the Massachusetts Institute of Technology commanded in 1965.

Bill Gates once noted that, if technology advanced as fast in the car industry as it does in the computer industry, we would all be driving around in cars that cost $25 and did 1,000 miles to the gallon. Today that is beginning to happen. Uber, which was founded in 2009, has become a global giant, with revenues of $18 billion in 2014 and operations in 48 countries, by applying new technology to the hidebound taxi industry: apps allow you to summon taxis and satellite navigation systems allow anyone to become a taxi driver. Google is producing cars that can drive themselves. 3D printing is allowing us to print human organs. Intelligent robots are taking over office and even domestic functions.

The internet of things is turning physical objects into virtual slaves, fulfilling the wildest imaginings of ancient magicians and science-fiction writers. Before long traffic lights will route cars around traffic jams; buildings will adjust heating and air conditioning to the number of people in them; pill bottles will glow to alert forgetful patients to take a pill and pharmacists to make a refill; floors will alert hospitals when old people fall and fail to get up; watches will act as our personal coaches, recording the number of steps we take, urging us to take the stairs and watching our calories; virtual assistants will manage our diaries and arrange our business trips. It will not be long before we are able to send instructions to 3D printers that will then turn our plans into physical objects on the other side of the world. Nor will it be long before those 3D objects can be programmed to change shape.

Carpe diem

Management literature is full of metaphors that celebrate speed and agility. Business books glory in titles such as *Faster, Blur, Out of Control, Blown to Bits, Fast Forward, Speed of Thought* and *Wake Up*. The Boston Consulting Group (BCG) talks of companies adopting an "accelerator mindset". McKinsey urges companies to increase their "metabolic rate". Rita Gunther McGrath, of Columbia Business School, says that companies need to forget about trying to build sustained competitive advantage and focus instead on seizing momentary opportunities. The point is not to build a castle with a moat but to build a canoe that can navigate fast-changing waters.

The most successful companies are the inverse of the behemoths of old: people-short and asset-light. In 1901 US Steel employed a quarter of a million men, more than the army and navy combined. At the end of 2014, Google employed 51,564, Facebook 8,348 and Twitter 3,600. The top ten hedge funds regularly make more profits than the top six banks but only employ a few hundred people compared with more than a million. In 2012 Facebook paid $1 billion for Instagram, which employed 13 people and had yet to make a penny. Two years later it paid $20 billion for WhatsApp, which had 55 employees and revenues of $20 million.

Companies are getting cleverer at using information technology to reduce the number of full-time employees to a minimum: rather than employing a stock of workers and looking for something for them to do they rely on creating spot markets in talent. They strike deals between consumers who order a service via an app and only then summon up workers who are waiting for something to do. The rise of these on-demand companies has been most visible in the service sector: Uber provides drivers on demand; Handy provides house cleaners and handymen. SpoonRocket, a San Francisco-based food company, will deliver a meal to your door within ten minutes. Shyp will pick up a present, wrap it and post it.

On-demand companies are also proliferating in the knowledge economy. ODesk furnishes 3 million companies with 10 million freelancers every day. Quirky uses freelancers to develop new products. Tongal uses them to create advertisements, one of which has been shown at the Super Bowl, for a fraction of the cost of big advertising agencies. Companies have applied the contract-worker model to consulting (Eden McCallum), legal services (Axiom), medical services (Medicast) and the C-suite (Business Talent Group). These companies are quickly changing the nature of employment by applying contract labour to ever more sophisticated tasks. They are also changing the nature of firms – turning companies into deal-makers that specialise in matching buyers and sellers and providing guarantees of quality.

Even companies in the low-wage sector are slimming their workforces in order to remain agile. Foxconn, the world's largest contract manufacturer and the maker of most Apple computers, is introducing 1 million robots. Nike reduced the number of contract workers it employs by 106,000 – or 9% – between 2012 and 2013 at a time when it increased its profits by 16% and its revenues by 5%, despite the fact that it operates in some of the lowest-wage countries in the world.[4]

The best companies are constantly reinventing themselves, sucking in information about their environment and adjusting their profiles and strategies in the light of that information. Jeff Bezos, the founder of Amazon, begins every annual letter to shareholders with a phrase that he used in his first such letter in 1997, "It's still Day 1 of the internet", and says of Amazon.com:[5] "Though we are optimistic, we must remain vigilant and maintain a sense of urgency." When Facebook realised that it was falling behind in the race for the mobile internet in 2012 it turned on a dime: within a year it was gaining half of its advertising revenue from mobile. Netflix cannibalised its DVD business by embracing streaming. Infosys reorganises itself every two or three years from top to bottom in order to keep the organisation from atrophying. Today's winners have to be willing to disrupt themselves in order to avoid becoming tomorrow's losers.

Breakneck disruption is turning business models upside down and inside out, blurring the borders between industries and discombobulating long-established business strategies. We used to assume that publishers and internet companies belonged to different worlds. Ditto banks and mobile-phone companies, broadcasters and cable companies. Now they are all getting muddled up together: one enterprising Mexican phone company, Medical, is providing medical advice over the phone. We used to assume that business was basically about selling things or services. Now companies are pioneering collaborative business models that involve everything from renting things on a short-term basis (Zipcar for cars or Airbnb for rooms) to organising sharing. Couch surfing connects people who have a spare couch with people who are willing to pay for the privilege of using it. Flickr, Twitter and Linux specialise in taking the shared efforts of thousands or even millions of people and then using them to create communities. We used to assume that industrial production meant making things at scale and then putting them in the shops. Now "pull production" allows companies such as Hong Kong's Li & Fung to tell its suppliers to get to work only when they have a specific order.

Gutted guilds

The great disruption is reaching some of the most cosseted areas of society, areas where the educated and affluent once gathered for protection against Schumpeter's "perennial gale", the great professional guilds that were formed in the Middle Ages and revitalised themselves in the industrial era. These guilds all adopted similar business models. They recruited their members when they were young, subjected them to prolonged periods of apprenticeship, which often involved doing routine tasks which the guild masters did not want to do themselves, weeded out the weakest and least committed, and then rewarded the survivors with job security in the form of a partnership or tenured professorship, which allowed them to reap dividends from all their hard work when they were young. This model is being ripped apart. New technology is automating much of the routine work that once provided guilds with a steady source of income and new entrants with a form of training. Global companies are employing economies of scale and scope to drive out smaller players. And growing consumer demand is forcing them to reduce their prices.

Universities, perhaps the world's oldest guilds, are being transformed from communities of learning into highly stratified knowledge- and credential-producing machines: only 500,000 of the 1.4 million instructors in US universities have tenure, a group of ageing alphas who lord over an ever-expanding army of part-time and contingent gammas. This is only a taste of things to come. Digital technology will allow star lecturers to reach millions via pin-sharp video and, in no time at all, 3D holograms. Ancient chores like marking exams and classifying students will be done by computers. Such disruption will have costs: thousands of weaker universities are likely to close as students discover that they can get better value for money from MOOCs (or massive open online courses) that take content from elite universities such as Harvard and Stanford and deliver them at a fraction of the cost of second-tier universities.

Accountancy is being gobbled up by the big four global companies at the top end and disintermediated by new technologies such as TurboTax at the bottom. Law firms are being squeezed by demanding customers, particularly multinational corporations, undercut by on-demand companies such as Axiom and InCloudCounsel and shaken up by algorithms that can search millions of documents in a matter of minutes. The young can tell which way the wind is blowing: applications for US law schools have fallen by 40% since 2004.

The same pattern is being repeated in the new guilds that have emerged in the 20th century such as management consulting. Mid-sized consultancies are dying. Booz & Company has been gobbled up by PwC (PricewaterhouseCoopers) and lumbered with the name Strategy&. Monitor has gone out of business after selling its soul to Libya's former dictator, Muammar Gadhafi, among others. New entrants are challenging the old partnership model. Companies such as Eden McCallum and Business Talent Group can undercut traditional consultancies on price because they employ consultants on a freelance basis, put together ad-hoc teams for particular products and eschew expensive real estate in city centres. These new model consultancies are particularly appealing to women, who found the partnership model of traditional consultancies – work like a dog in your 20s and 30s in order to become a partner and obtain financial security – incompatible with looking after young children.[6]

The great disruption is also coming to the biggest guild of all, the public sector. Governments are being prodded by a combination of inherited debt, popular disaffection and resistance to further tax rises to get more productivity out of their public workers. At the same time, technological innovation arguably has even more dramatic implications for the service-intensive public sector than for the private sector. The essence of bureaucracy, for example, is the control and dissemination of information, the very stuff that is being revolutionised by Moore's law. State institutions will transform themselves from bureaucratic empires to platforms, working hand-in-hand with voluntary organisations, private businesses and active citizens. Schools will routinely use computers to "flip the classroom": pupils will get their basic instruction from their iPads and teachers will concentrate on delivering personal instruction. Doctors will monitor patients via remote sensors and call them into their surgeries when they spot something wrong.

If you think that this sounds far-fetched, you need only to look around the world at what is already happening. The UK's coalition government reduced the size of the permanent civil service by 17% between 2010 and 2014; it has also published more than 14,000 data sets (at data.gov.uk) to create the largest open data portal in the world. Estonia has rid itself of unsightly junk by using GPS devices to locate over 10,000 illegal dumps and unleashing an army of 50,000 people to clean them up. The Montefiore Medical Centre in New York has reduced hospital admissions for older patients by more than 30% by using remote monitors to keep a watch on patients.

This will inevitably prove socially as well as organisationally disruptive. The public sector is dominated by powerful interest groups who have traditionally been highly successful at protecting their turf and winning the general public over to their point of view. Attempts to reform public-sector guilds have already provoked big fights. They will provoke even bigger ones as the power of technology multiplies. Still, as populations age and private companies become more agile, the pressure to boost productivity in the public sector will prove irresistible.

From Keynes to Schumpeter

How can we make sense of this frenzy of change? Perhaps the easiest way is to look at the world that the baby-boomers inherited and see how it is being reshaped. The post-war order rested on three pillars: managerial capitalism, social-democratic politics and a Western-centric balance of power. Now managerial capitalism is giving way to entrepreneurial capitalism; social-democratic politics is coming apart; and the centre of economic activity is shifting inexorably to the emerging world, particularly Asia. These changes are unleashing some troublesome demons that were imprisoned during the years of managerial, social-democratic Western hegemony, in particular the demons of inequality, identity politics and existential despair.

The age of the entrepreneur

In the wake of the Great Depression traumatised governments replaced laissez-faire capitalism with managerial capitalism. The spirit of capitalism was disciplined by three "Bigs". Big businesses exploited economies of scale and scope to dominate industrial sectors: the seven sisters in oil; the big three in carmaking and television; the big two in computers. Big trade unions claimed to speak for the workers, with 30% of American workers and 80% of Swedish workers belonging to unions. Big government played the role of pump-primer-cum-referee, stimulating demand to keep the economy whirring and brokering deals between labour and capital. People differed in their reaction to the rule of giants. J.K. Galbraith, an economist, thanked the lord that big companies had replaced "the entrepreneur as the directing force of the enterprise with management". "No individual genius arranged the flight to the moon," he wrote triumphantly. "It was the work of organisation – bureaucracy."[7] Schumpeter lamented that capitalism was being bureaucratised just like the state. But most people agreed that it was simply a fact about the world. Averill Harriman, a descendant of one of America's great robber barons, reflected:[8]

> People in this country are no longer scared of such words as
> "planning" ... people have accepted the fact the government has to
> plan as well as individuals in this country.

The same was even truer outside the US.

Yet managerial capitalism hit the buffers in the late 1970s. Predictable growth turned into stagflation. Governments proved to be dismal entrepreneurs: state-owned companies such as British Leyland employed more and more people to produce lousier and lousier products. An army of innovators, particularly in the computer and finance industries, picked apart the old industrial corporation. Public opinion turned against trade unions. And economists increasingly realised, in Paul Romer's phrase, that economic growth "springs from better recipes, not more cooking". The age of the manager gave way to the age of the entrepreneur.

Entrepreneurs are in the driving seat of the new capitalism, just as managers-cum-bureaucrats were in the driving seat of the old. Cap Gemini, a consultancy, calculated that, in 2010, the most recent year for which it has produced figures, nearly half (47%) of the world's wealthy people were entrepreneurs. Entrepreneurs are not only in tune with the dominant technology of the day – the internet provides upstarts with the wherewithal to seize momentary opportunities and take on long-established businesses – they are also in tune with the anti-establishment mood. People who dislike corporate bureaucrats tend to idealise the likes of Steve Jobs or Richard Branson.

It is true that big companies remain important. The all-disrupting internet is increasingly dominated by leviathans. But the heads of big companies are having to act like entrepreneurs rather than bureaucrats in order to survive. Nokia, for example, imploded because it continued to act as if it lived in the world of managerial capitalism. Big companies are increasingly drawn from sectors such as IT, where innovation is at a premium. And boards in every area of business have little compunction about firing underperforming managers. In the 1950s governments instinctively looked to big companies such as General Motors for their template of capitalism. Today they rightly look at entrepreneurial start-ups.

This transition from managerial to entrepreneurial capitalism is forcing companies to rethink their contracts with their workers. In 1962 Earl Willis, General Electric's manager of employee benefits, spoke for his generation when he said that "maximising employee security is a prime company goal".[9] Today Reed Hastings, the founder and CEO of Netflix, spoke for a much more hard-headed generation when he told his employees, in a much-celebrated presentation on his company's culture, that "we're a team, not a family", advising them to ask themselves:[10]

> *Which of my people, if they told me they are leaving for a similar job at a peer company, would I fight to keep at Netflix? The other people should get a generous severance now so that we can open up a slot to try and find a star for that role.*

Though many companies continue to employ an inner circle of company loyalists who embody the corporate DNA, the size of that inner circle has been contracting, and it is surrounded by an expanding outer circle of workers who have a more tenuous link to the company either as temporary contractors or as short-term workers. Even the core workers can be outplaced with remarkable brutality if they become a burden on performance. In the 1960s the average person had four different employers by the time they were 65. Today the average person has eight by the time they are 30.

Breakout nations

The rise of emerging markets represents an equally radical change. For the past 400 years the West has been the crucible of economic activity, from brute growth to innovation and optimism. Today the world is turning upside down. For all the recent turbulence emerging markets still accounted for 68% of global growth in 2013. Oxford Economics projects that the GDPs of emerging-market countries will increase 2.2 percentage points faster than those of developed economies over the next four years. BCG notes that by 2020 Indonesia alone will add the equivalent of the population of the UK, 68 million people, to the middle class. McKinsey calculates that almost half of the world's GDP growth between 2010 and 2025 will come from 440 cities in emerging markets, many of them middle-sized or small. As hundreds of millions of consumers join the ranks of the middle class in coming years, buying their first televisions, fridges and cars and potentially establishing loyalties that will last a lifetime, managers will have to familiarise themselves with Tianjin (China), Porto Alegre (Brazil) and Jumasi (Ghana).

Emerging-market countries are producing ever-larger numbers of ambitious companies. In 2013, 124 of the global *Fortune* 500 companies had their headquarters in emerging markets – more than double the number in *Fortune*'s 2008 list. China's Haier has emerged as the world's largest appliance-maker, and Huawei is the largest telecoms equipment-maker. Mexico's Bimbo is aggressively expanding into the US baked-goods market. McKinsey calculates that the proportion will rise to 45% by 2025, and that China will be home to more big companies than either Europe or the US.

The emerging world is also challenging the West's monopoly on innovation. The world's biggest multinationals are relocating more of their research and development to emerging markets: cities such as Shanghai and Bangalore boast "electronic cities", oases of order in seas of disorder, where huge multinationals house R&D facilities. Some of these – such as General Electric's health-care arm and Cisco's Eastern headquarters, both in Bangalore, and Microsoft's Beijing R&D centre – are huge. Emerging-world companies are leaping over Western companies in many areas, most notably mobile money: in Kenya, for example, where 58% of adults do not have a bank account, 60% of people use the M-Pesa system of mobile payments. They are changing the balance of power in the cultural industries: Bollywood produces 1,100 films a year for an audience of 3.6 billion people, while Hollywood produces 600 for 2.6 billion. Most importantly, they are coming up with new products and services that are dramatically cheaper than their Western equivalents, such as $300 computers and $30 mobile phones that provide nationwide service for just 2 cents a minute.

The frugal revolution is being applied to some remarkable areas. Devi Shetty charges $3,000 for a heart operation compared with $20,000–100,000 in the US, but his success rates are as good as in the best US hospitals. It is also generating a stream of remarkable ideas from the bottom of the pyramid. In India, Mansukh Prajapati, a potter, has invented a fridge called MittiCool that is made entirely of clay and consumes no electricity. In Kenya, entrepreneurs have invented a device that enables bicycle riders to charge their mobile phones while pedalling along. In the Philippines, Illac Diaz has deployed a Liter of Light, a recycled plastic bottle containing bleach-processed water that refracts sunlight, producing the equivalent of a 55-watt light bulb and helping to light huts in off-the-grid shanty towns. In Peru, where the humidity is punishing and rainfall can be low, an engineering college has designed advertising billboards that can convert humid air into drinking water.

The emerging world is also caught up in the entrepreneurial revolution. Once upon a time most people in emerging markets dreamt of getting safe jobs in the civil service or big multinational organisations. Now they dream of joining start-ups or creating start-ups of their own. Young entrepreneurs can be found in entrepreneurial hot spots across the emerging world. They have created a network of entrepreneurial hubs, clubs and accelerators. They have also established a *cursus honorum*: a spell working in Silicon Valley, another spell working in Bangalore or Shanghai, a lucky meeting with a business partner and a venture capitalist, and, hey presto, an entrepreneur takes off.

The strange death of social democracy

The simultaneous rise of entrepreneurial capitalism and the shift in the balance of economic power from the old world to the new is posing an existential threat to the brand of politics that has ruled the West for much of the post-war period. This rested on consensus and compromise: the big organisations that dominated society divvied up the spoils of the capitalist economy and planned ahead for the sake of social stability. Bill Clinton and Tony Blair did a good job of putting this consensus back together after Margaret Thatcher and Ronald Reagan tried to tear it apart. But the great disruption is reshaping politics as profoundly as it reshapes the economy – and today's inheritors of the New Democratic and New Labour legacies are more inclined to indulge in nostalgia for a world that has been lost than to produce workable plans for taming the disruption.

The established order is losing its support. Voter turnout is falling: across the OECD the average turnout in national elections fell by 11 percentage points between 1980 and 2011. In the UK, one of the first countries to have a mass working-class electorate, only 57% of social classes D and E bothered to vote in 2012 compared with

76% for classes A and B. The limited franchise of the Victorian era is being reintroduced, this time by apathy rather than legislation. Party membership is declining across the developed world: only 1% of Britons are now members of political parties compared with 20% in 1950. Parties have lost their roots in civil society, becoming instead withered rumps run by a narrow political class: habitués of Westminster, Congress or *Borgen* who devote their lives to the dismal art of what Pete Mair, a political scientist, called "ruling the void". Politicians no longer represent ordinary people to the state but instead represent the state to ordinary people. The inevitable reaction is the rise of anti-politics. Anti-politics is shaping popular culture. Jon Stewart and Stephen Colbert have made brilliant careers out of mocking the political establishment. Russell Brand is guaranteed a huge audience whenever he launches a tirade against the establishment. It is also set to reshape politics itself: nationalists such as Alex Salmond and Nigel Farage in the UK and anti-establishment crusaders such as Beppe Grillo in Italy are reconfiguring the political landscape by claiming to speak for the people against the powerful.

Politics is becoming much more volatile: governments struggle to survive, popularity evaporates and new political actors challenge the system. Governments find it much harder to form majorities to push their measures through. As Moisés Naím pointed out in his book *The End of Power*, in 30 of the 34 members of the OECD, the head of state is opposed by a parliament controlled by the opposition. New parties appear on the scene like comets, powered by discontent, and specialising in disruption and protest rather than constructive change and creative problem solving.

The result is a weird impasse between public disgust and official stasis. In the 2014 European elections protest parties made huge gains across Europe: the National Front came first in France with 25% of the vote; the UK Independence Party (UKIP) came first in the UK, turning almost the whole country outside London purple; and populist parties did well in Sweden and Denmark. Astonishingly, the rulers of the void in Brussels continued as if nothing had happened and elected an unreconstructed Eurocrat, Jean-Claude Junker, to chairmanship of the European Commission.

The US has seen the rise of a fiery protest movement in the form of the Tea Party and a general public disillusionment with the working of the political system. In 1958 73% of Americans said that they trusted the government in Washington to "do what is right" either all the time or most of the time. In 2013 only 10% did. In 2014 only 7% said that they thought that Congress is doing a good job. More than three-quarters of Americans reported being frustrated or angry with the federal government.[11] Yet the political system continues with business as usual. There is a growing feeling that both Europe and the US are incapable of making serious decisions, paralysed by powerful interest groups, focused on the minutiae of political process, but out of touch with the forces that are remaking society around them: ripe for disruption but seemingly determined to ensure that that disruption takes the form of populist fury.

Three demons, uncaged

The great disruption is unleashing three demons upon the world that could yet end up severely damaging the very engine of all this disruption, the capitalist system; disrupting the disruptor, as it were.

The first demon is the rise of inequality: concentrations of wealth in the West are reaching levels that have not been seen since the late 19th and early 20th centuries. In the US the top 10% of the population now controls 70% of the country's wealth – exactly the same proportion that they controlled in 1870. In Europe the figure is slightly lower at 63% but is moving in the same direction.

There are many reasons for this rising inequality, from rising returns on capital (an explanation favoured by Thomas Piketty, an economist) to declining tax rates. But part of the explanation lies in the great disruption: the rewards of technological innovation are being scooped up by a tiny fraction of the population. Superstars are reaping huge rewards for their talent, thanks to a combination of technological innovation (which increases the rewards for brains and innovation) and globalisation (which expands the market). The majority of workers are being subjected to competitive pressure on their wages. In the US the mean living standard has stagnated since the late 1970s. In Europe structural unemployment has reached 10% or more of the population. But whatever the reasons for the change, the impact on the tenor of society is all too palpable. Chrystia Freeland, a Canadian journalist turned politician, calls this "the age of elites". Tyler Cowan, an economist, argues that "average is over". Walter Russell Mead, a foreign-policy specialist, worries that the West might be headed for a *Downton Abbey* version of the future.

This rising tide of inequality is eroding the foundations of the capitalist system: inequality is seen as legitimate only if people feel that they have an opportunity of getting ahead. But too many people think that the system is rigged in favour of insiders. The products of privilege get more than their fair share of places at elite universities: Piketty notes that the average income of the parents of Harvard students now surpasses $450,000 a year, and the university does all it can, including, at its most obscene, tipping the scales in the admissions process in favour of the children of alumni, to encourage this plutocratic trend. Companies are increasingly raising money from private markets, which inevitably favour a tiny group of insiders, rather than going public.

Growing inequality is eroding democracy as well as meritocracy. Louis Brandeis, a great American Supreme Court judge, argued:

> We can have a democratic society or we can have great concentrated wealth in the hands of a few. We cannot have both.

This contradiction was manageable in the post-war era, when economies were growing, educational opportunities were expanding and inequalities were relatively compressed. In today's era of rising inequality and cash-strapped government the super-rich are using their money to buy political influence, by contributing to campaigns and funding lobbyists, while ordinary people are becoming disillusioned with the political process. The Koch Brothers raised and distributed some $400 million to try to defeat Barack Obama in 2012. Sheldon Adelson, a gambling magnate, is so powerful that people talk of the "Adelson primary" (on one weekend no fewer than four Republican presidential candidates visited him in Las Vegas). One poll in 2011 found that only 17% of Americans believed that the government acted with their "consent", an astonishing result in a democracy.[12]

The second demon is the return of the disposable worker.

Managerial capitalism brought job security to much of the workforce: blue-collar workers spent their entire lives working for GM in Detroit or Fiat in Italy. The 1980s saw the destruction of job-protecting trade unions in the private sector. Now, this insecurity is being extended to brain-intensive professions and even to parts of the public sector. The retail sector presents a hair-raising picture of the future. The *New York Times* reports that, over the past two decades, retailers have reduced the proportion of full-time workers from 70% to 30%. The consequences for employees are, at best, a loss of benefits and predictable working hours and, at worst, a loss of their jobs, as companies replace tellers with machines.[13]

The rise of disposable workers is part of a more general change in the nature of work. Jobs are constantly being reorganised in the light of new technology and new management thinking. Reorganisation can be a problem in itself. At France Telecom there was a spate of suicides and attempted suicides after it slimmed down its management in 2007–08. One man stabbed himself in the middle of a business meeting (he survived). A woman leapt from a fifth-floor office window after sending a suicide e-mail to her father: "I have decided to kill myself tonight ... I can't take the new reorganisation." Reorganisation is also a sign of deeper changes. Work has been freed from the office and is invading every aspect of our lives. People find it hard to know when they are "on" and when they are "off". Knowledge work is suffering the fate of production work a century ago – it is being broken up into ever-smaller parts and redistributed across globe-spanning production chains. This is bringing huge improvements to some of the most self-indulgent and inefficient parts of business. But it also brings in its wake alienation and disorientation. Knowledge workers are losing one of the great satisfactions of their job – taking a job from start to finish – as tasks are broken up into their component parts.

The rise of smart machines is exacerbating these two trends. In his first novel, *Player Piano* (1952), Kurt Vonnegut foresaw that industry might one day resemble a "stupendous Rube Goldberg machine" (or as Brits would say, a Heath Robinson contraption). His story describes a dystopia in which machines have taken over brainwork as well as manual work, and a giant computer, EPICAC XIV, makes all the decisions. A few managers and engineers are still employed to tend their new masters. But most people live in homesteads where they spend their time doing make-work jobs, watching television and "breeding like rabbits".

In *Race Against the Machine*, two academics at MIT's Sloan Business School, Erik Brynjolfsson and Andrew McAfee, argue that the very thing that is driving the new economy – the ever-expanding application of IT – is producing both rising inequality and mass stagnation. Innovators reap huge rewards for inventing convenient devices and clever apps. But at the same time those new machines reduce the demand for routine labour. Carl Benedikt Frey and Michael A. Osborne, two researchers at Oxford University, argue that nearly half of US jobs are at "high risk" of being taken over by robots in the next decade or two.

The third demon is the rise of identity politics. The most grotesque form of identity politics can be found in the Islamic world where fanatics are trying to create a caliphate that is open only to people who share their version of Islam. But there is a resurgence of less extreme versions of identity politics in much of the rest of the world. Scottish nationalism is driven partly by a justified opposition to the centralisation of power in Westminster and partly by a sentimental celebration of Scotland's allegedly distinct identity. Russian nationalism is driven by a mixture of hostility to the West and atavistic longing for a simpler world. The more the capitalist system is dominated by the logic of disruption, the more people take refuge in old certainties such as national and ethnic identities.

What can be done?

The business world is in the grip of a rather glib cult of disruption at the moment, which takes Clay Christensen's brilliant work and reduces it to the level of corporate muzak. CNBC produces an annual "disruptor list" of the 50 companies that are doing the most to revolutionise the business landscape (the top three in 2014 were, in order: SpaceX, "the company that wants to send you to space and colonise Mars"; Warby Parker, "taking on the Luxottica eyewear machine"; and Etsy, "a big voice for small artisans"). Tech Crunch, a leading internet website, holds an annual festival of disruption called "DisruptSF". The festival features "custom disruptor awards", a start-up alley crawl and an official hackathon. I once met a teenager in DisruptSF's home town, San Francisco, who, to the innocent if banal question, "what do you do", replied that his start-up had just been disrupted out of existence but he had an idea for a disruptor that could disrupt the disruptor. The University of California has opened a new programme under the rubric "the degree is in disruption".

Glib indeed. It is important to remember that disruption brings huge costs in its wake, not only for the victims of disruption, who can lose their livelihoods, but also for society as a whole, which can lose its bearings. Familiar landmarks are swept aside. Deeply rooted habits are rendered obsolescent. People lose their bearings. Jaron Lanier, a computer scientist, once quipped that "people are the flies in the Moore's law ointment". People are the flies in the disruption ointment as well.

The price of change is worth paying if you can get some tangible reward: you can put up with moving house if you get a better job, an easier commute, or a nicer house. But what happens when you get the disruption without an appreciable improvement in your life? That is the case for a worrying proportion of the population today. Discontent with the status quo is mounting. The middle ground is crumbling. The political extremes are gaining strength. Anxiety is becoming part of our way of life. It is no longer absurd to fear the return of "the vast red whirlwind" of Marxism or the vast black whirlwind of bulldog nationalism. Disruption and stagnation make terrible bedfellows.

What can be done to ease the problem? Three middle-of-the-road solutions are gaining ground. Unfortunately, they are almost as wrong-headed as the red and black alternatives they are designed to pre-empt. The first calls for putting a break on all this creative destruction. This is a philosophy that unites sections of both the right and the left. François Hollande led the way on the left by raising taxes on the rich. Ed Miliband talks about fixing utility prices or taking industries such as the railways back into public ownership. Republicans talk about strengthening the fence on the southern border. France's National Front and the UK's UKIP want to withdraw from the European Union and restrict immigration. But jamming your feet on the brake will damage growth without bringing an end to disruption. Hollande's France is stuck with high unemployment, low growth, and a bloated and unproductive public sector: if you want to find a French entrepreneur you are better off going to London or New York rather than Paris. Protecting the motherland from immigrants or speculators will produce obvious problems, such as capital flight and labour shortages, while doing little to prevent new technologies from finding their way in through the back door.

The second solution emphasises the wonder-working powers of education. This is the classic third-way answer to every problem from unemployment onwards. The only sensible way to deal with the dynamism of capitalism, the argument goes, is to invest in education so that people can leap from one job to another, preferably higher up the value chain. There is much truth in this: unemployment is significantly lower among people with university degrees than the general population. Yet the argument has always been over-optimistic. It is exceedingly hard to turn 40-year-old miners into IT specialists, and it is becoming less persuasive by the year. The striking thing about the current wave of technological innovation is that it is destroying brainwork as well as manual work.

The third solution emphasises the conscience of capitalists. Companies should embrace corporate social responsibility (CSR); the rich should practise "philanthrocapitalism"; policymakers should support "inclusive capitalism". Most of the world's biggest companies trumpet their commitment to CSR. Some have even adopted a triple bottom line (people, planet, profits). The United Nations Global Compact for corporate responsibility, launched at Davos in 1999, has attracted more than 3,000 corporate supporters. The US has created a National Corporate Philanthropy Day (February 25th), which even has its own colours, blue and green. The UK's 2006 Companies Act requires companies to report on social and environmental questions. China has created a Chinese Federation for Corporate Social Responsibility.

There are numerous problems with this argument. CSR can be little more than decoration: companies produce glossy brochures about their good works, and unleash armies of PR people on unfortunate journalists, but continue with business as usual. BP's commitment to producing a world beyond petroleum did not prevent it from leaking millions of gallons of oil into the Gulf of Mexico. And even when it is more than corporate propaganda, that more can be counter-productive: CSR tends to go hand-in-hand with all sorts of regulations which can be handled by big companies but make it harder for innovators to produce better goods at lower prices. Inclusive capitalism can all too easily turn into its opposite: a cosy corporatism that excludes more dynamic new entrants from the market. Conscience-fuelled capitalism can have its most depressing impact on the most explosive subject in modern political economy: creating jobs. The more policymakers and business people embrace the case for minimum wages and enlightened regulation, the more they give a shove – sometimes gentle and sometimes quite vigorous – to the replacement of people with machines. It is worth applying a simple rule of thumb to all these attempts to produce a nicer version of capitalism: the more the adjectives ("inclusive", "responsible", and so on), the fewer the jobs.

So what can be done? The great disruption is doing two things simultaneously: increasing people's risks as the economy becomes more volatile; and imposing more of those risks on the individual. After the second world war institutions took on ever more responsibilities for dealing with the downside of capitalism. Now companies are shedding risks in an attempt to remain competitive. The challenge is to produce solutions that are as big as the problems: great ideas to match the great disruption.

Governments need to update their social policies to deal with a rapidly changing world. Government policies were designed in a world where most people went to work for (often large) organisations. Self-employed people can have a terrible time dealing with rules that vary from state to state and tax inspector to tax inspector: in 2010 one contract engineer was driven so mad by all this that he flew a plane into the IRS (Internal Revenue Service) office in Austin, Texas. In his suicide note he complained that the IRS had turned him into a "criminal and non-citizen slave".

The least governments need to do is to clean up this mess. But they also need to do far more: reinvent the great institutions of the welfare state, particularly health care and pensions, for a more disruption-prone age. The biggest problem is that some countries deliver welfare through workplaces rather than through the individual. The worst offender is the US, which adopted this system in peculiar historical circumstances (employers could not raise wages during the second world war so competed by offering benefits instead). It can also be found in many European countries. They need to break with this habit and deal more directly with individuals. The other great problem is that pension systems are not properly funded.

Some far-seeing governments have already begun to act. The UK and US governments have moved from defined benefit to defined contribution pension schemes. They have also given people more incentives to build up pension pots. The Obama government has introduced a health-care reform – Obamacare – that makes it easier for the self-employed to buy benefits (for all the right's indignation about Obama's "socialist" reform it is in fact a sensible adjustment to a more fluid economy). But more advanced countries need to do much more. And backward countries – particularly in southern Europe – desperately need to catch up or they their entitlement programmes will collapse.

Individuals need to change their expectations: the age of dependence on employers is going the way of the age of deference to social superiors. People have to come to terms with a world in which the only people they can really rely on are themselves. Reid Hoffman points out a billboard that appeared on the side of Highway 101 in the San Francisco Bay Area proclaiming bluntly: "1,000,000 people overseas can do your job. What makes you so special?" Today's workers need to repeat those words every night before they go to bed and then in the morning when they get up.

They need to focus on finding a niche – on providing services that nobody else is providing or, if they are in a crowded field, providing those services better, faster or cheaper than their competitors. They need to keep their skills up to date. They need to learn how to sell themselves to the market: this means cultivating their networks, advertising their skills and, if they are particularly successful, even turning themselves into brands. They will also need to learn how to manage "You Inc" – that is, how to choose between investment and expenditure, work and rest. Thanks to the great disruption everybody needs to be prepared to run themselves as a small business.

This is not to say that people are all alone. Established institutions can play an important role in helping them to manage their lives. Schools and universities can teach people to be entrepreneurs, capable of running their own lives, rather than employees, looking to big institutions to provide them with jobs. People can cope with the downside of the entrepreneurial society by coming together to form voluntary organisations that can pool risk or deal with problems like isolation. Victorian workers invented institutions such as Friendly Societies to try to protect themselves from the vicissitudes of a dynamic economy, institutions that were, unfortunately, elbowed out of existence by big government and big trade unions. Today's workers are beginning to create their post-modern equivalents. Freelancers are forming "virtual" guilds, such as LawLink (for lawyers), Sermo (for physicians) and H-Net (for social scientists). These guilds are sources of insurance and stability in a tumultuous world: they provide job hoppers and displaced workers with a way of keeping their skills up to date and their contacts fresh. Freelancers are also creating institutions that respond to the need for communal as well as intellectual connections: most big cities now have co-working offices (variously dubbed Hubs, Sandbox Suites and Citizen Spaces) that provide people with a place to work and socialise.

There is also a welcome paradox at the heart of the great disruption: the very forces that are making life more uncertain are also providing us with a way of coping with many of those uncertainties. Three of the biggest reasons for the stagnation of people's living standards are the rising relative costs of health care, education (particularly university education) and housing. Disruptive innovation offers the chance of addressing all three problems. The IT revolution can reduce the relative cost of education and health care by bringing the same productivity improvements to services that the Industrial Revolution brought to manufacturing. The IT revolution is an almost miraculous force. Almost everybody in the rich world has the equivalent of a super computer on their desk or in their pocket – they can consult a library of books from the comfort of their own homes or Google an obscure reference while they are travelling to work. Soon they will be able to employ a virtual assistant to do their office work or arrange their business travel. A growing number of people in the emerging world have similar advantages: thanks to the proliferation of mobile phones and cheap iPads (sometimes subsidised by foundations) people in the slums of Nairobi or Mumbai will be able to educate themselves via Kahn Academy or People's University. Provided it is imaginatively used, IT can be one of the most equalising as well as one of the most disruptive forces in the world.

The biggest reason to keep your foot on the accelerator rather than touching the brake or turning the steering wheel is that the benefits of all this change continue to outweigh the costs. Schumpeter's memorable phrase about creative destruction has actually done some harm: it implies that the destructive part of entrepreneurship is just as weighty as the creative part. In reality, creation outweighs the destruction. A great deal of creation is of the non-destructive variety: new cures for diseases or new technological delights. And when we do have to endure "creative destruction" it normally involves more of the latter than the former. The balance between creation and destruction may have been too close for comfort for people in the rich world in recent decades. But stand back and look at the world as a whole and there is no doubt that creation wins out easily. In the past 20 years more people than ever before have risen out of poverty. And in the next 20 years the living standards of middle-class Westerners may improve significantly as technology raises the productivity of the service sector. The gale that Schumpeter celebrated may blow a little roughly at times. But it is nevertheless blowing us to a better place.

A guide to this book

These columns, written over the past five years, were frequently inspired by discrete events: the death of a significant thinker, the appearance of an interesting book, the resignation of a CEO and so forth. But they were given a degree of unity by the theme of creative destruction. And that unity has been reinforced by the selection and arrangement of the columns. (The date it was published appears at the end of each column.) The result is that this selection, despite its origins in the weekly journalistic grind, is designed to address a coherent set of questions. Why is the world experiencing such turbulent times? Who are the winners and losers of all this turbulence? And what can we do to cope with the great disruption – as companies, governments and individuals? That said, turbulence is never the be all and end all of management: I have also thrown in a few columns, at the end, that deal with more perennial problems of power, work and philosophy.

The first part looks at the gurus of disruption. Peter Drucker shared many of the same qualities as his fellow product of the Austro-Hungarian Empire, Schumpeter: a capacity to spot big social trends combined with a gift for a telling phrase. Ronald Coase asked the most fundamental question in business: why do firms exist in the first place? Why do we need the visible hand of management when the invisible hand of the market can do so much? C.K. Prahalad and Clay Christensen invented entire sub-disciplines of business thinking – Prahalad by identifying the "fortune at the bottom of the pyramid" and Christensen by showing how mavericks armed with a disruptive idea can transform entire industries. But in January 2008 the great gurus of disruption found themselves with a new rival in the form of "the one who knocks", Walter White. *Breaking Bad* was not only the best show on television. It was also the best guide to how to turn a disruptive start-up into a giant business.

The second part examines the forces of disruption: emerging-market companies that are reshaping established industries; "crazy diamond" entrepreneurs who discover economic value in the worthless and near-impossible; robot managers and big data analysts who are rendering traditional managers redundant; and pre-industrial business models, such as private partnerships and state-owned companies, that are re-emerging to challenge public companies.

The third part argues that the winners and losers from all this change can be surprising. The fact that the rich are getting richer and the rest of us are treading water conceals some interesting facts. Some of the biggest winners are emerging-market entrepreneurs (particularly women), who can now treat the world as their oyster. Previously marginalised groups such as people who have Asperger's and ageing workers are also being given new leases of life. It would be going too far to classify CEOs as losers. But the headlines about extravagant pay packets conceal a darker story: CEOs have less time than ever before to make their mark and are hemmed in by powerful groups from boards to pension funds. The same can be said for universities: institutions that ought to be at the heart of the knowledge economy are looking increasingly like General Motors in the 1970s: charging ever-higher prices for ever-lazier products. Our intellectual elite should not be crawling around on the frontiers of knowledge with a magnifying glass.

The book then turns to the question of how we can survive and thrive in the age of disruption. Part four looks at companies. Some companies are thriving by sticking to old-fashioned methods: this is particularly true of Germany's *mittelstand* of middle-sized family companies. Others are experimenting with radical new business methods: some such as Airbnb and Zipcar are pioneering the sharing economy; and others such as General Electric and Unilever are acting on Prahalad's advice about the fortune at the bottom of the pyramid.

Too many big companies have responded to disruption by embracing airy-fairy management fads: giving employees inflated titles (chief creativity officer) to make them feel important. But a few big companies are treating the problems with the seriousness they deserve. Unilever's CEO, Paul Polman, argues that companies need to take a more long-term approach if they are to have a chance of addressing popular worries about capitalism. The danger of Polman's approach is that it allows capitalism's critics, in the form of non-governmental organisations (NGOs), to set the agenda. A better approach to the problem of legitimacy might be for business people to take their lead from Schumpeter and do more to fight their corner in the culture wars. Too many business people are content to remain silent while other people set the agenda, or else just to speak in corporate clichés. They need to be willing to make a stirring case for business – that it is the fruit of human creativity and the guarantee of political pluralism – if they are not to be overwhelmed by public hostility or government regulation. Business people had a striking impact on the debate about Scottish devolution when they spoke out in the last week. They would be foolish to wait until the last minute in the UK's even more important debate over its membership of the EU.

Part five turns to the depressing subject of governments. The news is not all bad. Governments have played an important role in creating the infrastructure of capitalism: the internet was nurtured by the US defence department. Some institutions are showing an appetite for innovation: Sweden, once the capital of big government socialism, is allowing private-sector entrepreneurs to bring new ideas into its welfare state. But the bad news is nevertheless overwhelming: governments have become far too intrusive over the post-war decades and companies have responded to this intrusiveness not by asserting the principles of liberalism but by trying to game the system. The news is particularly depressing in the US. Washington is becoming the capital of crony capitalism rather than republican government: paralysed when it comes to tackling collective problems such as investment in infrastructure but hyperactive when it comes to brokering deals between interest groups. Nor is the problem limited to Washington. In 1950, when organisation man supposedly ruled, only 5% of jobs required licences. Today 30% do. You cannot work as an interior designer in Florida without two years of expensive study – as if preventing people from having clashing colour schemes is any business of the government.

And what about the workers? Part six looks at the great disruption from the point of view of people who are at the sharp end. The most dramatic example of the revival of the class struggle can be found in San Francisco, where long-standing residents of that city have been protesting against the influx of technology workers, who are pushing up the price of real estate and establishing private bus services so that they do not have to mix with the masses. But much of the dark side of the great disruption can be found in silent despair rather than noisy resistance. Perpetual reorganisation can drive workers to suicide. Information technology can turn you into a wage slave 24 hours a day. Companies have embraced various solutions to these problems such as mindfulness (zoning out for a while) or, even worse, compulsory fun. But workers might be better advised to stick to a more time-honoured strategy – what the British call skiving and the Americans shirking. This might sound like an invitation to laziness. But in fact refusing to take part in pointless meetings or respond to make-work e-mails might be better described as a way of conserving our energy for more productive purposes.

This collection concludes with columns that address some perennial problems of management. How do you get power? And what does power do to those who hold it? Why do some creative duos such as Mick Jagger and Keith Richard continue to thrive while others such as John Lennon and Paul McCartney fall apart? And why do we continue to put off important tasks even though we know that the costs of delay can be ruinous? There is no doubt that the great disruption confronts us all with new and dramatic problems. But human nature never varies: you can give business people all the big data and artificial intelligence in the world but they will continue to be driven by personal feuds and childish vanity. The gurus of disruption demand our attention as never before. But business people also need to spend some time reading the great philosophers and meditating on timeless truths.

Notes

1 Davis, G., "The Rise and Fall of Finance and the End of the Society of Organizations", *Academy of Management Perspectives*, August 2009.

2 Tapscott, D. and Williams, A., *Macrowikinomics: Rebooting Business and the World*, Portfolio Hardcover, 2010.

3 Hoffman, R. and Casnocha, B., *The Start-Up of You*, Crown Business, 2012.

4 Jopson, B., "Nike to tackle rising Asian Labour Costs", *Financial Times*, June 27th 2013.

5 Hoffman and Casnocha, op. cit.

6 Christensen, C., Wang, D. and Van Bever, D., "Consulting on the Cusp of Disruption", *Harvard Business Review*, October 2013.

7 Galbraith, J.K., *The New Industrial State*, Houghton Mifflin, 1971.

8 Hobsbawn, E., *The Age of Extremes: A History of the World, 1914–1991*, Vintage Books, 1994.

9 Hoffman, R. et al., *The Alliance: Managing Talent in the Networked Age*, Harvard Business Review Press, 2014.

10 Hoffman et al., op. cit.

11 Schuck, P.H., *Why Government Fails So Often – and How it Can Do Better*, Princeton University Press, 2014.

12 Rasmussen Reports, "New Low: 17% Say US Government Has Consent of the Government", August 7th 2011.

13 Greenhouse, S., "A part time life as hours shrink and shift", *New York Times*, October 27th 2012.

PART 1

The gurus of disruption

Taking flight

On September 17th 2009, *The Economist* launched a new
business column. Why call it Schumpeter?

THERE IS SOMETHING ABOUT BUSINESS that prevents most people
from seeing straight. The rise of modern business provoked relentless
criticism. Anthony Trollope featured a fraudulent railway company in
The Way We Live Now (1875). Upton Sinclair dwelt on "the inferno of
exploitation" in Chicago's meat packing industry in *The Jungle* (1906).
Muckraking journalists denounced the titans of American business
as "robber barons".

A striking number of business people accepted this hostile
assessment. Friedrich Engels used some of the profits of his successful
textile business to support Karl Marx, the self-proclaimed gravedigger
of capitalism. Henry Frick's last message to his fellow steel magnate,
Andrew Carnegie, was "Tell him I'll see him in hell, where we both
are going." Many of the greatest business people threw themselves
into philanthropy to try to win back the souls that they had lost in
making money. Anti-business sentiment is still widespread today. For
many environmentalists, business is responsible for despoiling the
planet. For many apostles of corporate social responsibility, business
people are fallen angels who can only redeem themselves by doing
good works.

But anti-business sentiment is not as pervasive as it once was,
thanks to the Thatcher-Reagan revolution and the collapse of
communism. Instead there is new irritation to contend with – the
blandification of business. Companies are at pains to present
themselves as warm-and-fuzzy global citizens. Politicians praise
businessmen as job creators. The United Nations and the World Bank
celebrate businesses as all-purpose problem-solvers. Nicolas Sarkozy
makes a distinction between business people (who create things) and
financial speculators (who wreak havoc).

Joseph Schumpeter was one of the few intellectuals who saw
business straight. He regarded business people as unsung heroes:

men and women who create new enterprises through the sheer force of their wills and imaginations, and, in so doing, are responsible for the most benign development in human history, the spread of mass affluence. "Queen Elizabeth [I] owned silk stockings," he once observed. "The capitalist achievement does not typically consist in providing more silk stockings for queens but in bringing them within the reach of factory girls in return for steadily decreasing amounts of effort ...The capitalist process, not by coincidence but by virtue of its mechanism, progressively raises the standard of life of the masses." But Schumpeter knew far too much about the history of business to be a cheerleader. He recognised that business people are often ruthless monomaniacs, obsessed by their dreams of building "private kingdoms" and willing to do anything to crush their rivals.

Schumpeter's ability to see business straight would be reason enough to name a business column after him. But this ability rested on a broader philosophy of capitalism. He argued that innovation is at the heart of economic progress. It gives new businesses a chance to replace old ones, but it also dooms those new businesses to fail unless they can keep on innovating (or find a powerful government patron). In his most famous phrase he likened capitalism to a "perennial gale of creative destruction".

For Schumpeter the people who kept this gale blowing were entrepreneurs. He was responsible for popularising the word itself, and for identifying the entrepreneur's central function: of moving resources, however painfully, to areas where they can be used more productively. But he also recognised that big businesses can be as innovative as small ones, and that entrepreneurs can arise from middle management as well as college dorm-rooms.

Schumpeter was born in 1883, a citizen of the Austro-Hungarian empire. During the 18 years he spent at Harvard he never learned to drive and took the subway that links Cambridge to Boston only once. Obsessed by the idea of being a gentleman, he spent an hour every morning dressing himself. Yet his writing has an astonishingly contemporary ring; indeed, he seems to have felt the future in his bones. The gale of creative destruction blew ever harder after his death in 1950, particularly after the stagflation of the 1970s. Corporate raiders and financial engineers tore apart underperforming companies.

Governments relaxed their hold on the economy. The venture-capital industry exploded, the computer industry boomed and corporate lifespans shortened dramatically. In 1956–81 an average of 24 firms dropped out of the *Fortune* 500 list every year. In 1982–2006 that number jumped to 40. Larry Summers argues that Schumpeter may prove to be the most important economist of the 21st century.

A prophet and a role model

The prophet of capitalism's creative powers also understood the precariousness of the capitalist achievement. He pointed out that successful firms depend upon a complex ecology that has been created over centuries. He wrote extensively about the development of the joint-stock company and the rise of stockmarkets. He also understood that capitalism might be destroyed by its own success. He worried that a "new class" of bureaucrats and intellectuals were determined to tame capitalism's animal spirits. And he warned that successful business people were always trying to conspire with politicians to preserve the status quo.

Schumpeter was far from infallible. His ideas about long business cycles have not withstood the test of time. He was too sceptical about the case for using government spending to avert depressions. He underestimated the self-correcting power of democracy. But, 65 years after his death, this great champion of innovation and entrepreneurship surely got as close as anybody to identifying what a column on modern business should be about.

September 2009

Remembering Drucker

Peter Drucker remains the king of the management gurus

IN THE NORMAL RUN of things the management world is divided into dozens of mutually suspicious tribes – theoreticians versus practitioners, publicity-hogging gurus versus retiring academics, supporters of "scientific" management versus advocates of the "humanistic" sort. But in November 2009 there was unusual comity: the leaders of all the management tribes came together to celebrate the centenary of the birth of Peter Drucker, a man who is often described as "the father of modern management" and "the world's greatest management thinker".

The celebrations took place all around the world, most notably in Vienna, where Drucker was born, in southern California, where he spent his golden years, and in China, where he is exercising growing influence. The speakers were not limited to luminaries of management: they also included Rick Warren, the spiritual guru of the moment in America, Frances Hesselbein, a former head of the American Girl Scouts, and David Gergen, an adviser to both Republican and Democratic presidents.

To mark the centennial, *Harvard Business Review* put a photograph of Drucker on its cover along with the headline: "What Would Peter Do? How his wisdom can help you navigate turbulent times". Claremont Graduate University in California, where Drucker taught, boasts not one but two institutions that are dedicated to keeping the flame alive: the Peter Drucker and Masatoshi Ito Graduate School of Management and the Drucker Institute. The institute acts as the hub of a global network of Drucker societies that are trying to apply his principles to everything from schools to refuse collection. It also produces a "do-it-yourself workshop-in-a-box" called "Drucker Unpacked".

Why does Drucker continue to enjoy such a high reputation? Part of the answer lies in people's mixed emotions about management. The management-advice business is one of the most successful industries of the past century. When Drucker first turned his mind to the subject in the 1940s it was a backwater. Business schools were treated as poor relations by other professional schools. McKinsey had been in the management-consulting business for only a decade and the Boston Consulting Group did not yet exist. Officials at General Motors doubted if Drucker could find a publisher for his great study of the company, *Concept of the Corporation*, on the grounds that, as one of them put it, "I don't see anyone interested in a book on management."

Today the backwater has turned into Niagara Falls. The world's great business schools have replaced Oxbridge as the nurseries of the global elite. The management-consulting industry earns revenues of hundreds of billions a year. Management books regularly top the bestseller lists. Management gurus can command $60,000 a speech.

Yet the practitioners of this great industry continue to suffer from a severe case of status anxiety. This is partly because the management business has always been prey to fads and fraudsters. But it is also because the respectable end of the business seems to lack what Yorkshire folk call "bottom". Consultants and business-school professors are forever discovering great ideas, like re-engineering, that turn to dust, and wonderful companies, like Enron, that burst into flames.

Peter Drucker is the perfect antidote to such anxiety. He was a genuine intellectual who, during his early years, rubbed shoulders with the likes of Ludwig Wittgenstein, John Maynard Keynes and Joseph Schumpeter. He illustrated his arguments with examples from medieval history or 18th-century English literature. He remained at the top of his game for more than 60 years, advising generations of bosses and avoiding being ensnared by fashion. He constantly tried to relate the day-to-day challenges of business to huge social and economic trends such as the rise of "knowledge workers" and the resurgence of Asia.

But Drucker was more than just an antidote to status anxiety. He was also an apostle for management. He argued that management is one of the most important engines of human progress: "the organ that converts a mob into an organisation and human effort into performance". He even described scientific management as "the most powerful as well as the most lasting contribution America has made to Western thought since the 'Federalist Papers'." He relentlessly extended management's empire. From the 1950s onwards he offered advice to Japanese companies as well as American ones. He insisted that good management was just as important for the social sector as the business sector. He acted as an informal adviser to the Girl Scouts. He helped inspire the mega-church movement. The management school that bears his name recruits about a third of its students from outside the business world.

Scout's honour

The most important reason why people continue to revere Drucker, though, is that his writing remains startlingly relevant. Reading *Concept of the Corporation*, which was published in 1946, you are struck not just by how accurately he saw the future but also by how similar today's management problems are to those of yesteryear. This is partly because, whatever the theorists like to think, management is not a progressive science: the same dilemmas and difficult trade-offs crop up time and again. And it is partly because Drucker discovered a creative middle ground between rival schools of management. He treated companies as human organisations rather than just as sources for economic data. But he also insisted that all human organisations, whether in business or the voluntary sector, need clear objectives and hard measurements to keep them efficient. Drucker liked to say that people used the word guru because the word charlatan was so hard to spell. A century after his birth Drucker remains one of the few management thinkers to whom the word "guru" can be applied without a hint of embarrassment.

November 2009

Why do firms exist?

Ronald Coase, a Nobel prize-winning economist, asked the most fundamental question about business

FOR PHILOSOPHERS the great existential question is: "Why is there something rather than nothing?" For management theorists the more mundane equivalent is: "Why do firms exist? Why isn't everything done by the market?"

Today most people live in a market economy, and central planning is remembered as the greatest economic disaster of the 20th century. Yet most people also spend their working lives in centrally planned bureaucracies called firms. They stick with the same employer for years, rather than regularly returning to the jobs market. They labour to fulfil the "strategic plans" of their corporate commissars. John Jacob Astor's American Fur Company made him the richest man in America in the 1840s. But it never consisted of more than a handful of people. Today Astor's company would not register as a blip on the corporate horizon. Firms routinely employ thousands of workers and move billions of dollars-worth of goods and services within their borders.

Why have these "islands of conscious power" survived in the surrounding "ocean of unconscious co-operation", to borrow a phrase from D.H. Robertson, an economist? Classical economics had little to say about this question. Adam Smith opened *The Wealth of Nations* with a wonderful description of the division of labour in a pin factory, but he said nothing about the bosses who hired the pin-makers or the managers who organised them. Smith's successors said even less, either ignoring the pin factory entirely or treating it as a tedious black box. They preferred to focus on the sea rather than the islands.

Who knows the secret of the black box?

The man who restored the pin factory to its rightful place at the heart of economic theory celebrated his 100th birthday on December

29th 2010. The economics profession was slow to recognise Ronald Coase's genius. He first expounded his thinking about the firm in a lecture in Dundee in 1932, when he was just 21 years old. Nobody much listened. He published *The Nature of the Firm* five years later. It went largely unread.

But Mr Coase laboured on regardless: a second seminal article on "The Problem of Social Cost" laid the intellectual foundations of the deregulation revolution of the 1980s. Eventually, Mr Coase acquired an army of followers, such as Oliver Williamson, who fleshed out his ideas. In 1991, aged 80, he was awarded a Nobel prize. Far from resting on his laurels, Mr Coase published a new book in 2011, with Ning Wang of Arizona State University, on "How China Became Capitalist".

His central insight was that firms exist because going to the market all the time can impose heavy transaction costs. You need to hire workers, negotiate prices and enforce contracts, to name but three time-consuming activities. A firm is essentially a device for creating long-term contracts when short-term contracts are too bothersome. But if markets are so inefficient, why don't firms go on getting bigger for ever? Mr Coase also pointed out that these little planned societies impose transaction costs of their own, which tend to rise as they grow bigger. The proper balance between hierarchies and markets is constantly recalibrated by the forces of competition: entrepreneurs may choose to lower transaction costs by forming firms but giant firms eventually become sluggish and uncompetitive.

How much light does *The Nature of the Firm* throw on today's corporate landscape? The young Mr Coase first grew interested in the workings of firms when he travelled around America's industrial heartland on a scholarship in 1931–32. He abandoned his textbooks and asked businessmen why they did what they did. He has long chided his fellow economists for scrawling hieroglyphics on blackboards rather than looking at what it actually takes to run a business. So it seems reasonable to test his ideas by the same empirical standards.

Mr Coase's theory continues to explain some of the most puzzling problems in modern business. Take the rise of vast and highly diversified business groups in the emerging world, such as India's Tata group and Turkey's Koc Holding. Many Western observers dismiss these as relics of a primitive form of capitalism. But they make perfect sense when you consider the transaction costs of going to the market. Where trust in established institutions is scarce, it makes sense for companies to stretch their brands over many industries. And where capital and labour markets are inefficient, it makes equal sense for companies to allocate their own capital and train their own loyalists.

But Mr Coase's narrow focus on transaction costs nevertheless provides only a partial explanation of the power of firms. The rise of the neo-Coasian school of economists has led to a fierce backlash among management theorists who champion the "resource-based theory" of the firm. They argue that activities are conducted within firms not only because markets fail, but also because firms succeed: they can marshal a wide range of resources – particularly nebulous ones such as "corporate culture" and "collective knowledge" – that markets cannot access. Companies can organise production and create knowledge in unique ways. They can also make long-term bets on innovations that will redefine markets rather than merely satisfy demand. Mr Coase's theory of "market failure" needs to be complemented by a theory of "organisational advantages".

All this undoubtedly complicates "The Nature of the Firm". But it also vindicates the twin decisions that Mr Coase made all those years ago as a young student at the London School of Economics: to look inside the black box rather than simply ignoring it, and to examine businesses, not just fiddle with theories. Is it too much to hope that other practitioners of the dismal science will follow his example and study the real world?

December 2010

Exit Albert Hirschman

A great lateral thinker died on December 10th 2012

ALBERT HIRSCHMAN knew what he was talking about when he called one of his books *Essays in Trespassing*. He was an extraordinarily peripatetic practitioner of the dismal science. Born in Berlin in 1915, he fled the Nazis in 1933, studied in Paris, London and Trieste, joined the anti-Mussolini resistance, fought on the Republican side in the Spanish civil war, served in the French army until France's collapse in 1940, helped to organise an "underground railway" for refugees, emigrated to America, joined the army and was a translator at Nuremberg. He applied the cosmopolitan spirit that he had acquired in these years to everything he wrote.

He made his reputation as a development economist, focusing on Latin America, but he soon found himself trespassing obsessively – not only into other sub-disciplines such as the theory of the firm but also into other disciplines entirely such as political science and the history of thought. Mr Hirschman was never awarded the Nobel prize in economics he so richly deserved, perhaps because his writing was hard to classify. However, as if by way of recompense, Princeton University Press has published a 768-page biography by Jeremy Adelman.

Mr Hirschman's most famous book, *Exit, Voice and Loyalty: Responses to Decline in Firms, Organisations and States*, remains as suggestive today as it was when it first appeared in 1970, for managers and policymakers as well as intellectuals. Mr Hirschman argued that people have two different ways of responding to disappointment. They can vote with their feet (exit) or stay put and complain (voice). Exit has always been the default position in the United States: Americans are known as being quick to up sticks and move. It is also the default position in the economics profession. Indeed, when his book appeared, Milton Friedman and his colleagues in the Chicago School were busy extending the empire of exit to new areas. If public schools or public housing were rotten, they argued, people should be encouraged to escape them.

Mr Hirschman raised some problems with the cult of exit. Sometimes, it entrenches the status quo. Dictators may rule longer if their bravest critics flee abroad (indeed, Cuba uses emigration as a safety valve). Monopolies may have an easier life if their stroppiest customers find an alternative. Mr Hirschman got the idea for his book during a ghastly train journey in Nigeria: he concluded that the country's railways were getting worse because the most vocal customers were shifting to the roads.

Exit may also reinforce the cycle of decline. State schools may get worse if the pushiest parents take their custom elsewhere. Mr Hirschman worried that a moderate amount of exit might produce the worst of all worlds: "an oppression of the weak by the incompetent and an exploitation of the poor by the lazy which is the more durable and stifling as it is both unambitious and escapable." (Mr Hirschman wrote better in his third language than most economists do in their first.) Exit may also entail costs. If you have invested heavily in a company that starts performing badly, then you may be better off agitating for a change in management rather than selling your shares at a loss.

Mr Hirschman overstated his case. Plenty of evidence suggests that choice can act as an energiser, not a soporific. The most comprehensive study of school choice, in Sweden in 1988–2009, by Anders Bohlmark and Mikael Lindahl, found that "free schools" (private schools that are paid for by the state) were not only good for their own pupils but also forced ordinary state schools to shape up. But Mr Hirschman's overall point was not that exit is bad but that exit and "voice" work best together. Reformers are more likely to be able to fix an organisation if there is a danger that their clients will leave. The problem with Friedman *et al.* was that they focused only on exit and not on how exit and voice could be used to reinforce each other.

Modern technology is adding to the power of both exit and voice. Consumers can abandon expensive middlemen for electronic commerce. They can also organise online armies to protest against poor service. But companies are also fighting back – making exit more difficult by persuading people to sign long-term contracts (particularly with teaser rates) and encouraging loyalty by offering rewards such as air miles. They are also adding their own voices to the hubbub via social media.

Squawk or go

Mr Hirschman wrote so much about so many different subjects that it is easy to see why his biography stretches to 768 pages. He challenged the conventional wisdom among his fellow development economists that poor countries need "balanced growth"; he argued instead that the "disequilibria" generated by unbalanced growth might do a better job of mobilising resources. He also challenged the conventional wisdom among sociologists and historians that the Protestant ethic prepared the way for capitalism. He suggested, rather, that the starring role should be given to a group of thinkers, such as Montesquieu, who argued that the best way to prevent social disorder was to channel people's passions into moneymaking.

The Economist claims to engage in a "severe contest" with "an unworthy, timid ignorance obstructing our progress". Mr Hirschman was an eloquent ally. In The Rhetoric of Reaction he wrote that purveyors of "timid ignorance" rely on three types of argument: jeopardy (reforms will cost a lot and endanger previous gains); perversity (reforms will harm the people they are intended to help); and futility (problems are so huge that nothing can be done about them). That certainly describes the current debates about global warming, illegal drugs and countless other topics. With luck, Mr Hirschman's exit will not silence his voice.

December 2012

Ahead of the curve

Daniel Bell, who died on January 25th 2011, was one of the great sociologists of capitalism

ASKED WHAT HE SPECIALISED IN, Daniel Bell replied: "generalisations". Mr Bell lived a varied life. He grew up in New York City, so poor that he sometimes had to scavenge for food. Yet he ended his days in bourgeois comfort in Cambridge, Massachusetts. He spent 20 years as a journalist, mostly as *Fortune*'s labour editor, before decamping to academia. His boss, Henry Luce, desperate to keep his star writer, asked him why he was leaving. He gave four reasons: June, July, August and September.

His taste for generalisations grew with the eating. He produced three of the great works of post-war sociology: *The End of Ideology* (1960), *The Coming of Post-Industrial Society* (1973) and *The Cultural Contradictions of Capitalism* (1978). On the *Times Literary Supplement*'s list of the 100 most influential books since the second world war, two were by Mr Bell.

Many of Mr Bell's insights remain as relevant today as when he first broached them. For example, the transition from industrial to consumer capitalism, which he chronicled in America decades ago, is now happening in China and India. Even when he was wrong, Mr Bell was wrong in thought-provoking ways. A few hours with his oeuvre is worth more than a week in Davos (and is less likely to cause skiing injuries).

The End of Ideology described the political landscape of the post-cold-war world 30 years before the cold war ended. Mr Bell argued that the great ideological struggles that had defined the first half of the 20th century were exhausted. The new politics, he said, would be about boring administration, not the clash of ideals. His timing could hardly have been worse: the 1960s was one of the most ideologically charged decades in American history. Nonetheless, Mr Bell was right that the ideology of communism was doomed. In China it has given way to market Leninism. In Russia it has been replaced by kleptocracy.

Mr Bell spent the next decade and a bit working on a huge book, *The Coming of Post-Industrial Society*, a term he coined and which caught on. Many of the book's insights – about the shift from manufacturing to services, the rise of knowledge workers and the waning of the class struggle – have now become so familiar that it is easy to forget how fresh they were in 1973. However, Mr Bell failed to spot one of the revolutions that was whirling around him: the transition from the managerial capitalism that he witnessed at *Fortune* to a much more freewheeling entrepreneurial capitalism. Perhaps this was the price he paid for spurning Luce and moving to academia.

Many of his other insights still bite. He argued that the old-fashioned class struggle was being replaced by other, equally vexatious conflicts: for example, between the principles of equality and meritocracy in higher education. He also anticipated the current debate about happiness by pointing out that material progress cannot eliminate the frustrations inherent in the zero-sum competition for power, prestige and the attention of the sexiest person in the room. The more people are free to rise on their own merits, the more they will race on the treadmill for status.

Mr Bell's best book was *The Cultural Contradictions of Capitalism*. In it he raised the possibility that the material abundance that capitalism produces might destroy the very virtues that had made capitalism possible in the first place. Capitalism, as Max Weber said, depends on the Puritan virtues of hard work, thrift and deferred gratification. But modern consumerism was stimulating the appetite for instant gratification and irrational self-expression, Mr Bell worried. The Protestant ethic was being destroyed by the shopping mall and the counter-culture.

This argument is not watertight. Despite Mr Bell's cultural contradictions and Karl Marx's economic contradictions, capitalism is still going strong. In *Bobos in Paradise* David Brooks, a *New York Times* columnist, argued that a cocktail of bourgeois virtues and bohemian values can prove economically invigorating. Some of the most successful companies in recent years have been founded by such un-Puritanical figures as Sir Richard Branson (Virgin), Steve Jobs (Apple) and Ben Cohen and Jerry Greenfield (Ben & Jerry's). High-tech companies such as Google have no difficulty in combining the profit motive with the ethos of a campus. But in one area Mr Bell was prescient: he worried that consumerism was encouraging people to borrow more money than they could reasonably hope to repay.

He was even more prescient about what might be called "the cultural contradictions of the welfare state". This was the subject of passionate debate in the pages of The Public Interest, a journal he co-founded in 1965 with another poor-boy-made-good, Irving Kristol. The welfare state cannot last unless someone creates the wealth to pay for it. But interest groups demand ever more from the state, and politicians jostle to promise more goodies. As the welfare state expands, it can eventually undermine people's willingness to take risks or look after themselves.

Different strokes for different folks

One of Mr Bell's most provocative insights ran throughout his work. This was the idea that, contrary to what economic determinists such as Marx said, different "realms" of society could operate according to different principles. (Always wary of the neoconservative label that Kristol embraced with such enthusiasm, Mr Bell described himself as a "socialist in economics, a liberal in politics and a conservative in culture".) Capitalism might coexist just as happily with Chinese authoritarianism as with American democracy, he reckoned. In this, one hopes that the great polymath was wrong.

February 2011

The guru of the bottom of the pyramid

C.K. Prahalad's death on April 16th 2010 deprived the world of a great management thinker

COIMBATORE KRISHNARAO PRAHALAD, universally known as C.K., was the most creative management thinker of his generation. He revolutionised thinking on two big subjects, business strategy and economic development, and made a significant contribution to a third, innovation. His admirers were legion, including bosses of some of the world's biggest companies, heads of NGOs and founders of scrappy start-ups.

Mr Prahalad burst onto the management scene with two path-breaking articles in *Harvard Business Review*, "Strategic Intent" (1989) and "The Core Competence of the Corporation" (1990), and a bestselling book, *Competing for the Future* (1996), all co-written with his former pupil, Gary Hamel. "Core competence" remains one of the most frequently reprinted articles ever published by *Harvard Business Review*.

Mr Prahalad shifted the focus of strategic thinking dramatically. He believed firms should seek not simply to position themselves well within their existing markets but to capitalise on their advantages to redefine markets in their favour. That, he argued, involves identifying and developing strengths, such as logistics or miniaturisation, that cannot easily be imitated by competitors. Firms should then "stretch" those skills to the maximum, setting themselves ambitious and industry-transforming goals, and using those goals to galvanise their workers. He cited a long list of successful Japanese companies, such as Sony, Canon and Komatsu, which had done just that.

Mr Prahalad was particularly struck by the ability of these firms to harness the ideas of their humbler employees. And, later in his career, he became increasingly fascinated by innovation. He argued that company-centric innovation was giving way to "co-creation", in which firms collaborate with their customers and business allies. He also shifted his attention to the legion of small businesses that were redefining the corporate world.

Mr Prahalad's work on strategy and innovation turned him into a superstar. He sat on the board of several prominent companies, including Hindustan Unilever and Pearson (which is a part-owner of *The Economist*), and worked as a consultant for others, including AT&T, Citigroup, Oracle and Philips. He subjected these corporate titans to often coruscating questions about their ability to "compete for the future". He commanded huge speaking fees and lived in grand houses in Michigan and California.

But his native India always tugged at Mr Prahalad's heartstrings. He was a leading member of Indus Entrepreneurs, a self-help group for Indian entrepreneurs. He was haunted by the contrast between the rich world he inhabited and the poor world he had grown up in. This led him to veer off in a radically new direction – and to produce perhaps his most thought-provoking book. *The Fortune at the Bottom of the Pyramid: Eradicating Poverty Through Profits* (2004) was a counterblast against two types of intellectual laziness: that of corporate titans who were ignoring the bulk of humanity and that of humanitarians who regarded profit as a dirty word. He argued that the world's poor represented trillions of dollars' worth of pent-up spending power. And he demonstrated that a legion of innovative companies in the developing world, including several in his native India, were learning how to turn these people into paying customers.

The book proved to be perfectly timed. Companies were waking up to the fact that technological innovation and economic reform were opening up new markets in poorer countries. Firms from those countries were growing in confidence. And academics were recognising the limits of their state-sponsored view of development. Mr Prahalad was lionised in the emerging markets, particularly in India, and hailed by corporate philanthropists, notably Bill Gates. The United Nations gave him a seat on its commission on the private sector and development.

What made Mr Prahalad such a creative thinker? And why was he able to keep reinventing himself when his fellow gurus were happy to trot out the same ideas for ever-rising lecture fees? For all his success, he was an outsider in the American-dominated world of management theory. He was one of nine children of one of Chennai's leading judges and Sanskrit scholars, and spent a formative period in his youth working for Union Carbide, an American chemicals firm which later became infamous for the deadliest industrial accident in history, at a factory in India.

This outsider's view went hand in hand with intellectual restlessness. Mr Prahalad invariably worked with a collaborator and never wrote more than two articles on the same subject. This gave his work an unfinished air. He did not revisit the idea of "core competences" in the light of the poor performance of some of the Japanese Godzillas he once worshipped, or the idea of "stretch" in the wake of the epidemic of over-leveraging. Nor did he provide a satisfactory reply to critics who argued that the real promise of emerging markets lay in the middle of the pyramid.

Preaching, not practising

This impatience led to one of the few failures of Mr Prahalad's otherwise gravity-defying career. In 2000 he co-founded a software company, Praja, which was meant to act as a test bed for his ideas, particularly his commitment to bringing information to ordinary people. Instead, it ate up millions of his own dollars and was sold off two years later. He concluded that he was no good at the "blocking and tackling" that fills most managers' days.

But then Mr Prahalad's core competence lay in big ideas rather than in dotting the "i"s and crossing the "t"s. He taught the world's biggest companies to think of themselves anew, as a "portfolio of competencies" rather than as a "portfolio of businesses". He taught everyone to see the developing world not as an also-ran but as a vortex of innovation and creativity. The world of management theory has more than its fair share of charlatans, but C.K. Prahalad was the genuine article.

April 2010

Think different

Clay Christensen lays down some rules for innovators. But can innovation be learned?

INNOVATION IS TODAY'S EQUIVALENT of the Holy Grail. Rich-world governments see it as a way of staving off stagnation. Poor governments see it as a way of speeding up growth. And businesspeople everywhere see it as the key to survival.

Which makes Clay Christensen the closest thing we have to Sir Galahad. In 1997 Mr Christensen, a knight of Harvard Business School, revolutionised the study of the subject with *The Innovator's Dilemma*, a book that popularised the term "disruptive innovation". In 2011 he published a study, *The Innovator's DNA*, co-written with Jeff Dyer and Hal Gregersen, which tries to take us inside the minds of successful innovators. How do they go about their business? How do they differ from regular suits? And what can companies learn from their mental habits?

Mr Christensen and his colleagues list five habits of mind that characterise disruptive innovators: associating, questioning, observing, networking and experimenting. Innovators excel at connecting seemingly unconnected things. Marc Benioff got the idea for Salesforce.com by looking at enterprise software through the prism of online businesses such as Amazon and eBay. Why were software companies flogging cumbersome products in the form of CD-ROMs rather than as flexible services over the internet? Salesforce.com is now worth $19 billion.

These creative associations often come from broadening your experience. Mr Benioff had his lucrative epiphany while on sabbatical – swimming with dolphins, he says. Joe Morton, co-founder of XANGO, got the idea for a new health drink when he tasted mangosteen fruit in Malaysia. Mr Christensen and co reckon that businesspeople are 35% more likely to sprout a new idea if they have lived in a foreign country (a rather precise statistic). But this is not a recipe for just hanging loose: IDEO, an innovation consultancy, argues that the best innovators are "T-shaped" – they need to have depth in one area as well as breadth in lots.

Innovators are constantly asking why things aren't done differently. William Hunter, the founder of Angiotech Pharmaceuticals, asked doctors why they didn't cover the stents they use in heart operations with drugs to reduce the amount of scar tissue (which accounts for 20% of rejections). David Neeleman, the founder of JetBlue and Azul, wondered why people treated airline tickets like cash, freaking out when they lose them, whereas customers could instead be given an electronic code?

This taste for questions is linked to a talent for observation. Corey Wride came up with the idea for Movie Mouth, a company that uses popular films to teach foreign languages, when he was working in Brazil. He noticed that the best English speakers had picked it up from film stars, not school teachers. But people without a flair for languages find the "Brad Pitt" method tricky – actors speak too fast. So Mr Wride invented a computer program that allows users to slow films down, hear explanations of various idioms and even speak the actors' lines for them.

For all their reputation as misfits, innovators tend to be great networkers. But they hang around gabfests to pick up ideas, not to win contracts. Michael Lazaridis, the founder of Research in Motion, says he had the idea for the BlackBerry at a trade show, when someone told him how Coca-Cola machines used wireless technology to signal that they needed refilling. Kent Bowen has turned CPS Technologies into one of the world's fizziest ceramics companies by encouraging his employees to network with scientists who are confronted with similar problems in different fields: for example, the company eliminated troublesome ice crystals by talking to experts on freezing sperm (really).

Innovators are also inveterate experimenters, who fiddle with both their products and their business models. Jeff Bezos, the founder of Amazon, now sells e-readers and rents out computer power and data storage (by one estimate a quarter of small and medium-sized companies in Silicon Valley use the company's cloud). These experiments are frequently serendipitous. IKEA never planned to base its business on self-assembly. But then a marketing manager discovered that the best way to get some furniture back into a lorry, after a photo-shoot, was to take its legs off, and a new business model was born.

Listen to mommy

Messrs Christensen, Dyer and Gregersen argue that companies that have the highest "innovation premiums" (calculated by looking at the proportion of their market value that cannot be accounted for by their current products) display the same five habits of mind as individual innovators. They work hard to recruit creative people. (Mr Bezos asks job applicants to tell him about something they have invented.) They work equally hard at stimulating observation and questioning. Keyence Corporation, a Japanese maker of automation devices for factories, requires its salespeople to spend hours watching its customers' production lines. Procter & Gamble and Google have found that job swaps provoke useful questions: the Googlers were stunned that P&G did not invite "mommy bloggers" – women who write popular blogs on child-rearing – to attend its press conferences.

For all their insistence that innovation can be learned, Mr Christensen and co produce a lot of evidence that the disruptive sort requires genius. Nearly all the world's most innovative companies are run by megaminds who set themselves hubristic goals such as "putting a ding in the universe" (Steve Jobs). During Mr Jobs's first tenure at Apple, the company's innovation premium was 37%. In 1985–98, when Mr Jobs was elsewhere, the premium fell to minus 30%. When Mr Jobs returned, the premium rose to 52%. The innovator's DNA is rare, alas. And unlike Mr Jobs's products, it is impossible to clone.

August 2011

Built to last

Jim Collins has stayed at the top by practising what he preaches

WHY DO SOME COMPANIES FLOURISH for decades while others wither and die? Jim Collins got his start as a management guru puzzling about corporate longevity. Given that Mr Collins has remained at the top of his profession for almost two decades, it is worth applying the same question to him.

How has he produced one bestseller after another? His latest book, *Great by Choice*, is piled high in every bookstore. A previous one, *Good to Great*, sold more than 4 million copies. And how has he achieved such oracular influence over bosses? In 2009, for example, Akio Toyoda, the president of Toyota, stunned the car industry by announcing that he had been reading Mr Collins's *How the Mighty Fall* and had concluded that his company was in the fourth of Mr Collins's five stages of decline.

Part of the answer lies in timing. *Built to Last* (1994) was a counterblast to the craze for ripping firms apart and "re-engineering" them. *Good to Great* (2001) was an antidote to the despair that gripped America in the wake of September 11th 2001 and the dotcom bust. *How the Mighty Fall* (2009) appeared as Lehman Brothers disintegrated and General Motors faced bankruptcy.

Another part of the answer lies in Mr Collins's mastery of the dark arts of the management guru. He bases his arguments on mountains of data. His recent books come with several appendices in which he discusses his methodology and challenges possible objections. But he also produces an entire lexicon of – often cringe-making – buzzwords. Mr Collins's favourites include "big hairy audacious goals", "the hedgehog concept", "the flywheel effect" and "level-five leaders". (Don't ask.)

His central message, which has remained the same through global booms and recessions, is admirably humdrum. He seeks to describe, in detail, how great bosses run their companies. After decades of minute observation, he concludes that hard work and perseverance matter more than genius. His heroes are self-effacing company men who spend years patiently building their organisations, rather than self-promoting egomaniacs who leap from fad to fad and firm to firm. In essence, Mr Collins is repackaging the universal message of self-help literature. Everybody can be successful, he argues, so long as they stick to a set of demanding but not impossible rules. For most company men and women, few of whom are geniuses, this is heartening news.

Mr Collins practises what he preaches. He rejected careers in both academia and consulting in order to focus exclusively on the question of what makes great companies tick. He moved back to his home town of Boulder, Colorado, collected a group of helpers who shared his fascination and set about producing a new book every four or five years. On a spreadsheet Mr Collins religiously logs how much time he spends on creative work, and how much on mundane tasks. He applies the same relentless determination to his hobby, mountain climbing, as he does to writing. He once climbed El Capitan, in Yosemite, in 24 hours – a feat that takes most experienced climbers three days.

His most recent book, *Great by Choice*, co-written with Morten Hansen, looks at how America's most successful companies (ie, companies that have outperformed the stockmarket average for their industry by a factor of ten) have dealt with turbulence and chaos. Mr Collins studies an era, 1972–2002, that might seem calm compared with today (he likes to study decades' worth of solid data). But he has chosen his companies from businesses such as information technology, drugs and airlines, which all suffered from extreme disruption.

Mr Collins challenges some common beliefs. Do turbulent times call for bold and risk-loving leaders, as so many people think? Probably not. Most of Mr Collins's leaders are risk-averse to the point of paranoia. Bill Gates hung a picture of Henry Ford in his office to remind people that even geniuses can mess up, as Ford did in later life. Andy Grove, a co-founder of Intel, was constantly looking for "the black cloud in the silver lining".

A second myth that Mr Collins punctures is that innovation is the only virtue that counts. Mr Collins's companies were usually "one fad behind" the market. Southwest Airlines was almost a carbon copy of a pioneer that later stumbled, Pacific Southwest Airlines. Intel dominates the chip market because it delivers products efficiently, not because it generates original ideas. (Mr Grove kept a McDonald's hamburger box on his desk, with the logo McIntel, to remind himself of this.)

Good to great to … Fannie Mae?

Mr Collins's love of vanilla virtues is as refreshing as a bowl of ice cream. Other gurus who encourage companies to tear themselves apart in the name of "transformation" have caused terrible harm. Few companies have suffered much from trying to be more methodical. Yet it is hard to read Mr Collins's latest work without feeling doubts. Are his conclusions as reliable as he implies? Some of the companies that he has celebrated over the years – Hewlett-Packard and Motorola in *Built to Last* and Circuit City and Fannie Mae in *Good to Great* – have fallen from grace. Circuit City, an electronics retailer, went bust. Fannie Mae, a mortgage giant backed by the American government, is worse than bust, having burned up tens of billions of dollars of taxpayers' cash. Mr Collins is allergic to egomaniacs, but how else can you describe the late Steve Jobs, perhaps the most successful businessman of his era?

This is not to say that Mr Collins's insights are worthless; merely that they are less robust than he suggests. Most business books would profit from a bit more rigour. Mr Collins's might profit from a bit more willingness to admit that, like all management gurus, he is dealing in clever hunches rather than built-to-last scientific discoveries.

November 2011

The *Breaking Bad* school

The best show on television is also a first-rate primer on business

THERE ARE OBVIOUS REASONS for watching *Breaking Bad*: for once the Hollywood hype surrounding the television series is justified. But there is also a less obvious reason: it is one of the best studies available of the dynamics of modern business. A Harvard MBA will set you back $90,000 (plus two years' lost income). You can buy a deluxe edition of all five seasons of *Breaking Bad*, complete with a plastic money barrel, for $209.99, or a regular edition for less than $80.

Breaking Bad, whose finale aired on September 29th, takes place in a recession-ravaged America where most people are struggling to get by on stagnant incomes but a handful of entrepreneurs live like kings. The hero, Walter White, is a high-school chemistry teacher with a second job in a car wash. When he is diagnosed with cancer he is also shaken out of his lethargy: he decides to go into the highly lucrative methamphetamine business to pay for his cancer treatment and leave his family a nest-egg.

Mr White's subsequent career embraces both sides of the entrepreneurial life: dramatic success and equally dramatic failure. He quickly discovers his inner businessman. "Do you know what would happen if I suddenly decided to stop going into work?" he asks his wife. "A business big enough that it could be listed on the NASDAQ goes belly up." But he then discovers that running a big business is rather different from launching a start-up – and, like so many before him, becomes the victim of the compromises that he has made in his entrepreneurial salad days.

The first lesson from *Breaking Bad* is that high-growth businesses come from unexpected places. Mr White uses his skills as a chemist to revolutionise the slapdash meth industry (he was a researcher before becoming a teacher). He is not alone. William Thorndike of Harvard Business School (HBS) studied eight bosses whose firms outperformed the S&P 500 index more than 20-fold over their business careers. He found that they were all outsiders who brought fresh perspectives on their industries. Clayton Christensen, also at HBS, argues that great entrepreneurs look at the world through a "marginal lens". It so happens that Bill Gates, a university drop-out working in a then marginal bit of the computer industry, started Microsoft in Mr White's home-town, Albuquerque, before moving to Seattle.

Three things help our chemistry teacher turn an insight into a flourishing business. The first is huge ambition. He is not in the "meth business" or the "money business", he says. He is in the "empire business". The second is product obsession. Other dealers might peddle "Mexican shoe-scrapings" on the ground that addicts care little about quality. He produces the king of meth, so pure that it turns blue, and would rather destroy an entire batch than let an inferior product be traded under his brand. The third is partnerships and alliances. He spots talent in a former pupil turned drug-dealer, Jesse Pinkman, and forms a strong working relationship with him. He also contracts distribution to a succession of local gangs so that he can concentrate on the higher-value-added part of the business: cooking and quality control.

Again Mr White is not alone. There is a reason people talk of business empires: tycoons like Rupert Murdoch are latter-day Caesars, fixated on conquering new territories. Steve Jobs eventually outcompeted Microsoft because he was so painstaking in perfecting Apple's products. Partnerships are the heart of a striking number of businesses: whether Larry Page and Sergey Brin or Warren Buffett and Charlie Munger – or indeed Goldman and Sachs or Hewlett and Packard. As for contracting out distribution, it is de rigueur for high-growth start-ups.

Breaking Bad is even sharper on the forces of destruction in business. Mr White's relationship with his partner falls apart. He is regularly in conflict with his distributors. And he sucks at work-life balance. Being in the meth business gives a unique twist to all these problems. His relationship with his partner is shattered by his leaving one of Mr Pinkman's girlfriends to die of an overdose and poisoning a subsequent girlfriend's son. His relationship with his best distributor is undermined by the man's scheme to engineer him out of the supply chain by learning his skills and killing him. His work-life balance is complicated by his reluctance to tell his wife he has become a meth dealer.

The big lie, and the hubris

Yet these are twists on common themes. The breakdown of relations between business partners, thanks to the acids of ego, greed and paranoia, is a perennial business problem: think of the tension between Michael Eisner and Michael Ovitz at Disney or the noisy implosions of the Beatles or dozens of other pop groups. Strained relations between companies and distributors are common: in one survey 80% of executives said that they had worries about "exclusivity, control and resource protection". In one of his books Mr Christensen notes that whenever he has attended a university reunion he was struck by how many of his contemporaries suffered from terrible work-life balance: "Their personal relationships had begun to deteriorate, even as their professional prospects blossomed." Mr White is even typical in telling himself the "big lie" that he is doing everything he does for his family.

Mr White's biggest failing is also a common one in business: hubris. The more successful he becomes, the more invulnerable he feels. The more rules he breaks, the more righteous he feels. And the more wealth he accumulates, the more he wants. An impressive volume of social-science studies suggests that leaders are more willing to break the rules than followers. There is no shortage of corporate examples, from Enron to Olympus, to illustrate this. Walter White is a thoroughly odd character: Mr Chips turned Scarface, as the show's creator, Vince Gilligan, puts it. But he also holds a worrying mirror to the business world.

September 2013

PART 2

Forces of disruption

An emerging challenge

Antoine van Agtmael thinks that firms in the rich world have
not fully digested the rise of the emerging markets

EMERGING MARKETS have been exceedingly kind to Antoine van
Agtmael. His company, Emerging Markets Management, controls
some $13 billion-worth of investments in them. His name guarantees
him access to their most powerful politicians and businessmen. He is
such a respected figure in America that he has been made chairman
of the National Public Radio Foundation, the local equivalent of being
given a seat in the House of Lords. This is only as it should be: Mr
van Agtmael was the man who coined the term "emerging markets".

These days the market in business catchphrases is saturated. Every
business writer wants to produce a rival to *The World is Flat* or *The
Long Tail*. Every management consultancy wants to coin the follow-up
to "re-engineering" or "total quality management". Such famous turns
of phrase are the gurus' equivalent of brands: they burnish their
reputations for original thinking and ensure that they stand out in a
crowd. A brilliant catchphrase can be worth millions in book sales
and speaking fees.

"Emerging markets" is one of those terms that has buried itself
so deeply in our brains that we have no idea that it once represented
a bold challenge to conventional thinking. Before Mr van Agtmael
coined the phrase in 1981 the region was referred to as either "the
third world" or "the developing world".

Bankers regarded the "third world" as little more than the
financial equivalent of a rat hole. The term conjured up images
of "flimsy polyester, cheap toys, rampant corruption, Soviet-style
tractors and flooded rice paddies", as Mr van Agtmael puts it. Western
governments regarded "the developing world" as an object of largesse
– an area that could be rescued from poverty only by a combination
of donations from the rich world and better economic planning by
developing countries' governments.

Mr van Agtmael argues that his idiosyncratic background gave him the wherewithal to challenge conventional thinking. He grew up in the Netherlands. His schoolteachers frequently talked about the country's historical ties with Indonesia. He even owned a few shares in global Dutch giants such as Philips and Unilever. He spent a decade working in the private sector – including a stint at a Thai subsidiary of an American bank, Bankers Trust – before eventually ending up at the World Bank's investment arm, the International Finance Corporation.

He was uncomfortable with the banking industry's contempt for the developing world. (One of his bosses at Bankers Trust once told him, "There are no markets outside the United States.") But he was equally unhappy with the World Bank's obsession with state-driven development. He became an evangelist for the power of private investment to turbocharge growth. But how could you persuade wary bankers to invest in the third world? He had a eureka moment after making an investment pitch to Salomon Brothers: why not replace the depressing-sounding phrases used to describe poorer countries with the more upbeat "emerging markets"?

Almost 30 years later Mr van Agtmael remains as bullish about emerging markets as ever. He has seen the category grow to include formerly closed economies such as China and Vietnam. He has seen emerging-market champions go from welcoming the term as uplifting to rejecting it as condescending. (His publisher in China changed the title of his latest book from *The Emerging-Market Century* to *The World is New*.) Most striking of all, he has seen the developing world start to produce some of the world's biggest and best companies, a legion of giants that are shaking up the West's comfortable assumption that it will continue to lead the world in global reach, technology, design and marketing. Mexico's CEMEX is the largest cement company in America, the second largest in Britain and the third largest in the world. Acer of Taiwan is vying to become the world's second-biggest manufacturer of personal computers. Brazil's Aracruz is the world's largest and most profitable producer of pulp for paper and tissues. He even cites Russia's Gazprom, which controls more gas reserves than all the West's big oil firms combined.

Just as the West once underestimated the potential of emerging markets, now it underestimates the power of the region's corporate champions, Mr van Agtmael believes. These companies are no longer content to be mere followers. They have built global brands: South Korea's Samsung is one of the world's best known makers of electronic goods (Mr van Agtmael still classifies South Korea as an emerging market), for example, and Mexico's Grupo Modelo produces one of the most recognised brands of beer in the world, Corona.

Emerging and upstaging

Reconciling the rich world to the rise of these powerhouses will be as difficult as integrating the third world into the global market, Mr van Agtmael argues. He knows as well as anybody that global trade can benefit all involved – that the emerging world's gains do not have to be paid for by the rich world's losses. Where Samuel Huntington predicted a "clash of civilisations", he hopes for a "creative collision" that will lead to innovation. He points out that some of the most fraught economic rivalries in recent history – the space race of the 1960s and Japan's rise in the 1980s – provoked creative rather than defensive responses.

But he is nevertheless worried about the sirens of protectionism. Mr van Agtmael points out that America and its allies have been on top of the world for so long that it will take a huge psychological adjustment to treat the likes of India and China as economic equals (his office has a spectacular view over the centre of Washington, DC, with its many monuments to America's glorious past). He also thinks that most people have no idea how serious the challenge from the emerging world has become. Perhaps the very phrase "emerging markets" may end up blinding people to the fact that many of these markets have already emerged.

April 2010

Mall of the masses

The traders in Dubai's Dragon Mart are kitting out the emerging world's new middle class

DUBAI BOASTS SOME of the world's most spectacular shopping malls, including the Mall of the Emirates with its indoor ski slope and the Dubai Mall with its 33,000-creature aquarium. But for anyone with an eye to the future the most interesting mall is one that few tourists visit: 20 minutes' drive from downtown, through scrubland and past abandoned building projects.

The embellishments on the Dragon Mart are feeble by Dubai standards. The architects did try to make the building look like a dragon; at least, they gave it some curves and stuck scalelike spikes into the roof. There is also a dragon coiled around a giant golden globe near the main entrance. Yet the mart is resolutely utilitarian. The most colourful decorations are giant Chinese flags. The first thing the visitor encounters upon entering the dragon's mouth is the Zhong Dong Sanitary Ware Centre, "the largest sanitary ware centre in the Middle East".

But what the mart lacks in bling it makes up for in size and vitality. Dragon Mart is the biggest Chinese shopping mall outside the Chinese mainland: it is 1.2km (0.75 miles) long and contains 3,950 shops. Here you can buy everything from mock Roman pillars to "development cream for the intimate parts of man", tablet computers to mobile phones shaped like handguns. Girls in tight jeans and T-shirts sell hijabs and prayer mats. Chinese immigrants who cannot speak a word of Arabic flog talking Korans: you trace a pen over the Arabic words and a computerised voice renders them in any one of a dozen languages.

Both the shops that fill the mall and the products that fill the shops bear unfamiliar brand names. Most of the world's malls are full of things made by Chinese hands but designed and branded by Western brains. The Dragon Mart provides an insight into a different world: of Chinese-owned companies that are injecting their cut-price products into the world's commercial bloodstream, often via the Dragon Marts springing up across the Middle East and Africa. Companies such as JZX Double Goats Grinding Wheel Manufacturing (which sells building machinery), Snow White Princess Trading (carpets), Yongde Shoes and Wen Ling Better Shoes (which respectively sell wallpaper and handbags). Or innumerable electronics companies that sell cut-price gadgets bearing names such as Wintouch and Titanium.

The mart is dedicated to efficiency and cheapness. The China Ocean Shipping Company (COSCO) has a huge logistics centre next to the mall allowing new goods to be brought straight off the ship from China and wholesale purchases to be exported anywhere in the world. The workers who man the stores live in the Chinese section of the International City that abuts the mart.

The hideous plastic tat of the East

The customers are wholesalers and bargain-hunting migrant workers. This is the mall where the people who build and maintain Dubai shop. They include a fast-growing Chinese population. The bargains are enticing – a digital camera for 99 dirhams ($27) or a treadmill for 700 dirhams ($190) if you pay the advertised price; less if you haggle.

It is easy to make fun of Dragon Mart. It sells some of the most hideous things devised by man – polyester Persian carpets, plastic executive desks and plastic gilded bookshelves. Many companies specialise in producing cheap knock-offs of Juicy Couture or Barcelona Football Club paraphernalia. Others peddle slimming soap or slimming navel magnets or Touch Me Please Breast Enlarging Cream. It is hard to see Boil Fashion becoming a challenger to Zara or Zhejiang Best Plastic becoming a global leader in its signature product, wallpaper.

Yet it would be foolish to dismiss these frugal Chinese manufacturers. They cater for the world's most exciting group of consumers, the emerging middle class, a group that McKinsey, a consultancy, estimates includes two billion people who spend $6.9 trillion a year. These people cannot afford to shop in the Mall of the Emirates; yet they are greedy for the trappings of middle-class life. Many of the goods displayed, like children's desks and patio furniture, represent a dream of upward mobility. Plastic tat to Western eyes may be luxuries to the offspring of slum-dwellers.

The Dragon Mart is evidence of the symbiotic relationship between state and entrepreneurial capitalism. It is tempting to think of these as polar opposites: the more you have of one the less you have of another. But the mart suggests they can advance together. It is owned by a local state-owned company, Nakheel, a subsidiary of Dubai World, and fed with daily shipments by a Chinese state-owned company, COSCO. But the mart is home to thousands of independent "bamboo capitalists", its Chinese retailers.

The Dragon Mart is also evidence of the rebirth of one of the world's oldest trading routes, the silk road. The old silk road specialised in luxuries like silk. The new silk road specialises in everything, albeit with a stress on plastic. Dubai boasts two of the most important nodes on this road: the world's ninth-biggest container port and one of its busiest airports. It is also building a new airport close to the port which will reduce the time it takes to transport goods from port to airport from seven hours to an hour.

The trading route will increasingly bypass Europe and take goods from China to Africa. So too the products: rather than providing labour for Western companies, the rising Chinese companies will produce their own designs. Some of the firms hawking goods in the Dragon Mart, such as Haier in kitchen goods and Go Baby in prams, have already gone global. Others will follow.

These new global champions will have no shortage of space in Dubai. The builders have already started work on a second mart right next to the first that will provide another 175,000 square metres of space and 4,500 parking spaces. The dragon's coils encircling the world are getting tighter by the day.

April 2012

Asian innovation

Frugal ideas are spreading from East to West

THE TATA NANO, the world's cheapest car, became a symbol before the first one rolled off the production line in 2009. The Tata group, India's most revered conglomerate, hyped it as the embodiment of a revolution. Frugal innovation would put consumer products, of which a $2,000 car was merely a foretaste, within reach of ordinary Indians and Chinese. Asian engineers would reimagine Western products with all the unnecessary frills stripped out. The cost savings would be so huge that frugal ideas would conquer the world. The Nano would herald India's arrival just as the Toyota once heralded Japan's.

Alas, the miracle car was dogged with problems from the first. Protesting farmers forced Tata Motors to move production out of one Indian state and into another. Early sales failed to catch fire, but some of the cars did, literally. Rural customers showed little desire to shift from trucks to cars. The Nano's failure to live up to the hype raises a bigger question. Is frugal innovation being oversold? Can Western companies relax?

Two books – *Reverse Innovation* by Vijay Govindarajan and Chris Trimble, and *Jugaad Innovation* by Navi Radjou, Jaideep Prabhu and Simone Ahuja – suggest that the answer to both questions is No. Mr Govindarajan, of Tuck Business School at Dartmouth College, has advised General Electric on frugal innovation and co-written a path-breaking article on the subject with GE's boss, Jeff Immelt. *Jugaad Innovation* is the most comprehensive book yet to appear on the subject (*jugaad* is a Hindi word meaning a clever improvisation). The books show that frugal innovation is flourishing across the emerging world, despite the gurus' failure to agree on a term to describe it. They also argue convincingly that it will change rich countries, too.

Multinationals are beginning to take ideas developed in (and for) the emerging world and deploy them in the West. Harman, an American company that makes infotainment systems for cars, developed a new system for emerging markets, dubbed "Saras", the

Sanskrit word for "flexible", using a simpler design and Indian and Chinese engineers. In 2009 Harman enrolled Toyota as a customer. GE's Vscan, a portable ultrasound device that allows doctors to "see" inside patients, was developed in China and is now a hit in rich and poor countries alike. (Mr Immelt believes that these devices will become as indispensable as stethoscopes.) Wal-Mart, which created "small mart stores" to compete in Argentina, Brazil and Mexico, is reimporting the idea to the United States.

The standard worry among Western firms is that this strategy will cannibalise the existing market for expensive technology. Why buy a $10,000 device if the same firm makes a slightly simpler one for $1,000? This is too pessimistic. GE opened up a new market among doctors for its cheap electrocardiograms; previously only hospitals could afford the things. Besides, standing still is not an option. Whether or not Western firms sell frugal products in the West, Asian firms will.

India's Mahindra & Mahindra sells lots of small tractors to American hobby farmers, filling John Deere with fear. China's Haier has undercut Western competitors in a wide range of products, from air conditioners and washing machines to wine coolers. Haier sold a wine cooler for half the price of the industry leader. Within two years, it had grabbed 60% of the American market. Some Western companies are turning to emerging markets first to develop their products. Diagnostics for All, a Massachusetts-based start-up that has developed paper-based diagnostic tests the size of a postage stamp, chose to commercialise its idea in the developing world so as to circumvent America's hideously slow approval process for medical devices.

Entrepreneurs everywhere are seizing on the idea of radical cost-cutting. Zack Rosenburg and Liz McCartney are rethinking house-building from the ground up; they hope to reduce the cost by 15% and the construction time by 30%. Vivian Fonseca collaborated in the development of a system for sending SMS messages to poor and elderly diabetics to help them control their disease. Jane Chen, the boss of Embrace, sells low-cost infant warmers for premature babies in India and several emerging markets.

This trend will surely accelerate. The West is doomed to a long period of austerity, as the middle class is squeezed and governments curb spending. Some 50 million Americans lack medical insurance; 60 million lack regular bank accounts. Such people are crying out for new ways to save money. A growing number of Western universities are taking the frugal message to heart (at least when it comes to thinking about things other than their own tuition fees). Santa Clara University has a Frugal Innovation Lab. Stanford University has an (unfrugally named) Entrepreneurial Design for Extreme Affordability programme. Cambridge University has an Inclusive Design programme. Even the Obama administration has an Office of Social Innovation and Civic Participation to encourage grassroots entrepreneurs in health care and energy.

Fighting frugality with frugality

Globalisation is forcing Western firms to provide more value for money. Logitech, an American firm, had to create a top-class wireless mouse for bottom-of-the-range prices when it took on Rapoo, a Chinese company, in China. John Deere had to do the same with its small tractors when it took on Mahindra in India. At the same time, globalisation gives Western firms more tools. Some are building innovation centres in the emerging world. PepsiCo, for example, established one in India in 2010. Some Western firms routinely fish in a global brain pool. Renault-Nissan asked its engineers in France, India and Japan to compete to come up with ideas for cutting costs. The Indians won. The Tata Nano may not have changed the world, but frugal innovation will.

March 2012

Getting on the treadmill

A South African company has some bright ideas for promoting health

THE THORNIEST PROBLEM facing the health-care profession is how to strike the right balance between promoting health and curing illness. As is routinely pointed out, prevention is better than cure – and cheaper too. But the forces ranged against this benign cliché are formidable. The sick require immediate treatment. The medical profession values surgeons more than dieticians. And most of us are greedy and short-sighted: why forgo the instant ecstasy of a Mars bar, or the joy of unprotected sex, when the rewards of restraint are so distant?

This is one reason why it is so hard to curb health-care inflation. Insurance premiums have surged 9% in America since 2010. In emerging economies, too, greater prosperity means people are eating more and slouching behind desks instead of sweating in fields. So these countries are increasingly suffering from rich people's illnesses, such as heart disease and diabetes. The World Health Organisation expects the incidence of such non-communicable diseases to rise by 17% over the next decade.

Some policymakers are reaching for a new tool: behavioural economics. Behavioural economists are mapping out ways to "nudge" people to drop the cream pie and chew an apple instead. Cass Sunstein, the co-author of *Nudge: Improving Decisions About Health, Wealth and Happiness*, works in Barack Obama's White House. David Cameron, Britain's prime minister, has established a "nudge unit" in Downing Street. Mr Obama's health-care law encourages employers to offer wellness programmes.

At the same time technology is making it easier for people to look after themselves. Monitoring equipment is becoming cheaper and easier to use: Philips has developed an app which uses the camera in an iPad2 to measure heart and respiration rates. You can keep your health records up to date with programmes such as Microsoft's

HealthVault. You can also use social media to shame yourself into shaping up. It is remarkable how much more effective a new year's resolution to lose weight is if you make it public – and agree to a forfeit if you fail.

America is beginning to embrace nudges. Some of the biggest health insurers are introducing incentives of one kind or another. Most reward people for having their vital signs tested and hitting goals such as lowering blood pressure or burning off flab. Some have added interesting bells and whistles to this basic formula. Aetna offers discounts for gym equipment and medical devices that can be used at home. Anthem provides e-mail access to a health coach. SonicBoom uses a combination of high-tech and peer pressure: members can monitor vital signs with tiny devices attached to their shoes and join groups such as Weight Warriors. A new type of health-care firm helps companies design incentive systems. Examples include IncentOne and Anderson Performance Improvement, both based in America.

Perhaps surprisingly, the most interesting incentives have been developed in an emerging economy: South Africa. The Discovery group, based in Johannesburg, has crafted a programme called Vitality that applies the "air miles" model to health care. You earn points by exercising, buying healthy food or hitting certain targets. You rise through various levels, from blue to gold, as you accumulate points (rewards are adjusted to your starting level of fitness to give everybody a chance of making progress). And you are given a mixture of short- and long-term rewards ranging from reduced premiums to exotic holidays.

Discovery has formed alliances with a host of companies to provide rewards linked to your "vitality level". Pick 'n' Pay, a South African grocery chain, provides discounts of up to 25% on 10,000 "healthy foods". Airlines such as Kulula offer discounted flights. Discovery can measure whether people actually go to the gym, rather than just join, by swiping their membership cards. It says it has solid evidence that participation in the programme more than pays for the rewards: active participants are less likely to fall ill and, if they do, they spend a shorter time in hospital.

This model has taken Discovery from "one man and a desk" in 1992 to become South Africa's largest health insurer, with 5,000 employees. The company is now entering new markets. It has formed partnerships with Humana, an American health insurer, and Prudential, a British company. It has also taken a 20% stake in Ping An Health, one of China's largest private health insurers. The model has even been stretched to other industries, including a credit card that offers discounts linked to well-being and car insurance that offers cheaper petrol to people who drive safely (a telemetric device installed in your car monitors aggressive driving, like harsh acceleration or sharp cornering).

Medical necessity

The Discovery story is another reminder of how quickly new ideas are starting to flow out of emerging markets. In the past 30 years Indian firms have become experts in processing information and Chinese firms masters of frugal manufacturing. Discovery may be a harbinger of another wave which challenges the West's lead in health care and other sophisticated services. Adrian Gore, Discovery's founder and chief executive, says the company was forced to concentrate on prevention because there are so few doctors in South Africa to effect cures: even those with private insurance share one GP between 1,000 people.

The Discovery story also poses a challenge to emerging markets. How can they apply the same spirit of innovation to their fledgling welfare states? Since they are building more or less from scratch, they can experiment with public systems, private ones and a mixture of both. Emerging-market governments can learn from Discovery and other firms that are using judicious incentives to nudge people towards sensible behaviour. Their people will be the healthier for it, as will their budgets.

October 2011

The case against globaloney

At last, some sense on globalisation

GEOFFREY CROWTHER, editor of *The Economist* from 1938 to 1956, used to advise young journalists to "simplify, then exaggerate". He might have changed his advice if he had lived to witness the current debate on globalisation. There is a lively discussion about whether it is good or bad. But everybody seems to agree that globalisation is a fait accompli: that the world is flat, if you are a (Tom) Friedmanite, or that the world is run by a handful of global corporations, if you are a (Naomi) Kleinian.

Pankaj Ghemawat of IESE Business School in Spain is one of the few who has kept his head on the subject. For more than a decade he has subjected the simplifiers and exaggerators to a barrage of statistics. He has now set out his case – that we live in an era of semi-globalisation at most – in a single volume, *World 3.0*, that should be read by anyone who wants to understand the most important economic development of our time.

Mr Ghemawat points out that many indicators of global integration are surprisingly low. Only 2% of students are at universities outside their home countries; and only 3% of people live outside their country of birth. Only 7% of rice is traded across borders. Only 7% of directors of S&P 500 companies are foreigners – and, according to a study a few years ago, less than 1% of all American companies have any foreign operations. Exports are equivalent to only 20% of global GDP. Some of the most vital arteries of globalisation are badly clogged: air travel is restricted by bilateral treaties and ocean shipping is dominated by cartels.

Far from "ripping through people's lives", as Arundhati Roy, an Indian writer, claims, globalisation is shaped by familiar things, such as distance and cultural ties. Mr Ghemawat argues that two otherwise identical countries will engage in 42% more trade if they share a common language than if they do not, 47% more if both belong to a trading block, 114% more if they have a common currency and 188% more if they have a common colonial past.

What about the "new economy" of free-flowing capital and borderless information? Here Mr Ghemawat's figures are even more striking. Foreign direct investment (FDI) accounts for only 9% of all fixed investment. Less than 20% of venture capital is deployed outside the fund's home country. Only 20% of shares traded on stockmarkets are owned by foreign investors. Less than 20% of internet traffic crosses national borders.

And what about the direction rather than the extent of globalisation? Surely Mr Friedman (author of *The World is Flat*) and company are right about where we are headed even if they exaggerate how far we have got? In fact, today's levels of emigration pale beside those of a century ago, when 14% of Irish-born people and 10% of native Norwegians had emigrated. Back then you did not need visas. Today the world spends $88 billion a year on processing travel documents and in a tenth of the world's countries a passport costs more than a tenth of the average annual income.

That FDI fell from nearly $2 trillion in 2007 to $1 trillion in 2009 can be put down to the global financial crisis. But other trends suggest that globalisation is reversible. Nearly a quarter of North American and European companies shortened their supply chains in 2008 (the effect of Japan's disaster on its partsmakers will surely prompt further shortening). It takes three times as long to process a lorry-load of goods crossing the Canadian-American border as it did before September 11th 2001. Even the internet is succumbing to this pattern of regionalisation, as governments impose a patchwork of local restrictions on content.

Mr Ghemawat also explodes the myth that the world is being taken over by a handful of giant companies. The level of concentration in many vital industries has fallen dramatically since 1950 and remained roughly constant since 1980: 60 years ago two car companies accounted for half of the world's car production, compared with six companies today.

He also refutes the idea that globalisation means homogenisation. The increasing uniformity of cities' skylines worldwide masks growing choice within them, to which even the most global of companies must adjust. McDonald's serves vegetarian burgers in India and spicy ones in Mexico, where Coca-Cola uses cane sugar rather than the corn syrup it uses in America. MTV, which went global on the assumption that "A-lop-bop-a-doo-bop-a-lop-bam-boom" meant the same in every language, now includes five calls to prayer a day in its Indonesian schedules.

Spot the difference

Mr Ghemawat notes that company bosses lead the pack when it comes to overestimating the extent of globalisation. Nokia, for example, spent years trying to break into Japan's big but idiosyncratic mobile-handset market with its rest-of-the-world-beating products before finally conceding defeat. In general companies frequently have more to gain through exploiting national differences – perhaps through arbitrage – than by muscling them aside.

This sober view of globalisation deserves a wide audience. But whether it will get it is another matter. This is partly because *World 3.0* is a much less exciting title than *The World is Flat* or *Jihad vs. McWorld*. And it is partly because people seem to have a natural tendency to overestimate the distance-destroying quality of technology. Go back to the era of dictators and world wars and you can find exactly the same addiction to globaloney. Henry Ford said cars and planes were "binding the world together". Martin Heidegger said that "everything is equally far and equally near". George Orwell got so annoyed by all this that he wrote a blistering attack on all the fashionable talk about the abolition of distance and the disappearance of frontiers – and that was in 1944, when Adolf Hitler was advancing his own unique approach to the flattening of the world.

April 2011

Crazy diamonds

True entrepreneurs find worth in the worthless and possibility in the impossible

ENTREPRENEURSHIP IS THE MODERN-DAY philosopher's stone: a mysterious something that supposedly holds the secret to boosting growth and creating jobs. The G20 countries hold an annual youth-entrepreneurship summit. More than 130 countries celebrate Global Entrepreneurship Week. Business schools offer hugely popular courses on how to become an entrepreneur. Business gurus produce (often contradictory) guides to entrepreneurship: David Gumpert wrote both *How to Really Create a Successful Business Plan* and *Burn Your Business Plan!*.

But what exactly is entrepreneurship (apart from a longer way of saying "enterprise")? And how should governments encourage it? The policymakers are as confused as the gurus. They assume that it must mean new technology; so they try to create new Silicon Valleys. Or that it is about small businesses; so they focus on fostering start-ups. Both assumptions are misleading.

Silicon Valley has certainly been the capital of technology-based entrepreneurship in recent decades. But you do not need to be a geek to be an entrepreneur. George Mitchell, the Texas oilman who pioneered fracking, did as much to change the world as anybody in the Valley. Nor do you need to be a conventional innovator. Miguel Dávila and his colleagues built a huge business by importing the American multiplex cinema into Mexico. Their only innovation, says Mr Dávila, "was putting lime juice and chili sauce on the popcorn instead of butter."

Equally, there is a world of difference between the typical small-business owner (who dreams of opening another shop) and the true entrepreneur (who dreams of changing an entire industry). Jim McCann, the creator of 1-800-flowers.com, is an entrepreneur rather than just a florist because, when he opened his first shop in 1976, he looked at the business "with McDonald's eyes", as he put it, and laboured for years to build the world's biggest flower-delivery business.

These misconceptions matter because they produce lousy policies. The world is littered with high-tech enclaves that fail to flourish. Malaysia's biotech valley has been nicknamed "Valley of the BioGhosts". The world is also full of small-business departments that fail to produce many jobs. The Kauffman Foundation, which researches such matters, has shown that the bulk of new jobs come from a tiny sliver of high-growth companies.

Daniel Isenberg has spent 30 years immersed in the world of entrepreneurship as a (sometimes failed) entrepreneur and venture capitalist as well as an academic (he previously taught at Harvard Business School and is now at nearby Babson College). He has also travelled the world accumulating examples – he is just as interested in Iceland's generic-drug industry as in Silicon Valley's giants. In his book *Worthless, Impossible, and Stupid*, he presents a new definition of entrepreneurship. In essence, entrepreneurs are contrarian value creators. They see economic value where others see heaps of nothing. And they see business opportunities where others see only dead ends.

There are plenty of striking examples of this: Mo Ibrahim, the founder of Celtel, saw the possibility of bringing mobile phones to sub-Saharan Africa when telecoms giants saw only penniless peasants and logistical nightmares. On a trip to Tobago Sean Dimin and his father Michael observed that fishermen were leaving tonnes of fish to rot, so they created a company, Sea to Table, to get the surplus fish to New York restaurants. As a student at Harvard Business School, Will Dean noticed that social media were irrigating a fashion for extreme sports. So he established a company, Tough Mudder, that charges people to subject themselves to pain and humiliation.

Mr Isenberg emphasises that successful contrarians also need the self-confidence to defy conventional wisdom (Mr Dean's professors told him that he was crazy) and the determination to overcome obstacles (it took the Dimins two years to get the fishermen to change their habits). Indeed, some of the best entrepreneurs are distinguished more by their ability to achieve the impossible than by the originality of their thinking. TCS is essentially a Pakistani version of FedEx. But to get it going, Khalid Awan had to overcome "insuperable" problems such as striking deals with the gangs that control the haulage industry and sweet-talking the politicians who can shut a new company at the drop of a hat.

In it for the money

Mr Isenberg has two important bits of advice for policymakers who genuinely want to foster entrepreneurship. First, they should remove barriers to entry, and growth, for all sorts of business, rather than seeking to build particular types of clusters. Second, they should recognise the importance of the profit motive. There has been much fancy talk of "social entrepreneurship" – harnessing enterprise to do good deeds – but in truth the main motivator for entrepreneurs is the chance of making big money. This is what drives people to take huge risks and endure years of hardship. And this is what encourages investors to take a punt on business ideas that, at first sight, look half-crazy.

Politicians and bureaucrats do not just confuse entrepreneurship with things they like – technology, small business – they also fail to recognise that it entails things that set their teeth on edge. Entrepreneurs thrive on inequality: the fabulous wealth they generate in America makes the country more unequal. They also thrive on disruption, which creates losers as well as winners. Joseph Schumpeter once argued that economic progress takes place in "cracks" and "leaps" rather than "infinitesimal small steps" because it is driven by rule-breaking entrepreneurs. It might be nice to think that we could have growth and job-creation without a good deal of Schumpeterian cracking. But, alas, some thoughts really are worthless, impossible and stupid.

July 2013

The wiki way

Two cyber-gurus take a second look at how the internet is changing the world

AFTER KENYA'S DISPUTED ELECTION in 2007 Ory Okolloh, a local lawyer and blogger, kept hearing accounts of atrocities. State media were not interested. Private newspapers lacked the money and manpower to investigate properly. So Ms Okolloh set up a website that allowed anyone with a mobile phone or an internet connection to report outbreaks of violence. She posted eyewitness accounts online and even created maps that showed where the killings and beatings were taking place.

Ms Okolloh has since founded an organisation called Ushahidi, which puts her original idea into practice in various parts of the world. It has helped Palestinians to map the violence in Gaza and Haitians to track the impact of the earthquake that devastated their nation in January 2010. It even helped Washingtonians cope with the "snowmaggedon" that brought their city to a halt in February 2010. Ushahidi's success embodies the principles of wikinomics.

Don Tapscott and Anthony Williams coined the term "wikinomics" in their 2006 tome of that name. Their central insight was that collaboration is getting rapidly cheaper and easier. The web gives amateurs access to world-class communications tools and worldwide markets. It makes it easy for large groups of people who have never met to work together. And it super-charges innovation: crowds of people can develop new ideas faster than isolated geniuses and disseminate them even faster.

Mr Tapscott and Mr Williams have now written a follow-up to their bestseller. They solicited 150 suggestions online for a snappy title. The result, alas, was a bit dull: *Macrowikinomics: Rebooting Business and the World.* But the book is well worth reading, for two reasons.

The first is that four years is an eternity in internet time. The internet has become much more powerful since "Wikinomics" was published. YouTube serves up 2 billion videos a day. Twitterers tweet

750 times a second. Internet traffic is growing by 40% a year. The internet has morphed into a social medium. People post 2.5 billion photos on Facebook every month. More than half of American teens say they are "content creators". And it is not only people who log on to the internet these days. Appliances do, too. Nokia, for example, has produced a prototype of an "ecosensor" phone that can detect and report radiation and pollution.

The second reason is that the internet's effects are more widely felt every day. In *Wikinomics* the authors looked at its impact on particular businesses. In their new book they look at how it is shaking up some of the core institutions of modern society: the media, universities, government and so on. It is a Schumpeterian story of creative destruction.

Two of the most abject victims of wikinomics are the newspaper and music industries. Since 2000, 72 American newspapers have folded. Circulation has fallen by a quarter since 2007. By some measures the music industry is doing even worse: 95% of all music downloads are illegal and the industry that brought the world Elvis and the Beatles is reviled by the young. Why buy newspapers when you can get up-to-the-minute news on the web? Why buy the latest Eminem CD when you can watch him on YouTube for free? Or, as a teenager might put it: what's a CD?

Other industries are just beginning to be transformed by wikinomics. The car industry is a model of vertical integration; yet some entrepreneurs plot its disintegration. Local Motors produces bespoke cars for enthusiasts using a network of 4,500 designers (who compete to produce designs) and dozens of microfactories (which purchase parts on the open market and then assemble them). Universities are some of the most conservative institutions on the planet, but the Massachusetts Institute of Technology has now put all of its courses online. Such a threat to the old way of teaching has doubtless made professors everywhere spit sherry onto the common-room carpet. Yet more than 200 institutions have followed suit.

Wikinomics is even rejuvenating the fusty old state. The Estonian government approved a remarkable attempt to rid the country of unsightly junk: volunteers used GPS devices to locate over 10,000 illegal dumps and then unleashed an army of 50,000 people to clean them up. Other governments are beginning to listen to more entrepreneurial employees. Vivek Kundra, Barack Obama's IT guru, designed various web-based public services for Washington, DC, when he worked for the mayor. Steve Ressler, another American, created a group of web-enthusiasts called Young Government Leaders and a website called GovLoop.

FixTheState.com

How can organisations profit from the power of the web rather than being gobbled up by it? Messrs Tapscott and Williams endorse the familiar wiki-mantras about openness and "co-creation". But they are less starry-eyed than some. They not only recognise the importance of profits and incentives. They also argue that monetary rewards can be used to improve the public and voluntary sectors. NetSquared, a non-profit group, introduced prizes for the best ideas about social entrepreneurship. Public-sector entrepreneurs such as Mr Kundra are excited by the idea of creating "app stores" for the public sector.

Messrs Tapscott and Williams sometimes get carried away with their enthusiasm for the web. Great innovators often need the courage to ignore the crowd. (Henry Ford was fond of saying that if he had listened to his customers he would have produced a better horse and buggy.) Great organisations need time to cook up world-changing ideas. Hierarchies can be just as valuable to the process of creative destruction as networks. But the authors are nevertheless right to argue that the web is the most radical force of our time. And they are surely also right to predict that it has only just begun to work its magic.

September 2010

Building with big data

The data revolution is changing the landscape of business

IN A SHORT STORY called "On Exactitude in Science", Jorge Luis Borges described an empire in which cartographers became so obsessive that they produced a map as big as the empire itself. This was so cumbersome that future generations left it to disintegrate. ("[I]n the western deserts, tattered fragments of the map are still to be found, sheltering some occasional beast or beggar.")

As usual, the reality of the digital age is outpacing fiction. In 2010 people stored enough data to fill 60,000 Libraries of Congress. The world's 4 billion mobile-phone users (12% of whom own smartphones) have turned themselves into data-streams. YouTube claims to receive 24 hours of video every minute. Manufacturers have embedded 30 million sensors into their products, converting mute bits of metal into data-generating nodes in the internet of things. The number of smartphones is increasing by 20% a year and the number of sensors by 30%.

The McKinsey Global Institute (MGI) has no Borges-like qualms about the value of all these data. In a suitably fact-packed report, "Big data: the next frontier for innovation, competition and productivity", MGI argues that data are becoming a factor of production, like physical or human capital. Companies that can harness big data will trample data-incompetents. Data equity, to coin a phrase, will become as important as brand equity. MGI insists that this is not just idle futurology: businesses are already adapting to big data.

Companies are assembling more detailed pictures of their customers than ever before. Tesco, a British retailer, collects 1.5 billion nuggets of data every month and uses them to adjust prices and promotions. Williams-Sonoma, an American retailer, uses its knowledge of its 60 million customers (which includes such details as their income and the value of their houses) to produce different iterations of its catalogue. Amazon, an online retailer, has claimed that 30% of its sales are generated by its recommendation engine ("you may also like"). The mobile revolution adds a new dimension to customer-targeting. Companies such as America's Placecast are developing technologies that allow them to track potential consumers and send them enticing offers when they get within a few yards of a Starbucks.

The data revolution is disrupting established industries and business models. IT firms are nosing their way into the health-care market: Google Health and Microsoft HealthVault both allow consumers to track their health and record their treatments. Manufacturers are hastening their transformation into service companies: all those sensors allow them to monitor their products and see if they need repairing long before they break down. BMW uses sensor-data to tell its customers when their cars need to be serviced, for example. Insurance firms can now monitor the driving styles of their customers and offer them rates based on their competence (or recklessness) rather than their age and sex.

This revolution is changing government, too. Tax authorities are getting better at spotting spongers (for example, by flagging people who claim unemployment pay as well as occupational-injury benefits). Health services are mining clinical data to gauge the cost-effectiveness of drugs. After a detailed study of its clients, the German Federal Labour Agency managed to cut its annual spending by €10 billion ($14 billion) over three years while also reducing the length of time people spent out of work.

MGI argues that the data deluge could create a new wave of productivity growth. Properly used, big data could save the American health-care system $300 billion a year and the European public sector €250 billion. It could also enable retailers to increase their operating margins by 60%. But it is hard to read these figures without succumbing to Borges-style doubts. Will big companies and big governments use big data to trample on the little man? And is this mountain of data really as useful as MGI's data-heads think?

Power to the little people

The McKinseyites provide good answers to the first question. The data revolution is clearly handing power to the little people as well as the big ones. You can now buy a device that will store all the world's recorded music for just $600. Shoppers can use their mobile phones to scan bar codes to see if there is a better deal elsewhere. Citizens can use publicly available information to demand better public services. Britain's Open Knowledge Foundation has used government databases to develop a useful site called wheredoesmymoneygo.org. Dr Foster Intelligence provides patients with information about the quality of health care.

But on the second question, they are silent. Big data has the same problems as small data, but bigger. Data-heads frequently allow the beauty of their mathematical models to obscure the unreliability of the numbers they feed into them. (Garbage in, garbage out.) They can also miss the big picture in their pursuit of ever more granular data. During the 2008 presidential campaign Mark Penn provided Hillary Clinton with reams of micro-data, thus helping her to craft micro-policies aimed at tiny slices of the electorate. But Mrs Clinton was trounced by a man who grasped that people wanted to feel part of something bigger. The winning slogans were vague and broad ("hope" and "change").

The sheer size of today's data banks means that companies need to be more careful than ever to treat data as a slave rather than a master. There is no substitute for sound intuition and wise judgment. But if firms can preserve a little scepticism, they can surely squeeze important insights from the ever-growing store of data. In the 1980s and 1990s retailers such as Wal-Mart used their mastery of retailing data to launch the "big-box" revolution (huge out-of-town stores with ultra-low prices). Today's big data will provide the raw material for further revolutions.

May 2011

I, robot-manager

Management thinkers need to ponder more about homo-robo relations

ROBOTS HAVE BEEN THE STUFF of science fiction for so long that it is surprisingly hard to see them as the stuff of management fact. A Czech playwright, Karel Capek, gave them their name in 1920 (from the Slavonic word for "work"). An American writer, Isaac Asimov, confronted them with their most memorable dilemmas. Hollywood turned them into superheroes and supervillains. When some film critics drew up lists of Hollywood's 50 greatest good guys and 50 greatest baddies, the only character to appear on both lists was a robot, the Terminator.

It is time for management thinkers to catch up with science-fiction writers. Robots have been doing menial jobs on production lines since the 1960s. The world already has more than 1 million industrial robots. There is now an acceleration in the rates at which they are becoming both cleverer and cheaper: an explosive combination. Robots are learning to interact with the world around them. Their ability to see things is getting ever closer to that of humans, as is their capacity to ingest information and act on it. Tomorrow's robots will increasingly take on delicate, complex tasks. And instead of being imprisoned in cages to stop them colliding with people and machines, they will be free to wander.

America's armed forces have blazed a trail here. They now have no fewer than 12,000 robots serving in their ranks. Peter Singer, of the Brookings Institution, a think-tank, says mankind's 5,000-year monopoly on the fighting of war is breaking down. Recent additions to the battlefield include tiny "insects" that perform reconnaissance missions and giant "dogs" to terrify foes. The Pentagon is also working on the EATR, a robot that fuels itself by eating whatever biomass it finds around it.

But the civilian world cannot be far behind. Who better to unclog sewers or suck up nuclear waste than these remarkable machines?

The Japanese made surprisingly little use of robots to clear up after the March 2011 earthquake, given their world leadership in this area. They said that they had the wrong sort of robots in the wrong places. But they issued a global call for robotic assistance.

As robots advance into the service industries they are starting to look less like machines and more like living creatures. The Paro (made by AIST, a Japanese research agency) is shaped like a baby seal and responds to attention. Honda's robot, ASIMO, is humanoid and can walk, talk and respond to commands. Roxxxy, an American-made "sex robot", can be programmed to appeal to all preferences, and (unlike many a real-life spouse) listens to its partner to try to improve its performance.

Until now executives have largely ignored robots, regarding them as an engineering rather than a management problem. This cannot go on: robots are becoming too powerful and ubiquitous. Companies may need to rethink their strategies as they gain access to these new sorts of workers. Do they really need to outsource production to China, for example, when they have clever machines that work ceaselessly without pay? They certainly need to rethink their human-resources policies – starting by questioning whether they should have departments devoted to purely human resources.

The first issue is how to manage the robots themselves. Asimov laid down the basic rule in 1942: no robot should harm a human. This rule has been reinforced by recent technological improvements: robots are now much more sensitive to their surroundings and can be instructed to avoid hitting people. But the Pentagon's plans make all this a bit more complicated: many of its robots will be, in essence, killing machines.

A second question is how to manage the homo side of homo-robo relations. Workers have always worried that new technologies will take away their livelihoods, ever since the original Luddites' fears about mechanised looms. That worry takes on a particularly intense form when the machines come with a human face: Capek's play that gave robots their name depicted a world in which they initially brought lots of benefits but eventually led to mass unemployment and discontent. Now, the arrival of increasingly humanoid automatons in workplaces, in an era of high unemployment, is bound to provoke a reaction.

Loving the alien

So, companies will need to work hard to persuade workers that robots are productivity-enhancers, not just job-eating aliens. They need to show employees that the robot sitting alongside them can be more of a helpmate than a threat. Audi has been particularly successful in introducing industrial robots because the carmaker asked workers to identify areas where robots could improve performance and then gave those workers jobs overseeing the robots. Employers also need to explain that robots can help preserve manufacturing jobs in the rich world: one reason why Germany has lost fewer such jobs than Britain is that it has five times as many robots for every 10,000 workers.

These two principles – don't let robots hurt or frighten people – are relatively simple. Robot scientists are tackling more complicated problems as robots become more sophisticated. They are keen to avoid hierarchies among rescue-robots (because the loss of the leader would render the rest redundant). So they are using game theory to make sure the robots can communicate with each other in egalitarian ways. They are keen to avoid duplication between robots and their human handlers. So they are producing more complicated mathematical formulae in order that robots can constantly adjust themselves to human intentions. This suggests that the world could be on the verge of a great management revolution: making robots behave like humans rather than the 20th century's preferred option, making humans behave like robots.

March 2011

The eclipse of the public company

Traditional listed firms are facing competition

FOR MOST OF THE PAST 150 YEARS public companies have swept all before them. Wall Streeters have dissolved their cosy partnerships to go public. Communists have abandoned their five-year plans in favour of stockmarket listings. And Silicon Valley entrepreneurs have bowed before the god of the IPO – the initial public offering that takes a start-up public and makes its founders rich.

But is the sun finally setting on the public company? Its rise came at the expense of two older kinds of organisation that had dominated business until the middle of the 19th century – private partnerships and chartered companies. Private partnerships were wonderfully flexible but lacked the vital ingredient of limited liability: partners could lose everything they owned if the business failed. Chartered companies offered limited liability but were controlled by governments. Liberal reformers combined the best of both models: they gave managers freedom from government control and investors the shield of limited liability. Their invention conquered the world.

Yet now both the private partnership and the state-controlled company are making a comeback. Two of the world's three largest banks by market capitalisation are state-directed Chinese ones. The world's biggest telecoms company, China Mobile, is state-run. State-owned energy firms such as Russia's Gazprom and Saudi Aramco now account for more than three-quarters of the world's oil production. Many of these state-run giants resemble old-style chartered companies. They have the trappings of the private sector, such as boards of directors and listings on a stockmarket. But they are essentially instruments of state power. The Chinese government deems minerals vital to national security. So, like the East India Company of old, Chinese state-owned companies roam the world in search of raw materials and then build the roads and rails to ship them out.

Private partnerships are also on the march. A succession of legal changes in the United States – starting with a law in Wyoming in the 1970s and culminating in an Internal Revenue Service ruling in 1996 – made life easier for them. Partnerships can now offer limited liability and issue tradable shares. They are more durable than before, since they are no longer destroyed when one partner leaves. They also escape from the double taxation that plagues the corporate sector: corporations have to pay corporate taxes and then their shareholders have to pay taxes on their dividends.

The result has been a revolution among small and mid-sized businesses in America. Larry Ribstein, a professor of law at the University of Illinois, calculates that about a third of American businesses large enough to file tax returns are now organised as partnerships or what he calls "uncorporations". Plenty of big businesses, too, are shunning the stockmarket, with its costly reporting requirements and impatient investors. Publicly traded partnerships and real-estate investment trusts mix and match features from corporations and uncorporations. Many big firms, such as Alliance Boots (a health-and-beauty group) have abandoned public stockmarkets and embraced private equity.

The most fashionable investment vehicles – leveraged buy-out firms, hedge funds and venture-capital funds – are spearheading the "uncorporate" revolution. These firms are usually organised as partnerships, though some, such as the Blackstone Group, are also listed. Corporate raiders often raise money by creating funds in the form of partnerships. Their targets are often restructured as partnerships. This makes managers behave like owners rather than hired hands: they can lose money as well as making it and they have years to turn their companies around rather than answering to the stockmarket every quarter. Hedge funds can make money by buying companies and selling underperforming assets. Venture capitalists make money in the long term by lending their names and expertise to start-ups. Hedge funds and venture-capital firms also make money in their different ways by getting fund managers to behave more like partners, with "skin in the game", as the modish phrase puts it.

So where does this leave the public company? State ownership comes with too many handicaps to pose a long-term threat. Politicians may lean on the board to hire their idiot nephews, chase visions of national greatness or mop up the jobless masses. The biggest state-owned firms are often big only because they are shielded from competition. It is hard to avoid making money if you have a monopoly over Saudi oil, for example.

Unlisted private firms pose a challenge of a different order. They have undoubtedly established themselves as an alternative corporate form. And that is no bad thing. Just as an ecosystem benefits from diversity, so the world is better off with a multitude of corporate forms. Many big companies periodically need to undergo the sort of patient restructuring that they can only get when they leave public markets. That said, private companies have disadvantages that will hamper their growth. They lack public firms' rigorous systems of corporate governance and financial reporting. They depend too heavily on borrowing: many drank themselves silly during the credit boom and now have throbbing heads.

The qualified bliss of being listed

In fact, the public and private models of ownership have a symbiotic relationship. The reward for those who take a company private often comes when, having revived it, they take it public again. Venture capitalists would not put so much money and effort into nurturing start-ups if they did not dream of a lucrative IPO. Public companies may have had their confidence shaken in the past few years and their territory shrunken a little. But the organisations that were launched on an unsuspecting world in the mid-19th century still have a healthy spark of life in them.

August 2010

Leviathan as capitalist

State capitalism continues to defy expectations of its demise

IT IS NOW 25 YEARS since Francis Fukuyama published *The End of History?* and ignited a firestorm of debate. Today there are many reasons for thinking that he was wrong about the universal triumph of liberalism and markets, from democracy's failure in the Middle East to the revival of religious fundamentalism. But one of the most surprising reasons is the continuing power of the state as an economic actor: far from retiring from the business battlefield in 1989, the state merely regrouped for another advance.

Survey the battlefield today and you can see state capitalism almost everywhere. In China companies in which the state is a majority shareholder account for 60% of stockmarket capitalisation. In Russia and Brazil companies in which the state has either a majority or a significant minority stake account for 30–40% of capitalisation. Even in such bastions of economic orthodoxy as Sweden and the Netherlands state-owned enterprises (SOEs) account for 5% of market capitalisation. The Chinese and Russian governments show little sign of wanting to surrender control of the commanding heights of the economy. Privatisation seems to have ground to a halt in Brazil and in India (though its new government may revive it). There has been talk of the French government taking a stake in Alstom or part of its business – adding to the stakes it and Germany hold in Airbus and the one France has taken in Peugeot.

What should one make of the revival of state capitalism? Opinions vary wildly. Some praise it as a superior form of capitalism while others treat it as a mere way-station on the road to proper capitalism. One of its most ardent proponents, Vladimir Putin of Russia, somehow keeps a straight face when claiming there is no state capitalism in his country. Some see SOEs as money pits whereas others think they are pretty good investments: Morgan Stanley, a bank, reckons that, together, shares in listed SOEs in Europe, the Middle East, Africa and Latin America did better than stockmarkets as a whole between 2001 and 2012.

Reinventing State Capitalism, a book by Aldo Musacchio of Harvard Business School and Sergio Lazzarini of Insper, a Brazilian university, sheds fresh light on the question. It notes that the old model of Leviathan-as-entrepreneur, in which the state owned companies outright and ran them by ministerial diktat, was largely swept aside by the privatisation wave of the 1980s and 1990s, when governments realised that they could make money out of their companies rather than constantly bailing them out. But instead of swimming off into the blue ocean Leviathan reappeared in three disguises – as a majority or minority shareholder and as an indirect investor.

In the first form, which is particularly popular in China, the state submits an SOE to the governance standards and investor scrutiny that come with a stockmarket listing while retaining the bulk of the shares. In the second, which accounts for about half of SOEs, the state retains just enough influence, through its minority stake, to swing some important decisions. In the third, the state seeks to invest in companies – including ones not previously government-linked – through public development banks (of which there are currently 286 in 117 countries), sovereign-wealth funds, pension funds and other vehicles. For instance, India's Life Insurance Corporation is the largest stockmarket investor in the country, with about $50 billion invested as of September 2011.

How successful has Leviathan been in these new incarnations? Messrs Musacchio and Lazzarini go out of their way to be fair. They point out that new-style SOEs more closely resemble true private-sector firms than old-fashioned nationalised industries: they are run by businesspeople not political hacks, and no longer have bloated workforces. The authors argue that good governance can overcome the classic problems of state ownership: Statoil of Norway is one of the world's best-run firms. And they observe that Leviathan can also bring benefits to the private sector: for example, it can provide long-term investment in countries that have shallow or dysfunctional capital markets.

But the authors nevertheless produce a lot of evidence that the new Leviathan retains some of the old one's weaknesses. This is especially clear in Brazil, where two successive presidents from the Workers' Party (PT), Luiz Inácio Lula da Silva and Dilma Rousseff, have trampled on other shareholders' rights in the name of the national interest. The government leant on Petrobras, the national oil company, to withdraw plans to raise the price of petrol in line with world prices. It engineered the removal of Roger Agnelli as boss of Vale, a privatised mining giant in which the national development bank, the BNDES, still owns a chunk, because it did not like his emphasis on exporting iron ore to China instead of building steel mills at home. This rise in interventionism has come just as the BNDES is losing its *raison d'être* because of the deepening of domestic capital markets. Messrs Musacchio and Lazzarini demonstrate that under the PT the bank has got into the habit of lending money to already successful businesses that could easily have raised it from the markets – companies that, by the by, are also generous contributors to political campaigns.

The importance of timing

The implication of all this is not so much that Mr Fukuyama was wrong about the market in 1989 but that he was premature. The development of state capitalism over subsequent years has undoubtedly been extraordinary. But there are good reasons for still hoping that it is a way-station to a more fully private economy, not a new form of capitalism. The best SOEs have demonstrated that they can thrive without the guiding hand of the state – and the worst have proved that, however many market disciplines you impose upon them, they will still find a way of turning state capitalism into its ugly sister, crony capitalism.

June 2014

The silver tsunami

Business will have to learn how to manage an ageing workforce

MARTIN AMIS AND CHRISTOPHER BUCKLEY are writers who are entering their silver years and are worried about the costs of an ageing population. Mr Amis compared the growing army of the elderly to "an invasion of terrible immigrants, stinking out the restaurants and cafés and shops". Mr Buckley devoted a novel, *Boomsday*, to the impending war of the generations. They have both touted the benefits of mass euthanasia, though Mr Amis favours giving volunteers "a martini and a medal" whereas Mr Buckley supports more sophisticated incentives such as tax breaks.

Novelists will have their jokes. But Messrs Amis and Buckley are right to warn about the threat of the "silver tsunami". Most people understand about the ageing of society in the abstract. But few have grasped either the size of the tsunami or the extent of its consequences. This is particularly true of the corporate world.

Companies in the rich world are confronted with a rapidly ageing workforce. Nearly one in three American workers will be over 50 by 2012, and America is a young country compared with Japan and Germany. China is also ageing rapidly, thanks to its one-child policy. This means that companies will have to learn how to manage older workers better. It also means that they will be confronted with a wave of retirements as the baby-boomers leave work in droves.

Most companies are remarkably ill-prepared. There was a flicker of interest in the problem a few years ago but it was snuffed out by the recession. The management literature on older workers is a mere molehill compared with the mountain devoted to recruiting and retaining the young.

Companies are still stuck with an antiquated model for dealing with ageing, which assumes that people should get pay rises and promotions on the basis of age and then disappear when they reach retirement. They have dealt with the burdens of this model by periodically "downsizing" older workers or encouraging them to take early retirement. This has created a dual labour market for older workers, of cosseted insiders on the one hand and unemployed or retired outsiders on the other.

But this model cannot last. The number of young people, particularly those with valuable science and engineering skills, is shrinking. And governments are raising retirement ages and making it more difficult for companies to shed older workers, in a desperate attempt to cope with their underfunded pension systems. Even litigation-averse Japan has introduced tough age-discrimination laws.

Companies will have no choice but to face the difficult problem of managing older workers. How do you encourage older people to adapt to new practices and technologies? How do they get senior people to take orders from young whippersnappers? Happily a few companies have started to think seriously about these problems – and generate insights that their more stick-in-the-mud peers can imitate. The leaders in this area are retail companies. Asda, a subsidiary of the equally gerontophile Wal-Mart, is Britain's biggest employer of over-50s. Netto, a Danish supermarket group, has experimented with shops that employ only people aged 45 and over.

Many industrial companies are also catching the silver wave. Some are rejigging processes to accommodate older workers. A forthcoming article in *Harvard Business Review* by Christoph Loch of INSEAD and two colleagues looks at what happened when BMW decided to staff one of its production lines with workers of an age likely to be typical at the firm in 2017. At first "the pensioners' line" was less productive. But the firm brought it up to the level of the rest of the factory by introducing 70 relatively small changes, such as new chairs, comfier shoes, magnifying lenses and adjustable tables.

Some companies, particularly in energy and engineering, are also realising that they could face a debilitating loss of skills when the baby-boomers retire en masse. Bosch asks all retirees to sit down for a formal interview in an attempt to "capture" their wisdom for younger workers. Construction companies such as Sweden's Elmhults Konstruktions and the Netherlands' Hazenberg Bouw have introduced mentoring systems that encourage prospective retirees to train their replacements.

Older and poorer

Companies will have to do more than this if they are to survive the silver tsunami. They will have to rethink the traditional model of the career. This will mean breaking the time-honoured link between age and pay – a link which ensures that workers get ever more expensive even as their faculties decline. It will also mean treating retirement as a phased process rather than a sudden event marked by a sentimental speech and a carriage clock.

There are signs that this is beginning to happen. A few firms have introduced formal programmes of "phased retirement", though they usually single out white-collar workers for the privilege. Some, notably consultancies and energy companies, have developed pools of retired or semi-retired workers who can be called upon to work on individual projects. Asda allows employees to work only during busy periods or take several months off in winter (a perk dubbed "Benidorm leave"). Abbott Laboratories, a large American health-care company, allows veteran staff to work for four days a week or take up to 25 extra days of holiday a year.

But there is one big problem with such seemingly neat arrangements: the plethora of age-discrimination laws that have been passed over the past few years make it harder for companies to experiment and easier for a handful of malcontents to sue. It would be an irony worthy of Messrs Amis and Buckley if laws that were passed to encourage companies to adapt to the demographic revolution ended up having the opposite effect.

February 2010

The father of fracking

Few businesspeople have done as much to change the world as George Mitchell

THE UNITED STATES has of late been in a slough of despond. The mood is reflected in a spate of books with gloomy titles such as *That Used to Be Us* (Thomas Friedman and Michael Mandelbaum) and *Time to Start Thinking: America in the Age of Descent* (Edward Luce). For the first time in decades the majority of Americans think their children will be worse off than they are. Yankee can-do optimism is in danger of congealing into European nothing-can-be-done negativism.

There are good reasons for this. The political system really is "even worse than it looks", as another doom-laden book puts it. Middle-class living standards have stagnated. The Iraq war turned into a debacle. But the pessimists are ignoring a mighty force pushing in the opposite direction: America's extraordinary capacity to reinvent itself. No other country produces as many world-changing new companies in such a variety of industries: not just in the new economy of computers and the internet but also in the old economy of shopping, manufacturing and energy.

George Mitchell, who died on July 26th 2013, was a one-man refutation of the declinist hypothesis. From the 1970s America's energy industry reconciled itself to apparently inevitable decline. Analysts produced charts to show that its oil and gas were running out. The big oil firms globalised in order to survive. But Mr Mitchell was convinced that immense reserves trapped in shale rock deep beneath the surface could be freed. He spent decades perfecting techniques for unlocking them: injecting high-pressure fluids into the ground to fracture the rock and create pathways for the trapped oil and gas (fracking) and drilling down and then sideways to increase each well's yield (horizontal drilling).

The result was a revolution. In an interview with *The Economist* in 2011 Mr Mitchell said he never had any doubt that fracking might turn the American energy market upside down. But even he was surprised by the speed of the change. Shale beds now produce more than a quarter of America's natural gas, compared with just 1% in 2000. America is on the way to becoming a net gas exporter. Traditional petro-powers such as Saudi Arabia and Russia are losing bargaining strength.

Mr Mitchell was the embodiment of the American dream. His father was a poor Greek immigrant, a goatherd who later ran a shoeshine shop in Galveston, Texas. Mr Mitchell had to work his way through university, but graduated top of his class. He left a fortune of more than $2 billion and a Texas landscape studded with examples of his philanthropy: he was particularly generous to university research departments and to Galveston.

Mr Mitchell was also the embodiment of the entrepreneurial spirit. He did not discover shale gas and oil: geological surveys had revealed them decades before he started. He did not even invent fracking: it had been in use since the 1940s. But few great entrepreneurs invent something entirely new. His greatness lay in a combination of vision and grit: he was convinced that technology could unlock the vast reserves of energy in the Barnett Shale beneath Dallas and Fort Worth, and he kept grappling with the unforgiving rock until it eventually surrendered its riches.

After studying petroleum engineering and geology Mr Mitchell served in the Army Corps of Engineers during the second world war. On returning to civvy street he displayed a mistrust of big organisations – he made a career with Texas's scrappy independents rather than with the local giants – and a gambler's cunning. In his early days he struck a deal with a Chicago bookmaker to buy rights to a piece of land known as "the wildcatter's graveyard", and quickly drilled 13 gushers.

His stubbornness was, though, his most important quality. Investors and friends scoffed, but he spent two decades poking holes in the land around Fort Worth. "I never considered giving up," he said, "even when everyone was saying, 'George, you're wasting your money'." Then, in 1998, with Mr Mitchell approaching his 80s, his team hit on the idea of substituting water for gunky drilling fluids. This drastically cut the cost of drilling and turned the Barnett Shale into a gold mine.

An unlikely environmental warrior

Yet Mr Mitchell's story is more complicated than just a fable of hard work rewarded and a vision vindicated. It also shows how governments can help along the entrepreneurial spirit. His company counted on support from various government agencies, including those that mapped the shale reserves (demonstrating that they were plentiful) and promoted the development of technologies such as diamond-studded drill bits. Jimmy Carter's 1980 law to tax "windfall profits" at oil firms also included a tax credit for drilling for unconventional natural gas.

Greens now protesting against fracking, in Britain and elsewhere, may be surprised to learn that Mr Mitchell was also an early believer in environmentally friendly growth. In 1974 he built a planned community, The Woodlands, in the pine forests north of Houston, in a bid to tackle the problems of urban sprawl. It contains a mix of social housing and offices as well as million-dollar villas. In his later years he also campaigned for tight government regulation of fracking: he worried that the wild men who ran the independents might discredit his technique by cutting corners and damaging the environment.

Mr Mitchell's son, Todd, talked of "the Mitchell paradox": he believed in population control but had ten children; he championed sustainability but never invested in renewable energy. Reconciling the tension between Mr Mitchell's twin passions – fracking and sustainability – will be one of the great problems of the coming decades. But one thing is certain: the revolution he started by poking holes in the Texas dirt is changing the world just as surely as the algorithms being generated in Silicon Valley.

August 2013

The transience of power

The powerful do not stay that way for long

IF PARTISANS ON THE LEFT AND RIGHT agree on anything, it is that power is becoming more concentrated. Occupy Wall Street types protest against the all-powerful 1%. Tea-partiers rage against the cosmopolitan elite. Al Gore's presidential campaign in 2000 may have been inept, but his campaign slogan – "the people versus the powerful" – is defining the politics of the 21st century.

It is easy to see why. During the financial crisis governments used oceans of public money to rescue banks from the consequences of their own folly and greed. Bankers quickly went back to paying themselves fat bonuses. Inequality is growing in many countries. Plutocrats wax richer as the middle class is squeezed and the poor are trodden underfoot. Hedge-fund moguls and casino kings spend fortunes to sway American elections – and the Supreme Court tells them to carry on spending.

Such is the popular view of power. Moisés Naím says it is bunk. In *The End of Power* Mr Naím, a former Venezuelan cabinet minister now ensconced at the Carnegie Endowment for International Peace, a think-tank, argues forcefully that rigid pyramids of power are collapsing. Micropowers are learning how to frustrate macropowers. Bigwigs are finding it harder to wield power and harder to hold on to it. The barriers that used to protect insiders, such as economies of scale and long-established relationships, are crumbling.

In the 1950s and 1960s the corporate world was ruled by cabals of giants – by the "Big Three" in American cars and broadcasting and the "Seven Sisters" in global oil. C. Wright Mills, a sociologist, complained that America was ruled by a tiny elite. J.K. Galbraith, an economist, argued that there was not much difference between state planning as practised by the Russians and corporate planning as practised by General Motors.

Today's corporate world could hardly be more different. Time is being compressed: Google was incorporated only in 1998 but is now one of the world's biggest companies. Geography too is being tightened: who would have guessed in Galbraith's day that one of the world's leading aircraft-makers would be Brazilian (Embraer) or that one of its most innovative clothes brands would be Spanish (Zara)? In 1980 a corporation in the top fifth of its industry had only a 10% chance of falling out of that tier in five years. Eighteen years later that chance had risen to 25%.

Bosses, too, spend less time at the helm: the tenure of the average American chief executive has plunged from about ten years in the 1990s to five-and-a-half today. Those who disappoint are held to account: about 80% of CEOs of S&P 500 companies are ousted before retirement. Bosses must confront a growing army of critics from within the capitalist system: look at the way that Apple's head honcho, Tim Cook, has been roasted by angry investors. They also face a growing army of critics from outside. Even banks have been chided for sins such as interest-rate rigging (Barclays), money-laundering (HSBC) and illicit dealings with Iran (Standard Chartered).

The same pattern is being repeated in every walk of life. Take politics. In 2012 only four of the OECD's 34 countries had governments with an absolute majority in parliament. The Netherlands spent four months without a government in 2010. Belgium spent 541 days without one in 2010-11. Established parties are ceding ground to upstarts such as the UK Independence Party or Beppe Grillo's Five Star Movement in Italy. They are also constrained by rival power centres, both transnational and provincial. Or take organised labour. In America big labour's clout is waning faster than that of big business. Unionisation in the private sector has fallen from 40% in 1950 to less than 7% today. Old labour baronies such as the AFL-CIO have been challenged by upstarts such as the Service Employees International Union.

Why is power becoming more evanescent? Mr Naím is reluctant – too reluctant – to credit the internet, which is surely the most obvious force undermining hierarchy. He points instead to three revolutions: "more", "mobility" and "mentality". Global GDP has grown fivefold since 1950, so more people have access to more things than ever before. People are more mobile; the UN estimates that there are 214 million migrants in the world, 37% more than two decades ago.

People are also more self-directed (or egotistic). Even in Saudi Arabia 20% of marriages end in divorce.

There are obvious objections to Mr Naím's argument. The supposedly anarchic internet is now ruled by five big companies (except in China, where the state calls the shots). Among banks and accountancy firms, power is more concentrated than it was at the turn of the century. Amazon and eBay may grow more dominant than any of the giant retailers of the 1950s.

Look on my works, ye Mighty, and despair

But Mr Naím has good objections to the objections. His argument is not that companies are shrinking but that they are becoming more fragile. Internet giants can no longer rely on the economies of scale that kept General Motors and Sears on top for decades. Rather, they must constantly struggle to keep their products innovative and their brands fashionable – or fall prey to more agile upstarts. Powerful people are less secure than they were, too. The composition of the top 1% is constantly changing as CEOs lose their jobs and young go-getters outpace their elders.

Mr Naím celebrates the anti-power revolution for holding the mighty to account and providing ordinary people with opportunities. But he sees downsides, too. The more slippery power becomes, the more the world is ruled by short-term incentives and ever-changing fears. Politicians fail to tackle long-term problems such as climate change. Companies think of little besides the struggle for survival. Nonetheless, it would be worse if the populists were right and the 1% really did rule the world.

March 2013

PART 3

Winners and losers

The other demographic dividend

Emerging markets are teeming with young entrepreneurs

GLOBALS IS ONE OF THOSE FAST-GROWING Indian IT companies that Westerners simultaneously admire and fear. Founded in 2000, it already has offices in 11 countries and customers around the world. The chairman and chief executive, Suhas Gopinath, is just 24 years old. Most of his employees are also in their mid-twenties.

Mr Gopinath is an illustration of a striking business revolution. Emerging-world businesses have traditionally been obsessed with seniority. Ambitious youngsters in countries like India have been equally obsessed with job security. Well-paying jobs, preferably with multinational firms, are the key to success in the marriage market. But this is changing rapidly.

Nandan Nilekani, one of the founders of Infosys, reports that he now comes across mould-breaking young leaders wherever he goes in India. They are even to be found in big companies such as ICICI, a leading bank, Hindustan Unilever, a consumer-goods giant, and Comat Technologies, which provides information to rural Indians. Vivek Wadhwa, an American academic who studies entrepreneurship, says he is inundated with requests for meetings whenever he visits the emerging world.

The rise of young entrepreneurs is extending the meaning of the demographic dividend. Demographers have often noted that most of the emerging world will stay young while the rich world ages. In 2020 the median age in India will be 28, compared with 38 in America, 45 in western Europe and 49 in Japan. But the dividend will be paid not just in the form of more favourable dependency ratios but also in a more entrepreneurial business culture. Young people are innately more inclined to overthrow the existing order than are their elders. This predisposition is being reinforced by two big changes in the emerging world.

The first is the information-technology revolution. The Boston Consulting Group calculates that there are already about 610 million internet users in the BRICI countries (Brazil, Russia, India, China and Indonesia). BCG predicts that this number will nearly double by 2015. And in one respect many consumers in emerging markets are leapfrogging over their Western peers. They are much more likely to access the internet via mobile devices (which are ubiquitous in the emerging world) rather than PCs. That gives local entrepreneurs an advantage, says Rob Salkowitz, the author of *Young World Rising*. Whereas Western companies are hampered by legacy systems and legacy mindsets, they can build their companies around the coming technology.

The second is a pro-entrepreneurial revolution. Global institutions such as the World Bank and the World Economic Forum have helped to popularise entrepreneurialism. Mr Gopinath was encouraged to stick to his guns as an entrepreneur when the WEF elected him its youngest ever Young Leader. Several big companies have also encouraged the trend. Microsoft is helping local businesses and NGOs improve information-technology infrastructure. Goldman Sachs is spending $100 million on female entrepreneurs, many of them in emerging markets.

But even more important than these external nudges are internal changes. The rise of a cohort of highly successful local start-ups such as India's Infosys, Argentina's Globant and Ghana's SOFTtribe has had a dramatic effect on thinking across the region. These companies have demonstrated that young entrepreneurs can succeed mightily: the seven founders of Infosys were in their 20s when they set the company up. They have also created a group of middle-class people who have the wherewithal to bankroll risk: parents who have made money in Infosys or young people who decide to set up on their own after a few fat years in the corporate world.

Great expectations

These young entrepreneurs have already begun to shape some markets such as mobile video games and online karaoke. They have also demonstrated an impressive ability to identify gaps in other markets. Bright Simons, a young Ghanaian, came up with an ingenious idea for dealing with the epidemic of counterfeit drugs. He asked drug producers to tag their products with unique bar codes. Consumers can then use their mobile phones to send a copy of the bar code to the producers to make sure the drugs are authentic. Kamal Quadir turned his back on a career on Wall Street in order to found CellBazaar, which provides the 20 million subscribers to Bangladesh's GrameenPhone with a virtual marketplace where they can sell things as humble as sacks of potatoes.

This argument needs to be qualified. China, the emerging world's most powerful engine, is ageing rapidly, thanks to the one-child policy: by 2020 the average age in China will be 37, almost the same as in America. Young entrepreneurs have plenty of obstacles to mount. In Nigeria the fashion for cyber-crime has all but killed legitimate cyber-business: PayPal will not accept payments from people with a Nigerian internet address. In Latin America many young entrepreneurs operate in an informal economy where innovation is rare and capital hard to come by.

Yet entrepreneurial energies are moving eastward. The fact that many rich-world companies have responded to the economic slump by stopping hiring younger workers will only accelerate the shift. Americans are flocking to see *The Social Network*, a film about a group of young Harvard students who founded one of the world's fastest-growing companies, Facebook. The next Facebook is increasingly likely to be founded in India or Indonesia rather than middle-aged America or doddery old Europe.

October 2010

The daughter also rises

Women are storming emerging-world boardrooms

ZHANG YIN (also known by her Cantonese name, Cheung Yan) was the eldest of eight children of a lowly Red Army officer who was imprisoned during the Cultural Revolution for "capitalist offences". Today she is one of the world's richest self-made women, with an estimated fortune of $1.6 billion. In the early 1980s, as a dogsbody in a paper mill, she noted that the waste paper her superiors so casually discarded was actually worth something. She has been capitalising on her insight ever since. Nine Dragons Paper, which she founded with her husband in 1995, is now one of the world's largest paper recyclers.

The emerging world is home to many businesswomen like Ms Zhang. Seven of the 14 women identified on *Forbes* magazine's list of self-made billionaires are Chinese. Many firms in emerging markets do a better job of promoting women than their Western rivals, some surveys suggest. In China, 32% of senior managers are female, compared with 23% in America and 19% in Britain. In India, 11% of chief executives of large companies are female, compared with 3% of *Fortune* 500 bosses in America and 3% of FTSE 100 bosses in Britain. Turkey and Brazil come third and joint fourth (behind Finland and Norway) in the World Economic Forum's ranking of countries by the proportion of CEOs who are women. In Brazil, 11% of chief executives and 30% of senior executives are women.

Young, middle-class women are overtaking their male peers when it comes to education. In the United Arab Emirates 65% of university graduates are female. In Brazil and China the figures are 60% and 47% respectively. In Russia 57% of college-age women are enrolled in tertiary education; only 43% of men are. Business schools, those hothouses of capitalism, are feminising fast. Some 33% of students at the China Europe International Business School (CEIBS) in Shanghai and 26% at the Indian School of Business are female, a figure comparable with those of Western schools such as Harvard Business School and INSEAD.

In *Winning the War for Talent in Emerging Markets: Why Women are the Solution*, Sylvia Ann Hewlett and Ripa Rashid point out that businesswomen face steep obstacles in emerging markets. How can they stay on the fast track if, as in the UAE, they cannot travel without a male chaperone? And how can they be taken seriously if, as in Russia, the term "businesswoman" is synonymous with prostitute? In every emerging market women bear the lioness's share of family responsibilities. In many places, deals are sealed with booze and male bonding.

The workload for tiger businesswomen can be crushing. Rapid growth means exhausting change. Having customers in different time zones, as global Asian firms often do, makes it worse. More than a quarter of the female high-fliers surveyed by Ms Hewlett and Ms Rashid report working between eight and 18 hours more each week than they did three years ago. And horrible commutes are common. In IBM's ranking of the world's worst commutes, Beijing and Mexico City each scored 99 out of a possible 100 pain points. New Delhi, Moscow and São Paulo also did appallingly. Female commuters often have to put up with leering, groping men, particularly if they work late: 62% of Brazilian women say that they feel unsafe travelling to work.

Still, young women have no shortage of high-profile role models, from Indra Nooyi, the Indian-born boss of PepsiCo, to Dong Mingzhu, the author of one of the bestselling business books in China. In *Regretless Pursuit*, Sister Dong, as her fans call her, recounts her rise from saleswoman to boss of Gree Electric, the country's biggest manufacturer of air-conditioners.

Living in emerging markets offers many advantages for female professionals. Most obviously, there are plenty of cheap hands to cook and take care of children. And corporate culture is changing astoundingly fast, not least because companies are hiring so many young people. (Youngsters in India and China grew up steeped in capitalism; their parents did not.)

Skills shortages spur a battle for brains. In some countries, companies expect to lose a fifth of their highly skilled staff every year. So they will try anything that might help them hang on to the talent. This includes becoming more female-friendly. Many multinationals have created mentoring programmes and women's networks. Boehringer Ingelheim, a drug company, and Citi, a bank, have introduced short-term job placements to encourage women to travel. Goldman Sachs (India) pairs expectant mothers with seasoned working mothers. Infosys, an IT firm, provides "pregnancy yoga". Wipro, another IT company, arranges child-care camps on its campus during long holidays. GE India provides its female staff with assertiveness training.

Wise firms focus on the two biggest problems for working women in emerging markets: looking after their ageing parents, which is typically more of a problem than child care, and commuting. A growing number of companies provide flexi-time so that women can work from home. Ernst & Young holds family days to show parents what their daughters have achieved. It also offers medical cover for parents. Many companies provide their female staff with late-night shuttle buses – and female-only taxi companies are springing up in India, the UAE and Brazil.

A woman's place is in the boardroom

All this might sound a bit namby-pamby to pioneers like Sister Dong (who says that she hasn't had a holiday for 20 years) and Zhang Yin (who boasts that: "My success came from my character"). But namby-pambyism is a sign of progress. Heroines who build empires out of sweat and determination are rare in any culture. (As, indeed, are heroes.) Rapid growth in emerging markets is pulling more women into corporate life. And as they show their mettle, patriarchal attitudes are beginning to dissolve.

August 2011

Uncaging the lions

Business is transforming Africa for the better

FOR ONCE AN INVESTMENT FAD seems justified: the 21st century is shaping up to be that of the emerging markets, just as the 20th was America's century and the 19th Britain's. But that leaves open the question of which countries, exactly, will emerge. Will Asia and Latin America mark the limits of the spreading prosperity? Or will the boom reach the perennial laggard, Africa? Will a new pride of economic lions take their place beside the Chinese dragon and the Indian tiger?

Ten years ago *The Economist* dubbed Africa "the hopeless continent". Since then its progress has been remarkably hopeful. In 2000–08 Africa's annual output grew by 4.9% (adjusted for purchasing-power parity), twice as fast as in the 1980s and 1990s and faster than the global average of 3.8%. Foreign direct investment increased from $10 billion to $88 billion – more than India ($42 billion) and, even more remarkably, catching up with China ($108 billion). The Boston Consulting Group notes that, since 1998, the revenues of Africa's 500 largest companies (excluding banks) have grown at an average of 8.3% a year.

But is this growth sustainable? Or is the current fad for Africa just another bubble? The pessimists have always had three strong arguments. One is that African politics is dysfunctional. Warring strongmen can undo the progress of decades in weeks. A second is that the African economy is unduly dependent on the resource sector. A third is that Africa's growth does too little to benefit the poor. But over the past decade, all these objections have weakened.

The numerous examples of government failure can now be weighed against examples of success. The continent's inflation rate has been reduced from 22% in the 1990s to 8% since 2000. The World Bank's annual "Doing Business" report ranked Rwanda as the world's top reformer in 2010, based on the number and impact of steps to promote entrepreneurship there. Mauritius was ranked 17th of the 183 economies covered by the report, ahead of lots of richer places.

It is true that Africa has depended on its abundant natural resources; and they will be a growing advantage in years to come. The hectic pace of growth in the emerging world is not only pushing up commodity prices but also intensifying competition for the right to drill the continent's oil and mine its minerals. Chinese companies in particular are wooing African governments with lavish expenditure on infrastructure.

McKinsey points out that the natural-resource sector accounts for only about a third of the continent's growth. Africa is producing a growing number of world-class companies outside the resource industry, from South African giants such as SABMiller, the world's second-largest brewer, and Aspen Pharmacare, the largest generic-drugmaker in the southern hemisphere, to niche players such as Tunisia's Coficab, one of the world's most successful suppliers of wiring for cars.

As to the poor, McKinsey points out that, thanks to rising living standards, some 200 million Africans will enter the market for consumer goods in the next five years. The consultancy also notes that the continent's working-age population will double from 500 million in 2010 to 1.1 billion in 2040. Consumer-goods companies ranging from Western giants such as Procter & Gamble to emerging-market car companies such as China's Great Wall and India's Tata Motors are pouring into Africa. Foreign firms are likely to start using Africa as a base for manufacturing as well, as Europe's population shrinks and labour costs in India and China rise.

Africa is also seeing the benefits of "frugal innovation" – inventions that are designed to serve the poor. Mobile-phone companies, which have done more than anybody to improve the lives of poor Africans, are continuing to innovate. Kenya's Safaricom and its rivals are pioneering money-transfer by mobile phone; mobile savings and agricultural-insurance schemes are next. Companies from other emerging markets are also expanding into Africa. Bharti Airtel, which completed its $10.7 billion acquisition of Zain Africa, is a world-leader in improving services while reducing costs.

Nor is innovation confined to telecoms. Vijay Mahajan of the McCombs School of Business at the University of Texas, Austin, produces a long list of innovators in everything from the design to the distribution of products. Nakumatt, a Kenyan retailer, allows people living abroad to buy vouchers for its stores and then transfer them to their African friends and relatives, making remittance payments smoother. Other bottom-of-the-pyramid innovations include the Jiko, a portable charcoal stove that can reduce fuel consumption by 30%; the Q-drum, a doughnut-shaped plastic container that can be used to transport water by rolling it along the ground; the Weza, a foot-powered generator that can be used to charge cell phones and radios; and a $20 washing machine made from discarded motors and iron.

Lions and bulls

A decade of growth has also given Africa's business people a new elan. Mo Ibrahim, a mobile-phone pioneer, has established an index to measure governments' performance and an annual prize of $5 million, plus $200,000 a year for life, to an African leader who rules well and then stands down. He has also founded a venture fund which plans to invest $200 million in Africa in 2010.

Such successful entrepreneurs can point to countless examples of how business can improve people's lives. In Kenya, where the government has removed its dead hand from the telecoms market, mobile phones are ubiquitous; in next-door Ethiopia, where the government's grip is as tight as ever, only 2% of the population has phones. A few African lions are beginning to take their place next to the dragons and tigers.

June 2010

Flower power

The forces reshaping one of Africa's most successful industries

LONGONOT FARM IS A GIANT FACTORY for mass-producing roses: a model of efficiency in a country whose natural condition seems to be chaos. The roses are housed in enormous plastic greenhouses – 49 in all, some covering a hectare and a half – and planted in long troughs. Workers in neat uniforms bearing the legend "Growing in Harmony" harvest the flowers and deliver them to an on-site packaging facility. There they are graded and sorted, stripped of their thorns and leaves, packed, labelled "Marks & Spencer" or "Sainsbury's", loaded onto lorries, sent to the airport and delivered to Europe by the next day. The farm produces 72 million stems a year.

A couple of dozen farms like Longonot line the shore of Lake Naivasha, a 139-square-kilometre (54-square-mile) expanse of freshwater in the Rift Valley, north-west of Nairobi. These farms are in turn part of a Kenyan horticultural industry that produces fruit and vegetables as well as flowers.

Central Kenya is perfect for growing things, being blessed not only with 12 hours of tropical sunlight a day but also with a more temperate climate at higher elevations. The Rift Valley is full of lakes, and their water and surrounding volcanoes provide soil rich in nutrients. Nairobi airport has lots of flights to Europe every day. And the industry is thriving: it turned over $3.2 billion in 2012, up from $2.3 billion in 2011; it is one of Kenya's largest sources of foreign reserves; it employs 4.5 million people directly, and they support many millions more. But it is nevertheless being reshaped by three powerful forces – two applied by the West and a third by local conditions.

Western consumers are demanding two contradictory things from Kenyan producers: more value for money and more corporate social responsibility (CSR). Many shoppers' incomes have been stagnant since the financial crisis. But at the same time Westerners worry increasingly about labour conditions in poor countries and environmental degradation. Britain's supermarkets are particularly powerful conveyors of these messages: the four biggest, which control about 70% of the grocery market, are relentless in imposing their will on their suppliers. They are caught up in a fierce price war: even the posh ones, such as Waitrose, promise to match competitors' prices. They are also caught up in a CSR race to show they are model employers: a wallchart in an office in Longonot is jam-packed with the dates of inspections by NGOs and industry groups.

Local pressures add to these difficulties. Land and labour are becoming dearer. And the bleeding-heart Westerners are right, in that the industry's growth is straining the environment: Lake Naivasha almost ran out of water a few years ago and local towns are buckling under the weight of migrant labourers looking for jobs.

These three forces are producing a wave of consolidation and vertical integration, as economies of scale and close ties to retailers become more important. Large companies such as the VP Group (which owns Longonot Farm), Swire and Finlays are expanding while smaller family farms are going out of business. The big firms are creating production chains that stretch from seeds to cellophane and spawning subsidiaries to handle transport and marketing. They are also forming tight relationships with European retailers. The people who once dominated Kenyan horticulture – independent farmers, many of them white, and sharp-eyed middlemen, many of them Indians – are being displaced by company men who speak of scale economies and integrated supply chains.

The big companies are also moving into produce with higher margins, from vegetables to flowers, and into labour-intensive niches such as prepared meals: the VP Group has a 2-hectare complex near Nairobi airport where 2,000 shift-workers wash, chop, sort and pack vegetables every hour of every day. The firms' tendrils extend into skilful activities such as breeding new varieties of rose. Longonot Farm has large sections devoted to promising strains that are identified first by a mere number and then, when more advanced, by names such as Moody Blue.

The seeds of innovation

All this restructuring is releasing another powerful force: innovation. Big companies are rethinking every link in their production chains, both to squeeze costs and to hit their CSR targets. Planting roses in troughs rather than the ground allows them to enrich the soil with volcanic ash, pumice and coconut fibre while wasting less water. Unleashing hostile insects (miticides) on pests like red spiders allows them to cut their use of pesticides. The VP Group wants to use agricultural waste to produce energy, so it can power its own operations and sell the surplus to the grid. It is also mitigating risks and lowering costs by establishing farms in Ethiopia, Namibia and Tanzania (including Zanzibar), where land and labour are cheaper, and selling more to Africa's emerging middle class.

The Kenyan horticultural industry has provoked a predictable debate. Critics say it is folly to transport flowers, fruit and vegetables halfway across the world. Defenders retort that growing roses in Kenya, where it is hot and light all year round, produces fewer carbon-dioxide emissions than growing them in dank, dark Britain or the Netherlands. Critics complain that poor Kenyans are labouring long hours to produce salads for lazy Europeans. Defenders reply that horticulture is creating jobs in parts of Kenya where they are in short supply. But the most interesting thing about the industry is the way that it is shaking up ideological certainties. The West's demand that companies be good citizens is confounding many on the left by consolidating more power in the hands of giant agribusinesses. At the same time it is confounding many on the right: far from choking enterprise, it is encouraging firms to become more productive and innovative.

April 2014

Those bloody Scandinavians

What the Nordic crime-writing boom says about globalisation

BUSINESS IN THE NORDIC COUNTRIES has suffered a series of humiliations in recent years. Nokia is a shadow of its former self. Volvo has been passed from one foreign owner (Ford) to another (the Zhejiang Geely Holding Group), and Saab Automobile has collapsed. Iceland's banking industry has imploded. But in one business, at least, Scandinavia is sweeping all before it: the production of crime thrillers.

Two Swedes, Stieg Larsson and Henning Mankell, have established the region as world leader in this popular genre. Larsson's Millennium trilogy has sold more than 60 million copies and Mr Mankell's Wallander books have also sold tens of millions. Larsson died in 2004 before his novels went global and Mr Mankell has consigned his hero to Alzheimer's disease, but there are plenty of other claimants to their thrones across the region – most obviously Jo Nesbo (from Norway), but also Arnaldur Indridason (from Iceland) and Camilla Lackberg (from Sweden).

The northern crime boom is spreading from the written word to the screen. Martin Scorsese is planning to produce a version of Mr Nesbo's *The Snowman*, to add to the store of adaptations of Larsson and Mr Mankell. *The Killing*, a Danish television series, took Europe by storm in 2011. Scandinavian crime fiction has transformed itself into a global brand in much the same way that British rock 'n' roll did in the early 1960s, and become a global industry that stretches all the way from writers' garrets in Stockholm and Oslo to Hollywood studios. Like other worldwide success stories, it is worth drawing lessons from.

The first lesson is that the next big thing can come from the most unexpected places. Scandinavia is probably the most crime- and corruption-free region in the world: Denmark's murder rate is 0.9 per 100,000 people, compared with 4.2 in the United States and 21 in Brazil. Scandinavians are also lumbered with obscure and difficult languages. A succession of mainstream British publishers rejected *The*

Girl with the Dragon Tattoo, Larsson's first book, before Christopher MacLehose decided to publish it. Mr Indridason at first had poor sales because people found it hard to grapple with Icelandic names.

Yet Scandinavia has a number of hidden competitive strengths: a long tradition of blood-soaked sagas; an abundance of gloomy misfits; a brooding landscape; and a tradition of detective writing (Per Wahloo and Maj Sjowall, a husband-and-wife team, enjoyed local success in the 1960s with their ten-volume Martin Beck series). There are prizes and classes galore to help crime writers on their way: Ms Lackberg started by taking an all-female crime-writing class. Even before the current boom, crime writing was so remunerative that it sucked in talent from everywhere. Mr Mankell started out writing mainstream plays and novels. Mr Nesbo was a footballer, stockbroker and rock musician before creating his hard-bitten detective, Harry Hole.

The second lesson is that place matters more than ever in a globalised world. The conventional wisdom on globalisation is that it produces a flat world in which everybody consumes the same bland products in the same bland settings: a universal airport lounge. But the Nordic crime writers understand that the more interconnected the world is, the more people crave a sense of place – the more distinctive and unusual the better. Mr Nesbo provides us with maps of Oslo and obscure details of Norwegian history. Mr Indridason entertains us with descriptions of Icelandic delicacies such as sheep's head and pickled haggis. That Wallander copes with horrific crimes in small-town Ystad rather than a big nowhere like Los Angeles is essential to his appeal.

The third lesson is that innovation is the essence of global success. The Scandinavians have taken the convention of the defective detective to new heights: Wallander has all Philip Marlowe's gloom without any of his glamour. He is just as likely to douse his misery with meatballs as with scotch. But they have also added new elements. Larsson invented a completely new sort of detective – a tattooed, computer-hacking she-punk. The Scandinavians are in general more interested in the sociology of crime than in the goriness of it. Mr Mankell is obsessed by the way that the smug Swedes respond to disruptive forces like immigration and criminal gangs. "The Killing" focuses as much on the impact of a horrific crime on society as it does on solving the crime.

Planes and pants

These principles are as good as any for explaining recent business trends. Some of the great success stories of recent years have come from out-of-the-way places: who would have thought that Brazil would produce one of the world's most successful aircraft-makers (Embraer) or that New Zealand would give birth to a colossus of underwear (Icebreaker)? John Quelch of the China Europe International Business School in Shanghai argues that place matters more, not less, in a globalised and virtual world. Real Madrid has transformed itself into one of the world's most popular football teams by emphasising its *Madrileño* identity. Newcastle Brown beer has a silhouette of the Newcastle skyline on its label and features its local nickname – "a bottle of dog" – in its ads. And as for innovation being the secret sauce of success, Embraer demonstrated this by doing its more sophisticated work at home rather than in advanced America; and Icebreaker by producing underwear that you can wear for days without washing.

The final lesson is more uncomfortable for the Scandinavians: that success is more fleeting than ever. Their formula is already wearing a little thin: Mr Nesbo's Harry Hole is more resonant of Sylvester Stallone than Ingmar Bergman. Publishers are scouring the world for the next crime wave: a few summers hence we may all have forgotten about Oslo and Ystad, and be reading about *les flics* in Paris and Lyon instead.

September 2012

Bringing home the bacon

Tiny Denmark is an agricultural superpower

EVERY WEEKDAY 20,000 PIGS are delivered to the Danish Crown company's slaughterhouse in Horsens, in central Denmark. They trot into the stunning room, guided by workers armed with giant fly swats. They are hung upside down, divided in two, shaved of their bristles and scalded clean. A machine cuts them into pieces, which are then cooled, boned and packed.

The slaughterhouse is enormous, ten football pitches long with 11km of conveyor belts. Its managers attend to the tiniest detail. The fly-swatting workers wear green rather than white because this puts the pigs in a better mood. The cutting machine photographs a carcass before adjusting its blades to its exact contours. The company calibrates not only how to carve the flesh, but also where the various parts will fetch the highest prices: the bacon goes to Britain and the trotters to China.

Denmark is a tiny country, with 5.6 million people and wallet-draining labour costs. But it is an agricultural giant, home to 30 million pigs and a quiverful of global brands. In 2011 farm products made up 20% of its goods exports. The value of food exports grew from €4 billion ($5.5 billion) in 2001 to €16.1 billion in 2011. The government expects it to rise by a further €6.7 billion by 2020.

Why, in a post-industrial economy, is the food industry still thriving? Much of the answer lies in a cluster in the central region of the country. Policymakers everywhere are obsessed by creating their own Silicon Valleys. But Denmark's example suggests that the logic of clustering can be applied as well to ancient industries as to new ones. In central Denmark just as in California, innovation is in the air, improving productivity is a way of life, and the whole is much greater than the sum of the parts. Entrepreneurs see the future in meat and milk.

The cluster includes several big companies, which act as its leading investors: Danish Crown, Arla, Rose Poultry and DuPont Danisco.

(DuPont's purchase of Danisco in 2011, which created a great deal of anxiety about American multinationals buying up Denmark's crown jewels, was a sign of the agricultural sector's vitality.) Plenty of smaller firms are also sprouting, which act as indicators of nascent trends and incubators of new ideas.

Though the food industry, capital-intensive and tightly regulated, is rarely rich soil for entrepreneurs, in Denmark it is fertile. Several young companies are making information-technology tools for different bits of the business: LetFarm for fields, Bovisoft for stables, AgroSoft for pigs, Webstech for grain. ISI Food Protection focuses on dealing with organisms that spoil food or spread poisoning. InOMEGA3 specialises in food ingredients containing Omega-3 fatty acids, which are credited with various health-giving powers. Soy4you develops alternatives to meat products.

The cluster also has a collection of productivity-spurring institutions such as the Danish Cattle Research Centre and the Knowledge Centre for Agriculture. Danish universities remain at the forefront of the agro-industry: at Danish Technical University (DTU) 1,500 people work on food-related subjects. A tradition of public-private partnerships, which began with farmers forming co-operatives to improve production and marketing in the late 19th century, continues to flourish. An Agro Food Park near Aarhus, backed by the industry and the regional government, is nearing completion. It employs 800 people already and is expected to have 3,000 staff by 2020.

The Cattle Research Centre, for example, demonstrates that there are dozens of ways to boost bovine productivity. Robots can do everything from milking cows to keeping them washed and brushed to mucking out their living quarters. The milking robot can also act as a "lab in the farm" by analysing the milk for signs of health problems. Microchips can keep an eye on cows' behaviour. Carefully screened "Viking semen" can improve the quality of the stock.

The word on everyone's lips is "innovation". Big companies are building centres to develop new products. Arla is spending €36 million on one in the Agro Food Park. DuPont's centre in Aarhus is part of a global network with branches in America, Australia and China. They are also abandoning their insular ways, collaborating with start-ups and sponsoring food festivals and star chefs. Universities are adding departments: Aarhus now has a centre devoted to consumer behaviour in regard to food and DTU is focusing on "bio-silicon" – applying IT to food.

Land of milk and honey-roast ham

If all this spending on innovation is to pay off and Denmark's food industry is to continue to thrive, the country's farmers will have to overcome formidable challenges at home and abroad. Among the Danish public, distaste for "factory farming" is increasing. *Borgen*, a popular television political drama, devoted an entire episode to criticising pig farming. Demand is shifting from the European Union, which consumes more than 60% of Denmark's food exports, to emerging countries, some of which are becoming agricultural powers in their own right. Growing pressure on natural resources such as water and feedstock could render some of the industry unsustainable.

Against that, food is a growing industry: demand is set to rise by 60% by 2030, and Denmark's food cluster is as well placed as any to benefit. Its companies have lots of expertise in food safety, for example: China has identified Denmark as a model. Danish firms are thriving at the high as well as the low end of the business: Noma, a celebrated restaurant in Copenhagen, has helped to create a cult of Nordic food, including pigs' tails, supplied by Danish Crown. Above all, perhaps, Danes are remarkably hard-headed about making money out of blood and soil: the Danish Crown slaughterhouse organises regular tours for visitors, including schoolchildren, with views of the killing line.

January 2014

In praise of misfits

Why business needs people with Asperger's syndrome, attention-deficit disorder and dyslexia

IN 1956 WILLIAM WHYTE argued in his bestseller, *The Organisation Man*, that companies were so in love with "well-rounded" executives that they fought a "fight against genius". Today many suffer from the opposite prejudice. Software firms gobble up anti-social geeks. Hedge funds hoover up equally oddball quants. Hollywood bends over backwards to accommodate the whims of creatives. And policymakers look to rule-breaking entrepreneurs to create jobs. Unlike the school playground, the marketplace is kind to misfits.

Recruiters have noticed that the mental qualities that make a good computer programmer resemble those that might get you diagnosed with Asperger's syndrome: an obsessive interest in narrow subjects; a passion for numbers, patterns and machines; an addiction to repetitive tasks; and a lack of sensitivity to social cues. Some joke that the internet was invented by and for people who are "on the spectrum", as they put it in the Valley. Online, you can communicate without the ordeal of meeting people.

Wired magazine once called it "the Geek Syndrome". Speaking of internet firms founded in the past decade, Peter Thiel, an early Facebook investor, told the *New Yorker* that: "The people who run them are sort of autistic." Yishan Wong, an ex-Facebooker, wrote that Mark Zuckerberg, the founder, has "a touch of Asperger's", in that "he does not provide much active feedback or confirmation that he is listening to you." Craig Newmark, the founder of Craigslist, says he finds the symptoms of Asperger's "uncomfortably familiar" when he hears them listed.

Similar traits are common in the upper reaches of finance. The quants have taken over from the preppies. The hero of Michael Lewis's book *The Big Short*, Michael Burry, a hedge-fund manager, is a loner who wrote a stockmarket blog as a hobby while he was studying to be a doctor. He attracted so much attention from money managers that he quit medicine to start his own hedge fund, Scion Capital. After noticing that there was something awry with the mortgage market, he made a killing betting that it would crash. "The one guy that I could trust in the middle of this crisis," Mr Lewis told National Public Radio, "was this fellow with Asperger's and a glass eye."

Entrepreneurs also display a striking number of mental oddities. Julie Login of Cass Business School surveyed a group of entrepreneurs and found that 35% of them said that they suffered from dyslexia, compared with 10% of the population as a whole and 1% of professional managers. Prominent dyslexics include the founders of Ford, General Electric, IBM and IKEA, not to mention more recent successes such as Charles Schwab (the founder of a stockbroker), Richard Branson (the Virgin Group), John Chambers (Cisco) and Steve Jobs (Apple). There are many possible explanations for this. Dyslexics learn how to delegate tasks early (getting other people to do their homework, for example). They gravitate to activities that require few formal qualifications and demand little reading or writing.

Attention-deficit disorder (ADD) is another entrepreneur-friendly affliction: people who cannot focus on one thing for long can be disastrous employees but founts of new ideas. Some studies suggest that people with ADD are six times more likely than average to end up running their own businesses. David Neeleman, the founder of JetBlue, a budget airline, says: "My ADD brain naturally searches for better ways of doing things. With the disorganisation, procrastination, inability to focus and all the other bad things that come with ADD, there also come creativity and the ability to take risks." Paul Orfalea, the founder of Kinko's and a hotch-potch of businesses since, has both ADD and dyslexia. "I get bored easily; that is a great motivator," he once said. "I think everybody should have dyslexia and ADD."

Where does that leave the old-fashioned organisation man? He will do just fine. The more companies hire brilliant mavericks, the more they need sensible managers to keep the company grounded. Someone has to ensure that dull but necessary tasks are done. Someone has to charm customers (and perhaps lawmakers). This task is best done by those who don't give the impression that they think normal people are stupid. (Sheryl Sandberg, Mr Zuckerberg's deputy, does this rather well for Facebook.) Many start-ups are saved from disaster only by replacing the founders with professional managers. Those managers, of course, must learn to work with geeks.

Geekery in the genes

The clustering of people with unusual minds is causing new problems. People who work for brainy companies tend to marry other brainy people. Simon Baron-Cohen of Cambridge University argues that when two hyper-systematisers meet and mate, they are more likely to have children who suffer from Asperger's or its more severe cousin, autism. He has shown that children in Eindhoven, a technology hub in the Netherlands, are two to four times more likely to be diagnosed with autism than children in two other Dutch towns of similar size. He has also shown that Cambridge students who study mathematics, physics and engineering are more likely to have autistic relatives than students studying English literature. Most employers are leery of hiring severely autistic people, but not all. Specialist People, a Danish firm, matches autistic workers with jobs that require a good memory or a high tolerance for repetition.

More broadly, the replacement of organisation man with disorganisation man is changing the balance of power. Those square pegs may not have an easy time in school. They may be mocked by jocks and ignored at parties. But these days no serious organisation can prosper without them. As Kiran Malhotra, a Silicon Valley networker, puts it: "It's actually cool to be a geek."

June 2012

Of companies and closets

Being gay-friendly is cheap and good for business

IN *LITTLE BRITAIN,* a television comedy, Daffyd Thomas, who insists he is "the only gay in the village", tries to expose the homophobia of his fellow Welsh villagers by wearing outrageous clothes (bright red rubber shorts are a favourite) and picketing the local library. But he is constantly frustrated: the inhabitants of Llanddewi Brefi are all either tolerant or gay themselves.

The corporate world is not yet as gay-friendly as Llanddewi Brefi. But attitudes have changed dramatically. Some 86% of *Fortune* 500 firms now ban discrimination on the basis of sexual orientation, up from 61% in 2002. Around 50% also ban discrimination against transsexuals, compared with 3% in 2002. The Human Rights Campaign (HRC), an American pressure group, measures corporate policies towards sexual minorities in its annual "equality index". Of the 636 companies that responded to its 2012 survey, 64% offer the same medical benefits for same-sex partners as for heterosexual spouses. Some 30% scored a fabulous 100% on the group's index.

Progress has taken place in a wide range of industries. The 100% club predictably contains plenty of talent-driven outfits such as banks and consultancies (including Mitt Romney's old employer, Bain & Company). But it also includes industrial giants such as Alcoa, Dow Chemical, Ford, Owens Corning and Raytheon. Lord Browne, the boss of BP who resigned after his sex life made headlines in 2007, said he always remained in the closet because "it was obvious to me that it was simply unacceptable to be gay in business, and most definitely the oil business". Today Chevron, one of BP's toughest competitors, has a 100% rating.

Companies are competing with each other to produce the most imaginative gay-friendly policies. American Express has an internal "pride network" with more than 1,000 members. Cisco gives gay workers a bonus to make up for an anomaly in the American tax code. (If you are married, the cost of various insurance premiums is deducted from your pre-tax income, but if you are merely a partner it is deducted from your post-tax income.) Some companies vocally support gay marriage. In January 2012 Lloyd Blankfein, the boss of Goldman Sachs, accepted an invitation from HRC to become its first corporate spokesman for gay nuptials, and seven big companies, including Microsoft and Nike, have written to Congress to support the idea.

What caused this corporate revolution? Pressure groups such as HRC and Britain's Stonewall can take some of the credit. But mostly it happened because changing attitudes in society at large have reduced the cost of being gay-friendly, and raised the rewards. A generation ago in the West, creating a gay-friendly workplace might have upset heterosexual staff. Now it probably won't. But failing to treat gays equally is very likely to drive them to seek employment elsewhere. Since they are perhaps 5–10% of the global talent pool, bigotry makes a firm less competitive.

Being fair to gays is arguably simpler than being fair to women. Women really do differ from men in the amount of time, on average, that they take off to raise children. And there is no obvious answer to questions such as: "how much paid maternity leave should a small firm offer?" From an employer's perspective, gays do not differ from straights in any way that matters.

Sylvia Ann Hewlett and Karen Sumberg of the Centre for Work-Life Policy, a think-tank, have tried to quantify the benefits of inclusiveness to companies. They discovered that 47% of gays who have come out of the closet say that they are "very trusting" of their employers, compared with 21% who are still in the closet. Some 52% of closeted gays said that they felt stalled in their careers, compared with 36% of non-closeted gays.

This makes sense. It is hard to give your best if you have to conceal an important part of who you are. Straight workers routinely plaster their offices with pictures of their families, which not only creates a pleasant working environment but also broadcasts the message: "I have kids. Please don't sack me." Closeted gays find it harder to socialise with colleagues and build informal networks. They waste energy inventing excuses. "You have to watch everything you say and how you say it," says one closeted executive. "You have to be excellent at the pronoun game."

Being gay-friendly can attract gay customers, too. Witeck-Combs Communications, a consultancy, estimates that gay Americans spend $835 billion a year. In 2001 Merrill Lynch created a private-banking team that focused exclusively on the gay market, courting gay non-profits and providing seminars on financial planning for domestic partners. Within five years the group had brought in more than $1 billion of business.

Out of the closet and into a cubicle

The revolution is far from over. Nearly half of the respondents to the Centre for Work-Life Policy's survey are still in the closet. And even the most enlightened companies cannot make up for intolerance in the rest of the world. It is hard to reach the top of a big company without serving a stint abroad. But homosexuality is still illegal in 76 countries – including such vibrant business hubs as Dubai and Singapore – and is punishable by death in Saudi Arabia, Iran and parts of Nigeria.

Still, the gay revolution in the workplace is remarkable. In most places, companies are more liberal than governments. In America, for example, until 2011 soldiers could be kicked out of the army for being gay, and 29 states still allow discrimination on the basis of sexual preference. In the coming years, the revolution is likely to gather pace. Younger workers are far more relaxed about homosexuality than their parents were. Indeed, many young heterosexuals would feel uncomfortable working for a firm that failed to treat gays decently. Companies vying to recruit them will bear this in mind.

February 2012

Enterprising oldies

Founding new businesses is not a monopoly of the young, even if it seems so nowadays

"A LAZY BASTARD living in a suit" is Leonard Cohen's description of himself in his album, "Old Ideas". Mr Cohen is certainly fond of wearing a suit, on and off stage. But lazy seems a bit harsh: he was 77 when he released "Old Ideas" which is 12 years beyond the normal retirement age in Canada, where he was born. But there is no sign of his laying down his guitar. He spent 2008–10 on tour, performing on stage in Barcelona on his 75th birthday. "Old Ideas" has won widespread acclaim. Mr Cohen says he has written enough songs for another album.

In the 1960s pop was a young person's business. The Who hoped they died before they got old. Bob Dylan berated middle-aged squares like Mr Jones in "Ballad of a Thin Man". But today age is no barrier to success. The Rolling Stones are still touring in their 60s. Bob Dylan's songwriting skills, if not his vocal chords, have survived intact. Sir Paul McCartney warbles on.

It is time to do for enterprise what such ageing rockers have done for pop music: explode the myth that it is a monopoly of the young. This idea has been powerfully reinforced by the latest tech boom: Facebook, Google and Groupon were all founded by people in their 20s or teens. Mark Zuckerberg will soon be able to count his years on earth in billions of dollars. But the trend is not confined to tech: Michael Reger was a founder of one of America's most innovative energy companies, Northern Oil and Gas, aged 30.

The rise of the infant entrepreneur is producing a rash of ageism, particularly among venture capitalists. Why finance a 40-year-old (with a family and mortgage) when you can back a 20-year-old who will work around the clock for peanuts and might be the next Mr Zuckerberg? But it is not hard to think of counter-examples: Mark Pincus was 41 when he founded Zynga and Arianna Huffington was 54 when she created the *Huffington Post*.

Research suggests that age may in fact be an advantage for entrepreneurs. Vivek Wadhwa of Singularity University in California studied more than 500 American high-tech and engineering companies with more than $1 million in sales. He discovered that the average age of the founders of successful American technology businesses (ie, ones with real revenues) is 39. There were twice as many successful founders over 50 as under 25, and twice as many over 60 as under 20. Dane Stangler of the Kauffman Foundation studied American firms founded in 1996–2007. He found the highest rate of entrepreneurial activity among people aged between 55 and 64 – and the lowest rate among the Google generation of 20- to 34-year-olds. The Kauffman Foundation's most recent study of start-ups discovered that people aged 55 to 64 accounted for nearly 23% of new entrepreneurs in 2010, compared with under 15% in 1996.

Experience continues to count for a great deal, in business as in other walks of life – or, to borrow a phrase from P.J. O'Rourke, age and guile can still beat "youth, innocence and a bad haircut". It is one thing to invent a clever new product but quite another to hire employees or build a sales machine. And even when it comes to breakthrough ideas, age may still be an asset. Benjamin Jones of Northwestern University's Kellogg School of Management and Bruce Weinberg of Ohio State University examined the careers of Nobel prize-winners in chemistry, physics and medicine. They found that the average age at which these stars made their greatest innovations is now higher than it was a century ago. Mr Wadhwa speculates that many of the most promising businesses in future will result from the mating of two subjects that each take years to understand – robotics and biology, say, or medicine and nanotechnology.

Experience may be nothing if it is not linked to mould-breaking creativity. But there are plenty of older people who are capable of breaking moulds. Ray Kroc was in his 50s when he began building the McDonald's franchise system, and Colonel Harland Sanders was in his 60s when he started the Kentucky Fried Chicken chain. David Ogilvy worked as a chef and a spy before turning to advertising in his late 30s, an age when Bill Gates reinvented himself as a philanthropist. The late Steve Jobs was as creative in his second stint at Apple, from 1995 to 2011, as in his first.

This is not to say that the rise of young entrepreneurs like Mr Zuckerberg is insignificant. The barriers that once discouraged enterprise among the young are collapsing. Social networks make it easier to build contacts. Knowledge-intensive industries require relatively little capital. But the fact that barriers are collapsing for the young does not mean that they are being erected for greybeards. The point is that the creation of fast-growing businesses is now open to everybody regardless of age.

Back on the road again

The evidence that older people are if anything becoming more enterprising should help to calm two of the biggest worries that hang over the West (and indeed over an ageing China). One is that the greying of the population will inevitably produce economic sluggishness. The second is that older people will face hard times as companies shed older workers in the name of efficiency and welfare states cut back on their pensions.

Here, Mr Cohen is a man for our times. In 2004 he faced financial ruin when he discovered that his manager, Kelley Lynch, had misappropriated most of his savings. He sued successfully but could not lay his hands on the money. So he had no choice but to go back to work. Mr Cohen told the *New York Times* that reconnecting with "living musicians" and "living audiences" had "warmed some part of my heart that had taken a chill". Let us hope the same is true of the ageing boomers who will have little choice but to embrace self-employment as the West's welfare states discover that they cannot keep their promises.

February 2012

Ideas reinvenTED

TED has revolutionised the ideas industry, in part by putting old wine in new bottles

THE FIRST TED CONFERENCE in 1984 was such a damp squib that the organisers did not hold a second one for six years. Today TED (which for the uninitiated stands for Technology, Entertainment, Design) is the Goliath of the ideas industry. The heart of the enterprise is TED's twice-yearly conference at which big ideas are presented in short, punchy talks. On March 17th–21st 2014 around 1,200 TEDsters gathered in Vancouver to listen to the likes of Bill Gates and Nicholas Negroponte celebrating TED's 30th birthday and thinking great thoughts. The conference has also spawned an array of businesses, albeit not-for-profit ones.

The organisation has built an electronic warehouse of more than 1,700 previous talks, at TED.com. These are free to view and, so far, they have been watched nearly 2 billion times. It has generated a mass movement: volunteers have put on more than 9,000 TED-like events called TEDx in 150 or so countries since 2009. It has established a TED prize (worth $1 million), a TED fellowship programme and a line of TED e-books. And it has become a central part of the world's star-making machinery: an invitation to speak at TED can turn an obscure academic into a superstar guru and a struggling journalist into a celebrated writer.

Such success has inevitably produced a backlash. Critics dismiss TED as the Starbucks of intellectual life (though YO! Sushi may be a better comparison). Evgeny Morozov, a technology pundit, says it has become "something ludicrous, and a little sinister". Benjamin Bratton, a sociologist, goes further and suggests that TED is a recipe for "civilisational disaster". In his view TED really stands for "middlebrow, megachurch infotainment". The *Onion*, a satirical website, has produced a series of "*Onion* talks" including "A future where all robots have penises".

There is certainly some truth in these criticisms: any organisation that invites Sting to its 30th birthday party is in danger of jumping the shark. But criticism must be tempered by admiration for what TED has achieved. It does indeed have a weakness for celebrities. But it has also discovered hundreds of lights hidden under bushels: the most viewed TED video, with 25 million downloads, features Ken Robinson, a once-obscure British educationalist. It is true that TED shrinks big ideas into bite-like chunks. But it has also demonstrated that there is a huge market for big ideas.

TED is the perfect example of the power of disruptive innovation. The ideas business was already overcrowded when it began to flex its muscles. The BBC rejected an early TED talk on the ground that it was too intellectual. But TED has rewritten the rules. Conference regulars compare the corporate pabulum that they are served at Davos with the intellectual sustenance they receive at TED. Businesses now hire it to run their in-house conferences. Publishers compete to sign up its speakers. TED has done more to advance the art of lecturing in a decade than Oxford University has done in a thousand years.

The man at the heart of this disruption is Chris Anderson, a journalist turned entrepreneur who calls himself TED's curator. (He is unrelated to the namesake who used to edit *Wired* and before that wrote for *The Economist*.) Mr Anderson made his money publishing computer and business magazines. He bought TED in 2001 and set about turning a cult conference into a multimedia phenomenon, by bringing together the two worlds that he knew best: the journalistic one of storytelling and the high-tech world of disruptive change. And he provided TED with both a powerful business model and a pipeline of polished output.

TED uses a shrewd combination of paid-for and free products, the purpose of the latter being to generate buzz. Tickets to its five-day conferences cost at least $6,000. It sells an ever-growing array of TED-branded products. But it has also been generous with its intellectual capital – not only giving away videos on the internet but also granting licences to enthusiasts to stage TEDx events. To ensure quality it sends all speakers a stone tablet engraved with the "TED Commandments", starting with: "Thou shalt not simply trot out thy usual *schtick*". Talks must last for just 18 minutes – "Long enough to be serious and short enough to hold people's attention", as Mr Anderson puts it. Potential speakers are carefully auditioned and extensively trained – and subtly reminded that only successful talks will be put online.

TED is constantly striving to improve its products and expand its pipeline. It has invested heavily in camera crews and stagecraft. It has experimented with shorter formats such as "TED in three minutes". It has even introduced an *American Idol* element: about half of the speakers at each conference are chosen by competitive auditions that take place all over the world and are theoretically open to anyone.

Modern-day missionaries

TED has become the leading ideas festival of the digital world. It draws much of its audience as well as many of its star speakers from the technocracy. It champions tech solutions to problems: its talks tend to give the impression that there is no ill in the world that cannot be solved with a laptop and an internet connection.

But there is also something old-fashioned about it. TED meetings have a revivalist feel, from the preacher's promises of salvation to the happy-clappy congregation. It is revealing that Mr Anderson is the son of missionaries, and, in rather Victorian fashion, grew up in India before going to Oxford. TEDsters can also sound like modern versions of Dale Carnegie, the author of *The Art of Public Speaking* (1915) and *How to Win Friends and Influence People* (1936). A striking number of TED talks preach that you can have it all, a great career and a fulfilled life, if only you work hard and follow your passion. The ultimate secret of TED's success is not its commitment to disruptive innovation but its ability to repackage old-time religion for the digital age.

March 2014

The shackled boss

Corporate bosses are much less powerful than they used to be

EXHAUSTED AFTER A SHIPWRECK, the hero of *Gulliver's Travels* wakes up on the island of Lilliput to find that he has been tied down by lots of "slender ligatures". Gulliver is far stronger than his tiny captors; but by working together the Lilliputians subdue the giant.

The bosses who gathered in Davos on January 25th–29th 2012 are more like Gulliver than they care to imagine. They may feel big, as they hobnob with politicians and stride from one *soirée* to another (in sensible shoes, to avoid slipping on the Swiss resort's icy pavements). And pundits will fret, as they always do, that Davos Men are carving up the world. But when those bosses return to work they will discover that the tiny ligatures that non-Davosites have attached to them bind ever more tightly.

Two decades ago bosses were relatively unbound. American chief executives struck heroic poses on the covers of *Forbes* and *Fortune* and appointed pliable cronies to their boards. Europeans such as Percy Barnevik, the boss of ASEA Brown Boveri, a Swedish-Swiss conglomerate, imported the American cult of the CEO to the old continent. But since then a succession of catastrophes – most notably the implosion of Enron in 2001 and the financial crisis in 2007–08 – have empowered the critics of over-mighty bosses. In 2010 two legal academics, Marcel Kahan and Edward Rock, published a seminal article on "Embattled CEOs". Since then they have become ever more embattled.

One sign is that bosses don't last long these days. Among the world's 2,500 biggest public companies, the average job tenure for departing CEOs has fallen from 8.1 years in 2000 to 6.6 years today, according to Booz & Company, a consultancy. The fall would have been steeper but for the generosity of China's state companies. In 2010 CEO turnover worldwide was 11.6%, but in China it was half that. Booz also notes that shareholders give bosses very little time to prove themselves: Léo Apotheker lasted for seven months as the head of SAP (a software firm) and ten months as head of Hewlett-Packard (a computer giant).

Another sign that the Lilliputians are winning is that fewer chief executives now chair their own boards (the corporate equivalent of a schoolboy marking his own exam papers). In Booz's global sample the proportion of incoming CEOs who doubled as chairmen fell from 48% in 2002 to less than 12% in 2009. Even America is growing wary of imperial bosses: according to the Corporate Library, a pressure group, the proportion of CEOs of S&P 500 firms who mark their own exams fell from 78% in 2002 to 59% in 2010.

Bosses are still paid handsomely; but this is partly a reaction to rising job insecurity. And in much of the world CEO pay is rising more slowly than it did in the 1990s. In America it may even be declining. Moreover, the Lilliputians are forcing politicians to tie more strings. In 2010 America's Congress passed a say-on-pay law that gives shareholders a right to hold a (non-binding) vote on pay. David Cameron, Britain's prime minister, has suggested giving shareholders a binding vote on pay.

The rise of institutional investors (notably mutual funds) has changed the old equation whereby dispersed shareholders confronted concentrated managers. The proportion of stock in America's publicly listed companies that is held by institutions increased from 19% in 1970 to 50% in 2008. And the scandals of the 2000s have reignited shareholder activism.

To assess the bosses who work for them, shareholders have powerful new tools. For example, outfits such as RiskMetrics offer advice on proxy battles. Shareholders also have powerful new allies. Hedge funds intervene aggressively in corporate decision-making, browbeating such giants as McDonald's, Time Warner and Deutsche Börse.

At the same time boards of directors have grown more demanding. Gone are the days when a boss could put his golfing buddies on the board. ("A big glob of nothing" was how one observer described boards in the 1960s.) Today the vast majority of board members are outsiders. This has led to a huge improvement in their quality. Korn Ferry, a consultancy, notes that the 95 new directors who won seats on the boards of its sample of America's 100 biggest companies are remarkably rich in international experience: 21% hold foreign passports and 12% have worked in Brazil, Russia, India or China. It has also increased their willingness to act as stern monitors rather than chummy advisers. In his excellent book *Winning Investors Over*, Baruch Lev of New York University's Stern School of Business writes that in this new world "the lonely CEO now often faces a 'team of rivals', sometimes adversaries."

A proposal for modesty

All this is affecting bosses' behaviour. The latest buzz phrases in the C-suite are "humble leadership", "servant leadership" and "bottom-up leadership". But is it actually improving corporate performance? The academic literature suggests that it is. John Core and his colleagues have shown that companies with strong shareholder rights have higher operating profits than those with weak rights. Craig Doidge and his colleagues have shown that companies with stronger boards can raise capital more cheaply.

However, some CEOs are raising objections to the new regime. How can they focus on long-term growth, they ask, if they are constantly second-guessed by a team of rivals? Some are jumping ship for private companies. Anthony Thompson, formerly in charge of Asda's "George" brand of clothes, left to join Fat Face, a private clothing company, rejoicing that: "I no longer have to slavishly adhere to corporate nonsense and overbearing governance." Gulliver eventually persuaded his captors to untie him. CEOs will undoubtedly try to do likewise.

January 2012

Bumpkin bosses

Leaders of Western companies are less globally minded than they think they are

THE HEADS OF MULTINATIONAL COMPANIES like to think of themselves as generals in the globalisation wars. They dream of conquering fresh markets in the East. They boast about the diversity of their armies. And they love to mock politicians for their parochialism: why is Ed Miliband, the leader of the British Labour Party, making such a fuss about Pfizer's bid for AstraZeneca when the first is run by a Scotsman and the second by a Frenchman?

Which all makes a lot of sense: companies in developed countries do themselves nothing but harm if they fail to think globally. The biggest growth opportunities now are in the emerging world: McKinsey, a consultancy, calculates that people there will buy $20 trillion-worth of goods a year by 2020. So are the biggest threats: China's Huawei has grown rapidly from an improbable idea into one of the world's biggest telecoms companies.

But how good are these generals at applying the logic of globalisation to themselves? Pankaj Ghemawat, of Spain's IESE and NYU's Stern business schools, calculates that only 12% of the world's *Fortune* Global 500 – the largest corporations by revenue – are led by a CEO who hails from a country other than the one in which the company is headquartered. (By contrast, almost 50% of the managers of football clubs in England's Premier League were born abroad.) The figure for firms' senior management as a whole is 15%. These two numbers are highly correlated: in *Fortune* Global 500 companies with foreign CEOs, 50% of the management team is foreign as well, compared with only 10% at companies with native CEOs. The proportion of foreign CEOs rises to 30% if you look at the 100 biggest companies, but it quickly falls to single digits if you look beyond the largest 500.

European companies are the most cosmopolitan at the top: 23% of the bosses of European firms on the *Fortune* Global 500 list are foreigners, as are 28% of the senior managers. North America is just average, with 11% and 13% respectively. Japan comes a dismal third among rich-world countries: only 3% of CEOs and 5% of senior managers are non-Japanese. One of the leading "foreign" CEOs, Han Chang-Woo, of Maruhan, moved to Japan from South Korea in 1945 at the age of 14.

There are good reasons to think that leaders will become even more parochial in the future. Western companies are finding it harder to recruit "high potentials" in emerging markets. Two decades ago they had the field to themselves. Today they have to compete with fast-growing local companies and constantly confront the question, "Why should I work for a company that is run by people who look like you when I could work for one which is run by people who look like me?" Western firms are also cutting the number of people they send abroad: according to one study the proportion of expats in senior-management roles in multinationals in the biggest emerging markets declined from 56% to 12% between 1998 and 2008. And the Europeans and Americans are making poor use of those people: another study shows that staff who do a spell abroad take longer to move up the organisation than people who stay at headquarters. In other words, go-getting executives do better to spend their time politicking at central office than acquiring experience abroad.

Why does this matter? The obvious reason is that, in a globalising world, parochialism at the top can impose huge costs, in terms of reduced creativity, missed opportunities and cultural blundering. A growing body of research suggests that mixed teams are more likely than homogeneous ones to come up with creative solutions. Native CEOs tend to surround themselves with senior managers who resemble them. They are also more likely to fixate on a "native solution" to a strategic problem than to consider other options: Germans look to mechanical engineering for answers, Britons favour the financial sort.

Mr Ghemawat argues that C-suite parochialism helps to explain the relatively unimpressive performance of Western multinationals in emerging markets. Bain & Company, a consultancy, looked at the performance of 92 Western firms with listed subsidiaries in such markets. These companies increased their profits there by an average of 15% a year between 2005 and 2010. But comparable local companies boosted their profits by 23% a year.

McKinsey calculates that companies headquartered in emerging markets grew roughly twice as fast in those markets as those headquartered in developed economies – and two-and-a-half times as fast when both were competing on "neutral turf" in the emerging world. Given that traditional multinationals have better-established brands and longer histories as global companies than emerging rivals, a good deal of the difference must be explained by superior local knowledge.

Hit the road

How can multinationals avoid the evils of bumpkinism? One way is to move managerial functions to other parts of the world. Procter & Gamble relocated its global cosmetics and personal-care unit from its Cincinnati headquarters to Singapore. General Electric's health-care division is moving the headquarters of its X-ray business from Wisconsin to Beijing. Jean-Pascal Tricoire, the boss of France's Schneider Electric, has posted himself to Hong Kong. A second technique is to bring the rest of the world to headquarters. Bertelsmann posts successful local managers to bucolic Gütersloh in western Germany for a couple of years. Daimler has decreed that half the participants in its programmes for young high-flyers must come from outside Germany. A third technique is to give people from the rich world more opportunities to travel: IBM and FedEx encourage their executives to provide consulting to emerging-world subsidiaries. It is always tempting to think that multinational companies are cosmopolitan by nature; in fact, they have to work hard at debumpkinising themselves.

May 2014

Declining by degree

Will America's universities go the way of its car companies?

FIFTY YEARS AGO, in the glorious age of three-martini lunches and all-smoking offices, America's car companies were universally admired. Everybody wanted to know the secrets of their success. How did they churn out dazzling new models every year? How did they manage so many people so successfully (General Motors was then the biggest private-sector employer in the world)? And how did they keep their customers so happy?

Today the world is equally in awe of American universities. They dominate global rankings: on the Shanghai Ranking Consultancy's list of the world's best universities, 17 of the top 20 are American, and 35 of the top 50. They employ 70% of living Nobel prize-winners in science and economics and produce a disproportionate share of the world's most-cited articles in academic journals. Everyone wants to know their secret recipe.

Which raises a mischievous question. Could America's universities go the way of its car companies? On the face of it, this seems highly unlikely. Student enrolments were higher than ever in 2010, as Americans who cannot find jobs linger or return to education. Cambridge, Massachusetts, shows no outward sign of becoming Detroit. Yet there are serious questions about America's ivory towers.

Two right-wing think-tanks, the American Enterprise Institute (AEI) and the Goldwater Institute, have both produced damning reports about America's university system. Two left-wing academics, Andrew Hacker and Claudia Dreifus, have published an even more damning book: "Higher Education? How Colleges are Wasting Our Money and Failing Our Kids and What We Can Do About It". And *US News & World Report*, a centrist magazine, says in its annual survey of American colleges that: "If colleges were businesses, they would be ripe for hostile takeovers, complete with serious cost-cutting and painful reorganisations."

College fees have for decades risen faster than Americans' ability to pay them. Median household income has grown by a factor of 6.5 in the past 40 years, but the cost of attending a state college has increased by a factor of 15 for in-state students and 24 for out-of-state students. The cost of attending a private college has increased by a factor of more than 13 (a year in the Ivy League will set you back $38,000, excluding bed and board). Academic inflation makes medical inflation look modest by comparison.

As costs soar, diligence is tumbling. In 1961 full-time students in four-year colleges spent 24 hours a week studying; that has fallen to 14, estimates the AEI. Drop-out and deferment rates are also hair-curling: only 40% of students graduate in four years.

The most plausible explanation is that professors are not particularly interested in students' welfare. Promotion and tenure depend on published research, not good teaching. Professors strike an implicit bargain with their students: we will give you light workloads and inflated grades so long as you leave us alone to do our research. Mr Hacker and Ms Dreifus point out that senior professors in Ivy League universities now get sabbaticals every third year rather than every seventh. This year 20 of Harvard's 48 history professors will be on leave.

America's commitment to research is one of the glories of its higher-education system. But for how long? The supply of papers that apply gender theory to literary criticism remains ample. But there is evidence of diminishing returns in an area perhaps more vital to the country's economic dynamism: science and technology. The Kauffman Foundation, which studies entrepreneurship, argues that the productivity of federal funding for R&D, in terms of patents and licences, has been falling for some years. Funding is spread too thinly. It would yield better results if concentrated on centres of excellence, but fashionable chatter about the "knowledge economy" stirs every congressional backwoodsman to stick his fingers into the university pie.

The Goldwater Institute points to a third poison to add to rising prices and declining productivity: administrative bloat. Between 1993 and 2007 spending on university bureaucrats at America's 198 leading universities rose much faster than spending on teaching faculty. Administration costs at elite private universities rose even faster than at public ones. For example, Harvard increased its administrative spending per student by 300%. In some universities, such as Arizona State University, almost half the full-time employees are administrators. Nearly all university presidents conduct themselves like corporate titans, with salaries, perks and entourages to match.

At least the Naval Academy is free

Given the size and competitiveness of America's higher-education system, you might expect these problems to be self-correcting. Why don't some universities compete by hiring teaching superstars? And why don't others slash prices? The big problem is that high-status institutions such as universities tend to compete with each other on academic reputation (which is enhanced by star professors) and bling (luxurious dormitories and fancy sports stadiums) rather than value for money. This starts at the top: Yale would never dream of competing with Harvard on price. But it also extends to second-division universities: George Washington University has made itself fashionable by charging students more and spending lavishly on its facilities.

This luxury model is unlikely to survive what is turning into a prolonged economic downturn. Parents are much less willing to take on debt than they were and much more willing to look abroad for better deals. The internet also poses a growing threat to what Bill Gates calls "place-based colleges". Online, you can listen to the world's best lecturers for next to nothing.

America's universities lost their way badly in the era of easy money. If they do not find it again, they may go the way of GM.

September 2010

Angst for the educated

A university degree no longer confers financial security

EVERY AUTUMN MILLIONS of school-leavers in the rich world bid a tearful goodbye to their parents and start a new life at university. Some are inspired by a pure love of learning. But most also believe that spending three or four years at university – and accumulating huge debts in the process – will boost their chances of landing a well-paid and secure job.

Their elders have always told them that education is the best way to equip themselves to thrive in a globalised world. Blue-collar workers will see their jobs offshored and automated, the familiar argument goes. School dropouts will have to cope with a life of cash-strapped insecurity. But the graduate elite will have the world at its feet. There is some evidence to support this view. A recent study from Georgetown University's Centre on Education and the Workforce argues that "obtaining a post-secondary credential is almost always worth it". Educational qualifications are tightly correlated with earnings: an American with a professional degree can expect to pocket $3.6 million over a lifetime; one with merely a high-school diploma can expect only $1.3 million. The gap between more- and less-educated earners may be widening. A study in 2002 found that someone with a bachelor's degree could expect to earn 75% more over a lifetime than someone with only a high-school diploma. Today the premium is even higher.

But is the past a reliable guide to the future? Or are we at the beginning of a new phase in the relationship between jobs and education? There are good reasons for thinking that old patterns are about to change – and that the current recession-driven downturn in the demand for Western graduates will morph into something structural. The gale of creative destruction that has shaken so many blue-collar workers over the past few decades is beginning to shake the cognitive elite as well.

The supply of university graduates is increasing rapidly. The

Chronicle of Higher Education calculates that between 1990 and 2007 the number of students going to university increased by 22% in North America, 74% in Europe, 144% in Latin America and 203% in Asia. In 2007 150 million people attended university around the world, including 70 million in Asia. Emerging economies – especially China – are pouring resources into building universities that can compete with the elite of America and Europe. They are also producing professional-services firms such as Tata Consulting Services and Infosys that take fresh graduates and turn them into world-class computer programmers and consultants. The best and the brightest of the rich world must increasingly compete with the best and the brightest from poorer countries who are willing to work harder for less money.

At the same time, the demand for educated labour is being reconfigured by technology, in much the same way that the demand for agricultural labour was reconfigured in the 19th century and that for factory labour in the 20th. Computers can not only perform repetitive mental tasks much faster than human beings. They can also empower amateurs to do what professionals once did: why hire a flesh-and-blood accountant to complete your tax return when TurboTax (a software package) will do the job at a fraction of the cost? And the variety of jobs that computers can do is multiplying as programmers teach them to deal with tone and linguistic ambiguity.

Several economists, including Paul Krugman, have begun to argue that post-industrial societies will be characterised not by a relentless rise in demand for the educated but by a great "hollowing out", as mid-level jobs are destroyed by smart machines and high-level job growth slows. David Autor, of the Massachusetts Institute of Technology (MIT), points out that the main effect of automation in the computer era is not that it destroys blue-collar jobs but that it destroys any job that can be reduced to a routine. Alan Blinder, of Princeton University, argues that the jobs graduates have traditionally performed are if anything more "offshorable" than low-wage ones. A plumber or lorry-driver's job cannot be outsourced to India. A computer programmer's can.

A university education is still a prerequisite for entering some of the great guilds, such as medicine, law and academia, that provide secure and well-paying jobs. Over the 20th century these guilds did a wonderful job of raising barriers to entry – sometimes for good reasons (nobody wants to be operated on by a barber) and sometimes for self-interested ones. But these guilds are beginning to buckle. Newspapers are fighting a losing battle with the blogosphere. Universities are replacing tenure-track professors with non-tenured staff. Law firms are contracting out routine work such as "discovery" (digging up documents relevant to a lawsuit) to computerised-search specialists such as Blackstone Discovery. Even doctors are threatened, as patients find advice online and treatment in Wal-Mart's new health centres.

Dreaming spires, meet pin factory

Thomas Malone of MIT argues that these changes – automation, globalisation and deregulation – may be part of a bigger change: the application of the division of labour to brain-work. Just as Adam Smith's factory managers broke the production of pins into 18 components, so companies are increasingly breaking the production of brain-work into ever tinier slices. TopCoder chops up IT projects into bite-sized chunks and then serves them up to a worldwide workforce of freelance coders.

These changes will undoubtedly improve the productivity of brain-workers. They will allow consumers to sidestep the professional guilds that have extracted high rents for their services. And they will empower many brain-workers to focus on what they are best at and contract out more tedious tasks to others. But the reconfiguration of brain-work will also make life far less cosy and predictable for the next generation of graduates.

September 2011

PART 4

Surviving disruption: the case of companies

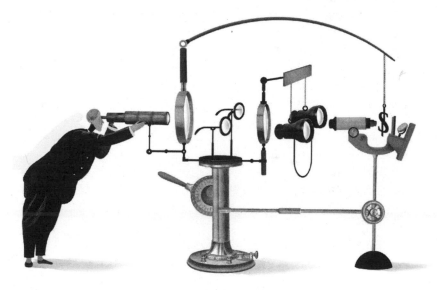

Measuring management

It is no longer just a plausible theory that good management boosts productivity

MANAGEMENT IS ONE of the most successful industries of the past century. In 1914 it was a mere infant. Harvard Business School (HBS) was just six years old. Management literature consisted of Frederick Taylor's *The Principles of Scientific Management* (1911) and a few other scraps. Today it is a loud-mouthed adult. A quarter of American graduate students study business. Some of the world's most profitable businesses peddle the modern equivalent of Taylor's "Principles".

But does management deserve its current elevated status? Or is it just a jargon-spouting con-trick? There is no shortage of sceptics. Matthew Stewart, a former management consultant, has written a book on *The Management Myth*. Philip Delves Broughton, an HBS alumnus, calls his fellow MBAs "masters of the apocalypse". This columnist co-wrote a book on management gurus called *The Witch Doctors*. Other critics argue that there is no such thing as "good management" – everything depends on context – or that it is impossible to measure how much difference something as nebulous as management makes.

For the past decade a group of economists, including Nicholas Bloom of Stanford University and John Van Reenen of the London School of Economics, have been trying to bring some rigour to the argument. They have focused on three commonly accepted management techniques – setting targets, rewarding performance and measuring results – and studied the performance of more than 10,000 organisations in 20 countries in the light of how well they implement these techniques. They have employed about 150 researchers and rigorous econometric methods to guarantee the robustness of their results. Their study is still a work in progress. But it nevertheless promises to be nothing less than the Domesday Book of the management age.

The economists conclude that good management is indeed tightly linked to improved corporate performance, measured in terms of productivity, profitability, growth and survival. Good management is more like a technology than merely an adjustment to circumstances. Certain successful management practices can be applied to many horses on many courses. Some of these are eternal, such as rewarding merit. Some are genuine innovations, such as the quality movement founded by W. Edwards Deming after the second world war.

In some respects Messrs Bloom and company's findings uphold conventional wisdom. America has the best-managed companies overall, followed by places like Germany and Japan. Rich-world laggards like Portugal and Greece, and big emerging markets, have a long tail of badly run firms. Big multinationals have the highest management scores, and public-sector bodies and firms run by their founders or their offspring have the lowest.

However, the researchers have put some hard figures on these common assumptions: they estimate that management accounts for roughly a quarter of the 30% productivity gap between America and Europe; so prophets of America's demise need to reckon with the size of its managerial superiority. They find that China's tail of poorly run firms is a lot shorter than India's or Brazil's. Britain's abnormally large number of poorly managed companies is in part the result of its tradition of primogeniture.

The findings have been subjected to two experiments. The first was accidental: when the 2007–08 financial crisis struck, in the worst-affected industries those businesses that implemented the "correct" management techniques properly did indeed fare better than the rest. The second was deliberate: the economists provided free management advice to a randomly chosen group of Indian textile plants and compared their performance with that of a set of control plants. A year later, those that implemented their advice had improved their relative productivity by 17%.

The researchers also made use of a mammoth survey by the US Census Bureau of management practices in more than 30,000 American factories. Again they found that their three chosen management techniques were tightly linked to superior performance. They found that companies in the south and mid-west are better managed than those in the west and the north-east. They also found that American management improved markedly between 2005 and 2010, particularly in data collection and analysis.

Why do good management practices spread in some areas and not in others? The economists have a simple answer: the quality of management seems to be clearly related to the competitiveness of the markets businesses operate in. That is why American firms are especially well-managed: the country's competitive business climate drives out badly run firms and rewards well-run ones. Multinationals that must cope with a wide variety of competitors tend to be well-run; public-sector firms, and family firms with strong political protection, do not.

Judgment and revelation

Some caveats are in order. Messrs Bloom and company may be a bit too quick to dismiss the idea of adjusting management principles to the circumstances. For example, the unthinking implementation of performance-related pay may be counter-productive in industries that rely on creativity and innovation – some of the most dynamic parts of the modern economy. And new management principles are constantly emerging; some may prove to matter more than the three the researchers base their studies on.

That said, the importance of this work should not be underestimated. Good evidence now exists that there is a body of management practices which is strongly associated with better performance, regardless of time or place. It is a body that can be expanded by the addition of new ideas such as, say, lean manufacturing or total quality management, but its core principles have demonstrably stood the test of time.

January 2014

Unpacking Lego

How the Danish firm became the world's hottest toy company

IT IS GETTING HARDER to go anywhere without stepping on a piece of Lego-related hype. *The Lego Movie* topped the charts at the box office. Model kits related to the film are piled high in the shops, adding to the already gigantic heap of Lego bits: 86 for every person on the planet. The toymaker has enjoyed ten years of spectacular growth, almost quadrupling its revenue. In 2012 it overtook Hasbro to become the world's second-largest toymaker. The number one, Mattel, is now seeking to buy the Canadian maker of Mega Bloks toy bricks, to fend off the challenge from Lego.

This is remarkable for many reasons. Lego's home town, Billund in rural Denmark, is so small that the company had to provide it with a hotel – an elegant one, unsurprisingly. The toy business is one of the world's trickiest: perennially faddish (remember Beanie Babies?) and, at the moment, convulsed by technological innovation. Children are growing up ever faster, and abandoning the physical world for the virtual. To cap it all, the company almost collapsed in 2003–04, having drifted for years, diversifying into too many areas, producing too many products and, in a fit of desperation, flirting with becoming a "lifestyle" company, with Lego-branded clothes and watches.

Lego's decade of success began when it appointed Jorgen Vig Knudstorp as chief executive. This was a risky move: Mr Knudstorp was a mere 35 years old and had cut his teeth as a management consultant with McKinsey rather than running a business. But it proved to be inspired. Mr Knudstorp decreed that the company must go "back to the brick": focusing on its core products, forgetting about brand-stretching, and even selling its theme parks. He also brought in stricter management controls, for example reducing the number of different pieces that the company produced from 12,900 to 7,000.

Under Mr Knudstorp Lego has struck a successful balance between innovation and tradition. The company has to generate new ideas to keep its sales growing: customers need a reason to expand their stock of bricks, and to buy them from Lego rather than cheaper rivals. But at the same time it must resist the sort of undisciplined innovation that almost ruined it. Lego produces a stream of kits with ready-made designs, such as forts and spaceships, to provide children with templates. But it also insists that the pieces can be added to the child's collection of bricks, and reused to make all sorts of other things.

Lego has got better at managing its relationships. *The Lego Movie* demonstrates how it can focus on the brick while venturing into the virtual world: Warner Bros. made the film while Lego provided the models. During its years of drift it relied too much on other firms' blockbuster franchises, such as Harry Potter and Star Wars. This time its intellectual property, not someone else's, is the star of the film. It has also got better at tapping its legion of fans – particularly adult fans of Lego, or AFOLs – for new ideas.

Can the company continue its winning streak? Its growth is slowing: its net profits grew by 9% in 2013 compared with 35% in 2012, and its revenues rose by 10% compared with 23% in 2012. Mr Knudstorp suggests that harder times are ahead: "When the company is getting bigger and the market isn't growing, it's a pure mathematical consequence that growth rates will have to reach a more sustainable level." Lego is now at an inflection point, building its organisational capacity and embracing globalisation to help it find new sources of growth.

In 2013 the company invested DKr2.6 billion ($478 million) in production facilities and added more than 1,300 full-time workers, a 13% increase. It is expanding two existing factories – in Kladno in the Czech Republic and Monterrey in Mexico – and building two new ones – in Nyiregyhaza in Hungary and, most important of all, in Jiaxing in China. Its management is being globalised too, with regional offices being opened in Singapore and Shanghai (as well as in London). The aim is twofold: to replicate in the rapidly growing East Lego's success in the West; and to transform a local company that happened to go global into a global company that happens to have its head office in Billund.

Late to the party

Globalisation is fraught with difficulties. Lego is relatively late in making its China play – jumping in when some other Western firms are jumping out with nothing but regrets to show for it. Lego also owes its identity to its roots in small-town Denmark: Ole Kirk Kristiansen, its founder, made up the name from the first two letters of two Danish words, leg godt, or play well, and committed his company to "nurture the child in each of us". An earlier attempt to move some of the responsibilities for designing products to an office in Milan proved to be a disaster. But the logic of globalisation is nevertheless compelling. The Chinese middle class is exploding, the toy business in the West is stagnant, and Lego needs a global workforce if it is to serve a global market.

Lego also has one important force on its side in its battle to globalise: parents in emerging markets, just like those in the rich world, are convinced that the company's products are good for their children. Grown-ups everywhere welcome it as a respite from the endless diet of videos and digital games that their offspring would otherwise consume. Chinese adults, including those very grown-up ones in government ministries, hope it will provide the secret ingredient that their education system sorely lacks: creativity. The Lego Movie may have provided the company with a welcome boost. But Lego's long-term success rests on the way adults feel reassured at buying a toy whose roots lie in an age before video games, mobile apps and toy-themed films.

March 2014

Taking the long view

The pursuit of shareholder value is attracting criticism – not all of it foolish

HE IS THE CHIEF EXECUTIVE of a multinational corporation, but Paul Polman sometimes sounds more like a spokesman for Occupy Wall Street. The boss of Unilever (an Anglo-Dutch consumer-goods firm with brands ranging from Timotei shampoo to Ben & Jerry's ice cream) agonises about unemployment, global warming and baby-boomer greed. He puts some of the blame for these ills on the most influential management theory of the past three decades: the idea that companies should aim above all else to maximise returns to shareholders.

He appears to mean it. Since taking charge in 2009, Mr Polman has stopped Unilever from publishing full financial results every quarter. He refuses to offer earnings guidance to equity analysts. He has introduced a lengthy "sustainable living plan" and attracted a new cadre of long-term investors, particularly in emerging markets. He even told an audience in Davos that hedge-fund managers would sell their own grandmothers to make a profit.

Mr Polman was one of several titans to decry the cult of shareholder value at the Peter Drucker Forum (an annual gathering of admirers of the late Austrian-born management guru) in Vienna on November 15th and 16th 2012. Roger Martin, the dean of Rotman School of Management at the University of Toronto, called it a "crummy principle that is undermining American capitalism". Georg Kapsch of the Federation of Austrian Industries urged the world to abandon it. Rick Wartzman, the director of the Drucker Institute, said its critics were gaining momentum.

The cult has certainly yielded perverse results. The fashion for linking pay to share prices has spurred some bosses to manipulate those prices. For example, a manager with share options gets nothing if the share price misses its target, so he may take unwise risks to hit it. Short-termism is rife on Wall Street: the average time that people hold a stock on the New York Stock Exchange tumbled from eight years in 1960 to four months in 2010. The emphasis on short-term results has tempted some firms to skimp on research and innovation, robbing the future to flatter this year's profits. "Long-term results cannot be achieved by piling short-term results on short-term results," Drucker once remarked.

One study shows that listed companies have invested only 4% of their total assets, compared with 10% for "observably similar" privately held companies. A second shows that 80% of managers are willing to reduce spending on R&D or advertising to hit the numbers. John Kay, a British economist (and author of a government report on short-termism), argues that the pursuit of short-term profit may have undermined two of Britain's greatest companies, ICI and GEC.

But hang on a second. Are the critics really right to argue that modern capital markets invariably put short-term results before long-term ones? Amazon has never found it hard to attract investors, despite the way it ploughs its profits into long-term plans for world domination. Plenty of other tech stocks are wildly popular despite negligible short-term returns. And are companies always foolish to react sharply to short-term warning signs? Nokia, a Finnish telecoms firm, would be much healthier today if it had reacted more swiftly to market warnings, rather than keeping a second-rate boss in place while Apple destroyed its business.

The critics make a distinction between long-term value (good) and short-term value (bad). But what is long-term value if not short-term results piled upon each other? And what is wrong with making regular checks on your performance? A company's quarterly results will probably tell you something about its long-term health as well as its performance over the previous quarter.

The critics have also failed to produce a viable alternative measure of success. One idea is to look at "customer satisfaction". But isn't the best way to please customers to give everything away for nothing? Another idea is to rely purely on the judgment of managers, but isn't this like allowing children to mark their own homework? Many critics of the shareholder model embrace a "stakeholder" model instead, but this is too vague to be much of a guide. Who are a company's stakeholders, and how should their competing interests be weighed against each other? No one knows. The great virtue of a share price is that it provides a clear external measure by which managers can be judged.

The stockmarket is not as short-sighted as some people think. Amazon is not the only firm it has rewarded for taking the long view, notes Baruch Lev of New York University's Stern School of Business. Others include Toyota, IBM and John Deere. Mr Lev also argues that most managers who manipulate their results to "hit the numbers" are caught. The problem is not that investors are fools, but that some managers think they are.

Mend it; don't end it

Rather than junking shareholder value, companies should tweak it. Some are getting better at this. Warren Buffett, like Mr Polman, adamantly refuses to provide earnings guidance to investors. IBM has produced a "2015 roadmap" to persuade investors that its big investments today will make money in the future. L'Oréal and Air Liquide have offered shareholders bonuses for holding shares longer than a certain period of time. Google, LinkedIn, Zynga and other tech companies have adopted dual-class voting structures that allow the founders to resist the pressure to produce short-term results.

Several companies allow their chief executives to exercise their share options only after retirement, to encourage long-term thinking. Giving managers ordinary shares (rather than options) which they cannot sell for several years aligns their interests even more closely with those of ordinary shareholders. As Bill Clinton once said of affirmative action, the best way to deal with the shortcomings of shareholder value is to "Mend it; don't end it."

November 2012

The silence of Mammon

Business people should stand up for themselves

HENRY HAZLITT, one of the great popularisers of free-market thinking, once said that good ideas have to be relearned in every generation. This is certainly true of good ideas about business. A generation ago Margaret Thatcher and Ronald Reagan did an excellent job of making the case in favour of business. Today it looks as though the case needs to be made all over again.

It is hardly surprising that business has fallen from grace in recent years. The credit crunch almost plunged the world into depression. The new century began with the implosion of Enron and other prominent firms. Some bosses pay themselves like princes while preaching austerity to their workers. Business titans who once graced the covers of magazines have been hauled before congressional committees or carted off to prison.

Business people have been at pains to point out that it is unfair to judge all of their kind by the misdeeds of a few. The credit crunch was the handiwork of bankers (who lent too much money) and policymakers (who fooled themselves into thinking that they had abolished boom and bust). Corporate criminals like WorldCom's Bernie Ebbers and Tyco's Denis Kozlowski were imprisoned for their crimes. Avaricious bosses like Angelo Mozilo, who pocketed more than $550 million during his inglorious reign at Countrywide, are exceptions. The average American boss is actually paid less today than he was in 2000.

This is all true enough but hardly sets the blood racing. More ambitious defenders of business have advanced two arguments. The first is that many firms are devoted to good works. They routinely trumpet their passionate commitment not just to their various stakeholders (such as workers and suppliers) but to the planet at large. Timberland puts "green index" labels on all its shoes. GlaxoSmithKline makes HIV drugs available at cost to millions of Africans. Starbucks buys lots of Fairtrade coffee.

The second argument is more hard-headed: that businesses have done more than any other institutions to advance prosperity, turning the luxuries of the rich, such as cars a century ago and computers today, into goods for the masses. General Electric's aircraft engines transport 660 million people a year and its imaging machines scan 230 million patients. Wal-Mart's "everyday low prices" save Americans at least $50 billion a year.

The problem with the first argument is that it smacks of appeasement. Advocates of corporate social responsibility suggest that business has something to apologise for, and thus encourage its critics to find ever more to complain about. Crocodiles never go away if you feed them. The problem with the second argument is that it does not go far enough. It focuses exclusively on material well-being, and so fails to engage with people's moral qualms about business.

This is doubly regrettable. It is regrettable because it has allowed critics of business to dominate the discussion of corporate morality. For all too many people it is now taken as a given that companies promote greed, crush creativity and monopolise power. And it is regrettable because it has deprived the business world of three rather better arguments in its defence.

The first is that business is a remarkable exercise in co-operation. For all the talk of competition "red in tooth and claw", companies in fact depend on persuading large numbers of people – workers and bosses, shareholders and suppliers – to work together to a common end. This involves getting lots of strangers to trust each other. It also increasingly involves stretching that trust across borders and cultures. Apple's iPod is not just a miracle of design. It is also a miracle of co-operation, teaming Californian designers with Chinese manufacturers and salespeople in all corners of the earth. It is worth remembering that the word "company" is derived from the Latin words "cum" and "pane" – meaning "breaking bread together".

Another rejoinder is that business is an exercise in creativity. Business people do not just invent clever products that solve nagging problems, from phones that can link fishermen in India with nearby markets to devices that can provide insulin to diabetics without painful injections. They also create organisations that manufacture these products and then distribute them about the world. Nandan

Nilekani, one of the founders of Infosys, put the case for business as well as anyone when he said that the computer-services giant's greatest achievement was not its $2 billion in annual revenue but the fact that it had taught his fellow Indians to "redefine the possible".

Enfranchising, not enslaving

A third defence is that business helps maintain political pluralism. Anti-capitalists are fond of arguing that companies account for half of the world's 100 biggest economies. But this argument not only depends on the abuse of statistics – comparing corporate turnover with GDP (which measures value added, not sales). It also rests on ignorance of the pressures of business life.

Companies have a difficult enough job staying alive, let alone engaging in a "silent takeover" of the state. Only 202 of the 500 biggest companies in America in 1980 were still in existence 20 years later. Anti-capitalists actually have it upside down. Companies prevent each other from gaining too much power, and also act as a check on the power of governments that would otherwise be running the economy. The proportion of the world's governments that can reasonably be called democratic has increased from 40% in 1980, when the pro-business revolution began, to more than 60% today.

Most hard-headed business people are no doubt reluctant to make these arguments. They are more concerned with balancing their books than with engaging in worthy debates about freedom and democracy. But they would do well to become a bit less reticent: the price of silence will be an ever more hostile public and ever more overbearing government.

December 2009

Mittel-management

Germany's midsized companies have a lot to teach the world

MANAGEMENT GURUS are constantly scouring the world for the next big idea. Thirty years ago they fixated on Japan. Today it is India. The more restless are already moving on to Peruvian or Zulu management. Yet in all this intellectual globe-trotting the gurus have sorely neglected the secrets of one of the world's great economies. Germany is the world's largest goods exporter after China despite high labour costs and a strongish euro. It is also stuffed full of durable companies that have survived hyperinflation and two world wars. Faber-Castell, a giant among pencilmakers, boasts that Bismarck was a customer.

Thankfully, a couple of management thinkers have defied the boycott on Germany. On November 18th 2010 Bernd Venohr, of the Berlin School of Economics and Law, gave a fascinating talk on the "secret recipe" of the country's *Mittelstand* at the second annual Peter Drucker Forum in Vienna. In 2009 Hermann Simon, of Simon-Kucher & Partners, a consultancy, published an even more gripping sequel to his 1996 book on *Hidden Champions*. Put the two together and you get a good idea of the management theory at the heart of Germany's success.

Although the term *Mittelstand* is sometimes applied to quite small, parochial firms, the most interesting ones are rather bigger and more outward-looking. Most shun the limelight: 90% of them operate in the business-to-business market and 70% are based in the countryside. They are run by anonymous company men, not hip youngsters in T-shirts and flip-flops.

They focus on market niches, typically in staid-sounding areas such as mechanical engineering rather than sexy ones like software. Dorma makes doors and all things door-related. Tente specialises in castors for hospital beds. Rational makes ovens for professional kitchens. This strategy helps them avoid head-to-head competition with global giants ("Don't dance where the elephants play" is a favourite *Mittelstand* slogan). It has also helped them excel at what they do.

Globalisation has been a godsend to these companies: they have spent the past 30 years of liberalisation working quietly but relentlessly to turn their domination of German market niches into domination of global ones. They have gobbled up opportunities in eastern Europe and Russia. They have provided China's "factory to the world" with its machine-tools.

The *Mittelstand* dominates the global market in an astonishing range of areas: printing presses (Koenig & Bauer), licence plates (Utsch), snuff (Pöschl), shaving brushes (Mühle), flycatchers (Aeroxon), industrial chains (RUD) and high-pressure cleaners (Kärcher). Kärcher's dominance of the high-pressure market is so complete that in 2005 Nicolas Sarkozy caused a scandal, after a spate of riots, by calling for a crime-ridden *banlieue* to be cleaned out "*au Kärcher*".

How durable is the *Mittelstand* model? Sceptics worry that it will eventually become the victim of globalisation: emerging-world companies will learn to produce their own clever machines at a fraction of the cost. They also worry that *Mittelstand* companies are too conservative. American start-ups can become global giants in a generation (Wal-Mart, now the world's biggest retailer, was not even listed on the stock exchange until 1972). German companies are content to remain relatively small.

The first criticism is overstated. *Mittelständler* have not only focused on sophisticated niches that are hard to enter. They have thrown their energies into building up ever more powerful defences. They constantly innovate to stay ahead of potential rivals. They are relentless about customer service. Their salespeople are passionate about their products, however prosaic, and dogged in their determination to open up new markets. Mr Simon's "hidden champions", mostly German *Mittelstand* firms, typically have subsidiaries in 24 foreign countries, offering service and advice. Many get the bulk of their revenues from service rather than products. Hako, which makes cleaning equipment, generates only 20% of its revenue from sales of its machines.

The second criticism has more substance. Germany has a poor record at generating start-ups or at quickly turning smallish firms into giants. *Mittelstand* firms are finding it increasingly difficult to persuade the world's best and brightest to make their careers in rural backwaters. But for all that, the record of the *Mittelstand* over the past three decades has been a history of global conquest rather than missed opportunities. Koenig & Bauer, for example, gets 95% of its revenue from outside Germany.

German lessons

So the *Mittelstand* is likely to keep powering Germany's export machine for years to come. But does it have any lessons for the rest of the world? Mr Simon says that although 80% of the world's medium-sized market leaders are based in Germany and Scandinavia, successful *Mittelstand*-style companies can be found everywhere from the United States (particularly the Midwest) to northern Italy, so the model does seem to be transferable.

Three general lessons – for politicians as well as corporate strategists – follow from this. First, you do not need to try to build your own version of Silicon Valley to prosper; it is often better to focus on your traditional strengths in "old-fashioned" industries. Second, niches that appear tiny can produce huge global markets.

The third lesson is that Western companies can preserve high-quality jobs in a vast array of industries so long as they are willing to focus and innovate. Theodore Levitt, one of the doyens of Harvard Business School, once observed that "sustained success is largely a matter of focusing regularly on the right things and making a lot of uncelebrated little improvements every day". That is a lesson that the Germans learned a long time ago – and that the rest of the rich world should take to heart.

November 2010

The corruption eruption

Saying "no" to corruption makes commercial as well as ethical sense

IT IS 15 YEARS since Moisés Naím coined the memorable phrase "corruption eruption". But there is no sign of the eruption dying down. Indeed, there is so much molten lava and sulphurous ash around that some of the world's biggest companies have been covered in it. Siemens and Daimler have recently been forced to pay gargantuan fines. BHP Billiton, a giant mining company, has admitted that it may have been involved in bribery. America's Department of Justice is investigating some 150 companies, targeting oil and drugs firms in particular.

The ethical case against corruption is too obvious to need spelling out. But many companies still believe that, in this respect at least, there is a regrettable tension between the dictates of ethics and the logic of business. Bribery is the price that you must pay to enter some of the world's most difficult markets (the "when in Rome" argument). Bribery can also speed up the otherwise glacial pace of bureaucracy (the "efficient grease" hypothesis). And why not? The chances of being caught are small while the rewards for bending the rules can be big and immediate.

When in Rome, behave like a Swede

But do you really have to behave like a Roman to thrive in Rome? Philip Nichols, of the Wharton School, points out that plenty of Western firms have prospered in emerging markets without getting their hands dirty, including Reebok, Google and Novo Nordisk. IKEA has gone to great lengths to fight corruption in Russia, including threatening to halt its expansion in the country, firing managers who pay bribes and buying generators to get around grasping officials holding up grid connections. What is more, Mr Nichols argues, it is misguided to dismiss entire countries as corrupt. Even the greasiest-palmed places are in fact ambivalent about corruption: they invariably have laws against it and frequently produce politicians who campaign against it. Multinationals should help bolster the rules of the game rather than pandering to the most unscrupulous players.

And is "grease" really all that efficient? In a paper published by the World Bank, Daniel Kaufmann and Shang-Jin Wei subjected the "efficient grease" hypothesis to careful scrutiny. They found that companies that pay bribes actually end up spending more time negotiating with bureaucrats. The prospect of a pay-off gives officials an incentive to haggle over regulations. The paper also found that borrowing is more expensive for corrupt companies, probably because of the regulatory flux.

The hidden costs of corruption are almost always much higher than companies imagine. Corruption inevitably begets ever more corruption: bribe-takers keep returning to the trough and bribe-givers open themselves up to blackmail. Corruption also exacts a high psychological cost on those who engage in it. Mr Nichols says that corrupt business people habitually compare their habit to having an affair: no sooner have you given in to temptation than you are trapped in a world of secrecy and guilt. On the other hand, the benefits of rectitude can be striking. Texaco, an oil giant now subsumed by Chevron, had such an incorruptible reputation that African border guards were said to wave its jeeps through without engaging in the ritual shakedown.

Moreover, the likelihood of being caught is dramatically higher than it was a few years ago. The internet has handed much more power to whistle-blowers. NGOs keep a constant watch on big firms. Every year Transparency International publishes its Corruption Perceptions Index, its Bribe Payers Index and its Global Corruption Barometer.

The likelihood of prosecution is also growing. The Obama administration has revamped a piece of post-Watergate legislation – the Foreign Corrupt Practices Act (FCPA) – and is using it to pursue corporate malefactors the world over. The Department of Justice pursued 150 cases in 2010 compared with just eight in 2001. And it is subjecting miscreants to much rougher treatment. Recent legislation has made senior managers personally liable for corruption on their watch. They risk a spell in prison as well as huge fines. The vagueness of the legislation means that the authorities may prosecute for lavish entertainment as well as more blatant bribes.

America is no longer a lone ranger. Thirty-eight countries have now signed up to the OECD's 1997 anti-corruption convention, leading to a spate of cross-border prosecutions. In February 2010 Britain's BAE Systems, a giant arms company, was fined $400 million as a result of a joint British and American investigation. Then a more ferocious Bribery Act came into force in Britain. On April 1st Daimler was fined $185 million as a result of a joint American and German investigation which examined the firm's behaviour in 22 countries.

Companies caught between these two mighty forces – the corruption and anti-corruption eruptions – need to start taking the problem seriously. A Transparency International study of 500 prominent firms revealed that the average company scored only 17 out of a possible 50 points on "anti-corruption practices" (Belgium was by far the worst performing European country). Companies need to develop explicit codes of conduct on corruption, train their staff to handle demands for pay-offs and back them up when they refuse them. Clubbing together and campaigning for reform can also help. Businesses played a leading role in Poland's Clean Hands movement, for example, and a group of upright Panamanian firms have formed an anti-corruption group.

This may all sound a bit airy-fairy given that so many companies are struggling just to survive the recession. But there is nothing airy-fairy about the $1.6 billion in fines that Siemens has paid to the American and German governments. And there is nothing airy-fairy about a spell in prison. The phrase "doing well by doing good" is one of the most irritating parts of the CSR mantra. But when it comes to corruption, it might just fit the bill.

April 2010

Fail often, fail well

Companies have a great deal to learn from failure – provided they manage it successfully

BUSINESS WRITERS have always worshipped at the altar of success. Tom Peters turned himself into a superstar with *In Search of Excellence.* Stephen Covey has sold more than 15 million copies of *The 7 Habits of Highly Effective People.* Malcolm Gladwell cleverly subtitled his third book, *Outliers,* "The Story of Success". This success-fetish makes the latest management fashion all the more remarkable. The April issue of *Harvard Business Review* is devoted to failure, featuring among other contributors A.G. Lafley, a successful ex-boss of Procter & Gamble (P&G), proclaiming that "we learn much more from failure than we do from success". The current British edition of *Wired* magazine has "Fail! Fast. Then succeed. What European business needs to learn from Silicon Valley" on its cover. IDEO, a consultancy, has coined the slogan "Fail often in order to succeed sooner".

There are good reasons for the failure fashion. Success and failure are not polar opposites: you often need to endure the second to enjoy the first. Failure can indeed be a better teacher than success. It can also be a sign of creativity. The best way to avoid short-term failure is to keep churning out the same old products, though in the long term this may spell your doom. Businesses cannot invent the future – their own future – without taking risks.

Entrepreneurs have always understood this. Thomas Edison performed 9,000 experiments before coming up with a successful version of the light bulb. Students of entrepreneurship talk about the J-curve of returns: the failures come early and often and the successes take time. America has proved to be more entrepreneurial than Europe in large part because it has embraced a culture of "failing forward" as a common tech-industry phrase puts it: in Germany bankruptcy can end your business career whereas in Silicon Valley it is almost a badge of honour.

A more tolerant attitude to failure can also help companies to avoid destruction. When Alan Mulally became boss of an ailing Ford Motor Company in 2006 one of the first things he did was demand that his executives own up to their failures. He asked managers to colour-code their progress reports – ranging from green for good to red for trouble. At one early meeting he expressed astonishment at being confronted by a sea of green, even though the company had lost several billion dollars in the previous year. Ford's recovery began only when he got his managers to admit that things weren't entirely green.

Failure is also becoming more common. John Hagel, of Deloitte's Centre for the Edge (which advises bosses on technology), calculates that the average time a company spends in the S&P 500 index has declined from 75 years in 1937 to about 15 years today. Up to 90% of new businesses fail shortly after being founded. Venture-capital firms are lucky if 20% of their investments pay off. Pharmaceutical companies research hundreds of molecular groups before coming up with a marketable drug. Less than 2% of films account for 80% of box-office returns.

But simply "embracing" failure would be as silly as ignoring it. Companies need to learn how to manage it. Amy Edmondson of Harvard Business School argues that the first thing they must do is distinguish between productive and unproductive failures. There is nothing to be gained from tolerating defects on the production line or mistakes in the operating theatre.

This might sound like an obvious distinction. But it is one that some of the best minds in business have failed to make. James McNerney, a former boss of 3M, a manufacturer, damaged the company's innovation engine by trying to apply six-sigma principles (which are intended to reduce errors on production lines) to the entire company, including the research laboratories. It is only a matter of time before a boss, hypnotised by all the current talk of "rampant experimentation", makes the opposite mistake.

Companies must also recognise the virtues of failing small and failing fast. Peter Sims likens this to placing "Little Bets", in a new book of that title. Chris Rock, one of the world's most successful comedians, tries out his ideas in small venues, often bombing and always junking more material than he saves. Jeff Bezos, the boss of

Amazon, compares his company's strategy to planting seeds, or "going down blind alleys". One of those blind alleys, letting small shops sell books on the company's website, now accounts for a third of its sales.

Damage limitation

Placing small bets is one of several ways that companies can limit the downside of failure. Mr Sims emphasises the importance of testing ideas on consumers using rough-and-ready prototypes: they will be more willing to give honest opinions on something that is clearly an early-stage mock-up than on something that looks like the finished product. Chris Zook of Bain & Company, a consultancy, urges companies to keep potential failures close to their core business – perhaps by introducing existing products into new markets or new products into familiar markets. Rita Gunther McGrath of Columbia Business School suggests that companies should guard against "confirmation bias" by giving one team member the job of looking for flaws.

But there is no point in failing fast if you fail to learn from your mistakes. Companies are trying hard to get better at this. India's Tata group awards an annual prize for the best failed idea. Intuit, in software, and Eli Lilly, in pharmaceuticals, have both taken to holding "failure parties". P&G encourages employees to talk about their failures as well as their successes during performance reviews. But the higher up in the company, the bigger the egos and the greater the reluctance to admit to really big failings rather than minor ones. Bosses should remember how often failure paves the way for success: Henry Ford got nowhere with his first two attempts to start a car company, but that did not stop him.

April 2011

The business of sharing

What do you do when you are green, broke and connected? You share

WHY BUY WHEN YOU CAN RENT? This simple question is the foundation stone of a growing number of businesses. Why buy a car (and pay for parking) when you can rent one whenever you need to load up at IKEA? Why buy a bike (and risk having it stolen) when you can pick one up at a bike rack near your home and drop it off at another rack near your office? Why buy a DVD when you can watch it and return it in a convenient envelope?

Renting is not a new business, of course. Hotel chains and car-hire firms have been around for ages, and the world's oldest profession, one might argue, involves renting. But for most of the past 50 years renters have been conceding ground to owners. Laundromats have been closing down as people buy their own washing machines. Home ownership was, until the financial crisis, rising nearly everywhere. Rental markets grew ossified: hotels and car-hire firms barely changed their business models for decades. All this is now changing dramatically, however, thanks to technology, austerity and greenery.

The internet makes it easy to compare prices, which makes rental cars and hotel rooms cheaper. It also allows new ways of renting and sharing to thrive. For example, car-sharing is booming even as car sales languish. Zipcar, an American firm, has 400,000 members who pay an annual fee and can then rent cars by the hour. They log on to find out where the nearest Zipcar is parked, and return it to one of many scattered parking bays rather than a central location. Netflix, a film-rental firm, made $116 million in 2011 by making it easy to hire movies by mail. Governments are joining in: London is one of several cities that rent bikes to citizens who take the trouble to fill out a few forms.

Trendy folk are applauding. "Sharing is clean, crisp, urbane, postmodern," says Mark Levine of the *New York Times*. "Owning is dull, selfish, timid, backward." ("Crisp"? Never mind.) The sharing craze spawned two books: *What's Mine is Yours: The Rise of Collaborative Consumption*, by Rachel Botsman and Roo Rogers, and *The Mesh: Why the Future of Business is Sharing*, by Lisa Gansky. The first book is much the better of the two. But the second, written by an internet entrepreneur, contains some valuable practical advice.

People are renting things they never used to rent, such as clothes and toys. Bag Borrow or Steal, for example, applies the Netflix principle to posh handbags. The firm boasts that it allows women to avoid "the emotional and financial sacrifices" of "the endless search for the 'right' accessory." Rent-That-Toy does the same for trikes for tikes. TechShop, in Menlo Park, California, rents tinkering space and equipment to amateur inventors.

Other pioneers of "collaborative consumption" have dispensed with inventories and act purely as brokers. Some help people sell their spare capacity in everything from parking spaces to energy. CouchSurfing connects people who have a spare sofa with travellers who wish to sleep on it, on the tacit understanding that the travellers will do the same for someone else in the network some day. There are 2.3 million registered couchsurfers in 79,000 cities worldwide. Other groups have created barter economies. thredUP specialises in exchanging children's clothes, but also has exchanges for everything from make-up to video games. Freecycle helps people give things away so that they do not end up in landfills: its website has 7.6 million members.

The moguls who run Zipcar may have different motives from the greens who run Freecycle, but they share the same faith: that access often matters more than ownership, and that technology will make sharing more and more efficient. The internet has always been good at connecting buyers and sellers; GPS devices and social networks are enhancing its power. GPS devices can connect you to people around the corner who want to share rides. Social networks are helping to lower one of the biggest barriers to "collaborative consumption" – trust. Couchsurfers, for example, can see at a keystroke what others in the network think of the stranger who wants to borrow their couch. If he is dirty or creepy, they need not let him in.

People are growing impatient with "idle capacity" (ie, waste). The average American spends 18% of his income on running a car that is usually stationary. Half of American homes own an electric drill, but most people use it once and then forget it. If you are green or broke, as many people are these days, this seems wasteful. Besides, "consumer philandering" sounds fun. "Today's a BMW day," purrs Zipcar, "Or is it a Volvo day?"

New ways to show off

Attitudes to conspicuous consumption are changing. Thorstein Veblen, who coined the term, argued that people like to display their status by owning lots of stuff. But many of today's conspicuous consumers – particularly the young – achieve the same effect by virtual means. They boast about what they are doing (on Twitter), what they are reading (Shelfari), what they are interested in (Digg) and whom they know (Facebook). Collaborative consumption is an ideal signalling device for an economy based on electronic brands and ever-changing fashions.

There are obvious limitations to this new model. Few people, besides tramps and journalists, will want to wear recycled underpants. Returning Zipcars on time can be a hassle. But the sharing stampede is nevertheless gathering pace. Zipcar has imitators in more than a thousand cities. Every week sees the birth of a business describing itself as the Netflix of this or that. Collective consumption is also disrupting established business models based on built-in obsolescence. The internet may be synonymous with novelty, but by encouraging people to reuse the same objects rather than buy new ones, it may revive the old virtue of building products that last.

October 2010

The bottom of the pyramid

Businesses are learning to serve the growing number of hard-up Americans

MANAGEMENT GURUS HAVE RHAPSODISED about "the fortune at the bottom of the pyramid" in emerging markets ever since C.K. Prahalad popularised the idea in 2006. They have filled books with stories of cut-price Indian hospitals and Chinese firms that make $100 computers. But when it comes to the bottom of the pyramid in the rich world, the gurus lose interest.

This is understandable. McDonald's and Wal-Mart do not have the same exotic ring as Aravind Eye Care and Tata Motors. The West's bottom-of-the-pyramid companies are an unglamorous bunch. Many rely on poorly educated shift workers. Some inhabit the nether world of loan sharks and bail bondsmen.

But even in one of the world's richest countries the hard-up represent a huge and growing market. The average American household saw its real income decline between 2005 and 2009. Millions of middle-class Americans have been forced to "downshift", as credit dries up and the costs of college and health care soar. Some 44 million Americans live below the official poverty line ($21,954 a year for a family of four in 2011). Consumer spending per household fell by 2.8% in 2009, the first time it had fallen since the Bureau of Labour Statistics started gathering data in 1984.

This is a challenge to the American dream. But it is also an opportunity for clever companies. Even the poorest Americans are rich by the standards of many other countries, so there is money to be made by serving them. McDonald's, for example, is booming. Since 2006 its restaurants have generated an annual increase in sales of 4%, despite rising food prices. (This figure excludes restaurants that have been open for less than a year.) In April 2011 the firm hired an astonishing 50,000 full- and part-time staff in America, at a time when many others were shedding hands.

Frugal shops have been thriving, too. Wal-Mart and Target are marching into new markets (such as basic medical care) and new places (such as inner cities). Aldi, a German discounter, has been doing surprisingly well in America, too. Unlike Wal-Mart, it specialises in small stores – the size of a basketball court rather than a football pitch. More than 90% of its goods are its own unfancy brands. To keep its supply chain simple, Aldi stocks barely 1,000 products; some of its rivals stock 100,000. Yet Aldi is not a grotty place to shop. It has wide aisles and bright decorations, unlike some of the discount stores that disfigure American inner cities.

Aldi's success highlights an interesting fact: that there is a lot of innovation in this market. Companies are reconfiguring themselves to appeal to the *nouveaux pauvres* as well as the old poor: middle-class people who enjoy lattes and salads but who are currently strapped for cash. Wal-Mart has vastly expanded its grocery section. McDonald's sells healthy fast food, such as fruit and walnut salad, as well as the usual slabs of meat and cheese in a bun. It also plans to remodel or rebuild 6,000 of its 14,000 American stores. And both McDonald's and Dunkin' Donuts are challenging Starbucks by offering drinkable coffee for less.

The rise of online pawn

Even that staple of the urban poor, the pawn shop, is being reinvented. Pawngo is putting pawn on the internet for the convenience of what it describes as "college-educated working professionals with temporary cashflow problems". Customers can send their college-graduation presents (for example) to Pawngo by FedEx and get a loan in the form of a bank transfer.

Entrepreneurs are also adjusting their business models to deal with the age of austerity. One popular model is paying for things upfront (which appeals to consumers who have poor credit or who want to curb their splurging). Pre-paid wireless providers such as Leap Wireless and MetroPCS have captured 90% of the growth in the market for mobile telephony. Houston's Direct Energy has just introduced a pre-paid plan for electricity. A second popular model is "collaborative consumption", which allows people to share or rent rather than own. Swap.com enables you to swap DVDs and videos with other sofa spuds. thredUp does the same for children's clothes. Jobless students can hitch lifts via Craigslist (a website for classified ads), or doss down in someone else's flat via CouchSurfing, another website.

Adjusting to this new world can be hard. Companies have long assumed that America would always be a land of mass affluence and upward mobility. But the American economy was undergoing a structural shift even before the 2007 financial crisis, with galloping rewards at the top and stagnation for many of the rest. Some economists expect the malaise to last for years. Few companies have thought much about the implications of this.

Wireless companies blithely assume that everyone will soon have smartphones and broadband connections, just as everyone now has a car and a television. But their confidence is probably misplaced, argues a new report on *The Poverty Problem* by BernsteinResearch, a consultancy. Broadband penetration may have plateaued, at nearly two-thirds of households. Pay-TV penetration is beginning to decline.

The optimists' complacency creates opportunities for nimbler and gloomier competitors. It also creates an opening for companies from the emerging world, many of which have frugal innovation in their DNA. TracFone Wireless, a subsidiary of Carlos Slim's América Móvil, has sold more than 3 million phones in America since 2008 to pre-paying customers. MedicallHome, a Mexican company that provides medical advice over the phone for $5 a month, as well as access to its network of 6,000 doctors, is expanding north of the border. Emerging giants such as India's Tata and China's Haier regard America as a natural market for their frugal products. The bottom of the pyramid is wider than most people realise. Firms that offer ultra-low prices will find themselves as much in demand in Detroit as in Delhi.

June 2011

The tussle for talent

The best companies are obsessed by "the vital few"

PLATO BELIEVED THAT MEN ARE DIVIDED into three classes: gold, silver and bronze. Vilfredo Pareto, an Italian economist, argued that "the vital few" account for most progress. Such sentiments are taboo today in public life. Politicians talk of a "leadership class" or "the vital few" at their peril. Schools abhor picking winners. Universities welcome the masses: more people now teach at British ones than attended them in the 1950s.

In the private sector things could hardly be more different. The world's best companies struggle relentlessly to find and keep the vital few. They offer them fat pay packets, extra training, powerful mentors and more challenging assignments. If anything, businesses are becoming more obsessed with ability.

This is partly cyclical. Deloitte and other consultancies have noticed that as the economy begins to recover, companies are trying harder to nurture raw talent, or to poach it from their rivals. When new opportunities arise, they hope to have the brainpower to seize them. The acceleration of the tussle for talent is also structural, however. Private-equity firms rely heavily on a few stars. High-tech firms, for all their sartorial egalitarianism, are ruthless about recruiting the brightest. Firms in emerging markets are desperate to find high-flyers – the younger the better – who can cope with rapid growth and fast-changing environments.

Few people know more about how companies manage talent than Bill Conaty and Ram Charan. Mr Conaty led the human-resources department at General Electric (GE) for 14 years. Mr Charan has spent the past few decades offering advice to some of the world's leading bosses. Their book, *The Talent Masters*, provides a nice mix of portraits of well-known talent factories, such as GE and Procter & Gamble (P&G), along with sketches of more recent converts to the cause.

"Talent masters" are proud of their elitism. GE divides its employees into three groups based on their promise. Hindustan

Unilever compiles a list of people who show innate leadership qualities (and even refers to them throughout their careers as "listers"). Talent masters all seem to agree on the importance of two things: measurement and differentiation. The best companies routinely subject their employees to "reviews" and "assessments" of one sort or another. But when it comes to high-flyers they make more effort to build up a three-dimensional picture of their personalities and to provide lots of feedback. Jeff Immelt, GE's boss, prides himself on his detailed knowledge of the 600 people at the top of his company, including their family circumstances and personal ambitions. Hindustan Unilever's managers build detailed dossiers on their listers. Novartis, a drug firm, asks high-flyers to produce "leader plans" and share them with their mentors and contemporaries.

They single out high-flyers for special training. GE spends $1 billion a year on training, much of it on its elite management college in Crotonville. Novartis sends high-flyers to regular off-site training sessions. Training courses are clearly powerful motivators. But they also help to form bonds between the future leaders of far-flung organisations.

Even more important than off-site courses is on-the-job training. Many companies speak of "stretch" assignments or "baptisms by fire". P&G refers to "accelerator experiences" and "crucible roles". The most coveted are foreign postings: these can help young managers understand what it is like to run an entire company, or force specialists to deal with a wide range of problems. Other tough tests include building a business in an isolated village (a popular challenge at Hindustan Unilever) or turning around a failing division.

Successful companies make sure that senior managers are involved with "talent development". Jack Welch and A.G. Lafley, former bosses of GE and P&G, claimed that they spent 40% of their time on personnel. Andy Grove, who ran Intel, a chipmaker, obliged all the senior people, including himself, to spend at least a week a year teaching high-flyers. Nitin Paranjpe, the boss of Hindustan Unilever at the time of writing and now president of Unilever's Home Care Business, recruits people from campuses and regularly visits high-flyers in their offices. Involving the company's top brass in the process prevents lower-level managers from monopolising high-flyers (and taking credit for their triumphs). It also creates a dialogue between established and future leaders.

Successful companies also integrate talent development with their broader strategy. This ensures that companies are more than the sum of their parts. Adrian Dillon, a former chief financial officer of Agilent, a firm that makes high-tech measuring devices, says he would rather build a "repertory company" than a "collection of world experts". P&G likes its managers to be both innovative and worldly: they cannot rise to the top without running operations in a country and managing a product globally. Agilent and Novartis like to turn specialists into general managers. Goodyear replaced 23 of its 24 senior managers in two years as it shifted from selling tyres to carmakers to selling them to motorists.

The risks of reaching for the stars

Elitism has its drawbacks. In their rush to classify people, companies can miss potential stars. Those who are singled out for special treatment can become too full of themselves. But the first problem can be fixed by flexibility: people who are average in one job can become stars in another. And people who become too smug can be discarded.

Their obsession with talent has served the likes of GE and P&G well. They have trained enough leaders for themselves, with plenty to spare. P&G's alumni include Meg Whitman (formerly of eBay), Scott Cook (Intuit) and Jim McNerney (Boeing). The world's public sectors could learn a lot from such talent masters.

January 2011

Age shall not wither them

Companies should start seeing older workers as assets rather than liabilities

THE NATIONAL RURAL ELECTRIC CO-OPERATIVE ASSOCIATION (NRECA) does not have the same ring to it as Google or Facebook. But in its own humble way the NRECA, based in Virginia, is helping to shape the future. It is a pioneer in coping with one of the biggest challenges facing business: managing older workers. It lets employees work flexible hours and telecommute up to three days a week. It gives them health checks and advice on managing stress, and regularly has ceremonies to congratulate long-serving staff. More than a third of its workers are over 50 and the average employee has been with the company almost 12 years.

Employers in the rich world have no choice but to learn how to deal with an ageing workforce, as the baby-boom generation gets older and life expectancies increase. Yet many are petrified of the changes. The Sloan Centre on Ageing and Work at Boston College found in a survey that 40% of employers worry that the ageing of the workforce will have a negative or very negative impact on their business. A 2010 survey by two British management institutes found that only 14% of managers think that their workplaces are prepared to cope with the greying of the workforce.

Peter Cappelli of the University of Pennsylvania's Wharton business school and Bill Novelli, a former boss of the AARP, America's indomitable grey-power lobby, delivered a powerful counterblast to such pessimism in a book, *Managing the Older Worker*. Not only do older workers nowadays want to go on working. They bring all sorts of benefits. They possess decades' worth of formal and informal knowledge, which risks being lost as the baby-boomers retire, creating an epidemic of skills shortages in aerospace, energy and health care. More often than not they are the repositories of a company's core values.

But don't older people bring lots of problems, too? Literature is full of examples of difficult-to-manage older people, from Shakespeare's King Lear to Charles Dickens's Jeremiah Flintwinch. However, today's oldies are in far better shape than those of earlier generations. If Mick Jagger and Keith Richards can go on touring into their late 60s, their contemporaries can at least be trusted with a desk and a computer. People's muscles do weaken with age. But few jobs require brawn these days: in America 46% of jobs make almost no physical demands on workers, reckons the Urban Institute, a think-tank. Some older workers are reluctant to embrace new technology (though that surely does not apply to Bill Gates, who is in his late 50s). But they make up for this in different ways. Studies suggest that older workers are better at jobs that require personal skills, a growing proportion of the total.

Employers may be mistaken if they assume that older workers lack the animal spirits to make a go of new ventures. A study by the Kauffman Foundation, a research body, found that Americans aged 55–64 have launched more businesses than those aged 20–34 in every year since 1996. Conscientiousness also tends to rise with age: older workers have lower levels of absenteeism than younger colleagues.

None of this means that adjusting to an ageing workforce will be easy. Companies will need to rethink the traditional career ladder that linked seniority to pay and power. This is proving easier in America, where people change jobs more often. But it still has a long way to go elsewhere in the world, especially in Europe, where people tend to cling to their jobs, and in hierarchical East Asian societies. The biggest barrier to change is psychological: young high-flyers find it hard to manage older workers, and older curmudgeons resent being bossed about by whippersnappers. Almost 90% of employers worry about hiring older workers because of such conflicts. Companies need to think harder about training high-flyers to manage their seniors. America's armed forces are ahead of the game here. The West Point military academy and the Marine Corps already have programmes to teach officer cadets how to work with older sergeants.

Sages and mentors

Companies also need to think harder about providing satisfying careers for older workers. Three techniques are already proving successful. The first is to treat them as mentors. Westpac, an Australian bank, has dubbed some older staff "sages" and asked them to codify the company's informal knowledge. The second is to recognise that they respond to different incentives: they may be less interested in money and promotion and more concerned with flexibility.

The third is to treat retirement as a process rather than a sudden event. Some employers offer older workers "bridge jobs" between full-time work and retirement. Mercy Health Systems gives them seasonal jobs that allow them to take long periods of leave without losing their benefits. They are also treating recently retired staff as a just-in-time workforce that can be used to cope with surges in demand or to fill in for absent colleagues. Northrop Grumman, a giant defence contractor, re-employs retired workers to teach new recruits about the company while Union Carbide, a chemicals company, asks retired executives to guide younger managers.

The nightmare that haunts many companies is that older workers spell rigidity. They will trap companies in the past and prevent them from riding the next wave of innovation. But this will be a problem only if companies let it be. Businesses cannot change long-term demographic trends. But they can change the way that they cope with those trends. If they refuse to rethink their hallowed practices, they might easily see the ageing workforce becoming a trap; but if they rethink those practices, as pioneers like the NRECA have done, they could turn older workers into the very model of a modern workforce.

April 2011

Womenomics

Feminist management theorists are flirting with some dangerous arguments

THE LATE PAUL SAMUELSON once quipped that "women are just men with less money". As a father of six, he might have added something about women's role in the reproduction of the species. But his aphorism is about as good a one-sentence summary of classical feminism as you can get.

The first generations of successful women insisted on being judged by the same standards as men. They had nothing but contempt for the notion of special treatment for "the sisters", and instead insisted on getting ahead by dint of working harder and thinking smarter. Margaret Thatcher made no secret of her contempt for the wimpish men around her. (There is a joke about her going out to dinner with her cabinet. "Steak or fish?" asks the waiter. "Steak, of course," she replies. "And for the vegetables?" "They'll have steak as well.") During America's 2008 presidential election Hillary Clinton taunted Barack Obama with an advertisement that implied that he, unlike she, was not up to the challenge of answering the red phone at 3am.

Many pioneering businesswomen pride themselves on their toughness. Dong Mingzhu, the boss of Gree Electric Appliances, an air-conditioning giant, says flatly, "I never miss. I never admit mistakes and I am always correct." Between 2006 and 2009 her company boosted shareholder returns by nearly 500%.

But some of today's most influential feminists contend that women will never fulfil their potential if they play by men's rules. According to Avivah Wittenberg-Cox and Alison Maitland, two of the most prominent exponents of this position, it is not enough to smash the glass ceiling. You need to audit the entire building for "gender asbestos" – in other words, root out the inherent sexism built into corporate structures and processes.

The new feminism contends that women are wired differently from men, and not just in trivial ways. They are less aggressive and more consensus-seeking, less competitive and more collaborative, less power-obsessed and more group-oriented. Judy Rosener, of the University of California, Irvine, argues that women excel at "transformational" and "interactive" management. Peninah Thomson and Jacey Graham, the authors of A *Woman's Place is in the Boardroom*, assert that women are "better lateral thinkers than men" and "more idealistic" into the bargain. Feminist texts are suddenly full of references to tribes of monkeys, with their aggressive males and nurturing females.

What is more, the argument runs, these supposedly womanly qualities are becoming ever more valuable in business. The recent financial crisis proved that the sort of qualities that men pride themselves on, such as risk-taking and bare-knuckle competition, can lead to disaster. Lehman Brothers would never have happened if it had been Lehman Sisters, according to this theory. Even before the financial disaster struck, the new feminists also claim, the best companies had been abandoning "patriarchal" hierarchies in favour of "collaboration" and "networking", skills in which women have an inherent advantage.

This argument may sound a little like the stuff of gender workshops in righteous universities. But it is gaining followers in powerful places. McKinsey, the most venerable of management consultancies, has published research arguing that women apply five of the nine "leadership behaviours" that lead to corporate success more frequently than men. Niall FitzGerald, the deputy chairman of Thomson Reuters [until 2011] and a former boss of Unilever, is as close as you can get to the heart of the corporate establishment. He proclaims, "Women have different ways of achieving results, and leadership qualities that are becoming more important as our organisations become less hierarchical and more loosely organised around matrix structures." Many companies are abandoning the old-fashioned commitment to treating everybody equally and instead becoming "gender adapted" and "gender bilingual" – in touch with the unique management wisdom of their female employees. A host of consultancies has sprung up to teach firms how to listen to women and exploit their special abilities.

The new feminists are right to be frustrated about the pace of women's progress in business. Britain's Equality and Human Rights Commission calculated that, at the current rate of progress, it will take 60 years for women to gain equal representation on the boards of the FTSE 100. They are also right that old-fashioned feminism took too little account of women's role in raising children. But their arguments about the innate differences between men and women are sloppy and counterproductive.

People who bang on about innate differences should remember that variation within subgroups in the population is usually bigger than the variation between subgroups. Even if it can be established that, on average, women have a higher "emotional-intelligence quotient" than men, that says little about any specific woman. Judging people as individuals rather than as representatives of groups is both morally right and good for business.

Caring, sharing and engineering

Besides, many of the most successful women are to be found in hard-edged companies, rather than the touchy-feely organisations of the new feminist imagination: in 2009, Areva (nuclear energy), AngloAmerican (mining), Archer Daniels Midland (agribusiness), DuPont (chemicals), Sunoco (oil) and Xerox (technology) all had female bosses. Cranfield School of Management's Female FTSE 100 Index reveals that two of the industries with the best record for promoting women to their boards are banking and transport.

Women would be well advised to ignore the siren voices of the new feminism and listen to Ms Dong instead. Despite their frustration, the future looks bright. Women are now outperforming men markedly in school and university. It would be a grave mistake to abandon old-fashioned meritocracy just at the time when it is turning to women's advantage.

December 2009

The art of management

Business has much to learn from the arts

ARTISTS ROUTINELY DERIDE BUSINESSPEOPLE as money-obsessed bores. Or worse. Every time Hollywood depicts an industry, it depicts a conspiracy of knaves. Think of *Wall Street* (which damned finance), *The Constant Gardener* (drug firms), *Super Size Me* (fast food), *The Social Network* (Facebook) or *The Player* (Hollywood itself). Artistic critiques of business are sometimes precise and well-targeted, as in Lucy Prebble's play *Enron*. But often they are not, as those who endured Michael Moore's *Capitalism: A Love Story* can attest.

Many businesspeople, for their part, assume that artists are a bunch of pretentious wastrels. Bosses may stick a few modernist daubs on their boardroom walls. They may go on corporate jollies to the opera. They may even write the odd cheque to support their wives' bearded friends. But they seldom take the arts seriously as a source of inspiration.

The bias starts at business school, where "hard" things such as numbers and case studies rule. It is reinforced by everyday experience. Bosses constantly remind their underlings that if you can't count it, it doesn't count. Quarterly results impress the stockmarket; little else does.

Managers' reading habits often reflect this no-nonsense attitude. Few read deeply about art. *The Art of the Deal* by Donald Trump does not count; nor does Sun Tzu's *The Art of War*. Some popular business books rejoice in their barbarism: consider Wess Robert's *Leadership Secrets of Attila the Hun* ("The principles are timeless," says Ross Perot) or Rob Adams's *A Good Hard Kick in the Ass: the Real Rules for Business*.

But there have been welcome signs of a thaw on the business side of the great cultural divide. Business presses are publishing a series of luvvie-hugging books such as *The Fine Art of Success*, by Jamie Anderson, Jörg Reckhenrich and Martin Kupp, and *Artistry Unleashed* by Hilary Austen. Business schools such as Rotman School of Management at the University of Toronto are trying to learn from the arts. New consultancies teach businesses how to profit from the arts. Ms Austen, for example, runs one named after her book.

All this unleashing naturally produces some nonsense. Madonna has already received too much attention without being hailed as a prophet of "organisational renewal". Bosses have enough on their plates without being told that they need to unleash their inner Laurence Oliviers. But businesspeople nevertheless have a lot to learn by taking the arts more seriously.

Mr Anderson & co point out that many artists have also been superb entrepreneurs. Tintoretto upended a Venetian arts establishment that was completely controlled by Titian. He did this by identifying a new set of customers (people who were less grand than the grandees who supported Titian) and by changing the way that art was produced (working much faster than other artists and painting frescoes and furniture as well as portraits). Damien Hirst was even more audacious. He not only realised that nouveau-riche collectors would pay extraordinary sums for dead cows and jewel-encrusted skulls. He upturned the art world by selling his work directly through Sotheby's, an auction house. Whatever they think of his work, businesspeople cannot help admiring a man who parted art-lovers from £70.5 million ($126.5 million) on the day that Lehman Brothers collapsed.

Studying the arts can help businesspeople communicate more eloquently. Most bosses spend a huge amount of time "messaging" and "reaching out", yet few are much good at it. Their prose is larded with clichés and garbled with gobbledegook. Half an hour with George Orwell's "Why I Write" would work wonders. Many of the world's most successful businesses are triumphs of story-telling more than anything else. Marlboro and Jack Daniels have tapped into the myth of the frontier. Ben & Jerry's, an ice-cream maker, wraps itself in the tie-dyed robes of the counter-culture. But business schools devote far more energy to teaching people how to produce and position their products rather than how to infuse them with meaning.

Studying the arts can also help companies learn how to manage bright people. Rob Goffee and Gareth Jones of London Business School point out that today's most productive companies are dominated by what they call "clevers", who are the devil to manage.

They hate being told what to do by managers, whom they regard as dullards. They refuse to submit to performance reviews. In short, they are prima donnas. The arts world has centuries of experience in managing such difficult people. Publishers coax books out of tardy authors. Directors persuade actresses to lock lips with actors they hate. Their tips might be worth hearing.

Corporations chasing inspiration

Studying the art world might even hold out the biggest prize of all – helping business become more innovative. Companies are scouring the world for new ideas (Procter & Gamble, for example, uses "crowdsourcing" to collect ideas from the general public). They are also trying to encourage their workers to become less risk averse (unless they are banks, of course). In their quest for creativity, they surely have something to learn from the creative industries. Look at how modern artists adapted to the arrival of photography, a technology that could have made them redundant, or how William Golding (the author of *Lord of the Flies*) and J.K. Rowling (the creator of Harry Potter) kept trying even when publishers rejected their novels.

If businesspeople should take art more seriously, artists too should take business more seriously. Commerce is a central part of the human experience. More prosaically, it is what billions of people do all day. As such, it deserves a more subtle examination on the page and the screen than it currently receives.

February 2011

PART 5

Surviving disruption: the case of governments

Beyond the start-up nation

Israel has become a high-tech superpower over the past two decades. Can the good news last?

ISRAELIS TELL A JOKE about a Jew who takes to reading Arab newspapers. A friend, puzzled, asks him why. If I read the Israeli papers, all I hear is bad news about the Jews, he replies; but the Arab papers constantly claim we are all rich and successful, and rule the world. These days the hero of the tale has another source of good news about Israel: the business press. Over the past two decades Israel has been transformed from a semi-socialist backwater into a high-tech superpower. Adjust for population and Israel leads the world in the number of high-tech start-ups and the size of the venture-capital industry. In 1990 Harvard Business School's leading guru, Michael Porter, devoted just one sentence of his 855-page *The Competitive Advantage of Nations* to Israel; today there is a growing pile of books on Israel's high-tech boom, most notably *Start-Up Nation: The Story of Israel's Economic Miracle*, by Dan Senor and Saul Singer.

Israelis are rightly proud of their high-tech miracle. They lap up books like *Start-Up Nation* and delight in talking about their country's successful IPOs. They are also proud of how it was one of the last countries to enter recession and among the earliest to exit: the economy grew by more than 4% in the year to September 2010. But for all its success the Israeli boom nevertheless raises a number of troubling questions.

First, does the economy rest on too narrow a base? High-tech industries employ only 10% of the workforce but account for 40% of exports. Second, why has Israel proved so bad at turning start-ups into domestic giants? It has 3,800 high-tech start-ups but only four high-tech companies with sales of more than $1 billion a year. Third, is Israel capable of producing content for the internet as well as just the hardware and software that constitutes its "plumbing"? And, fourth, why has the land of the high-tech miracle got one of the rich world's lowest labour-participation rates, just 55%? These questions all add up to one bigger one. Is the Israeli miracle sustainable? Or did it result from a peculiar combination of circumstances in the 1990s?

Israel's policymakers are well aware of all this, and are thinking hard about the solutions. They have identified a number of areas with high growth potential, such as water management, agricultural science, alternative energy and of course security, in which Israel already has world-beating technology. In the life sciences, the government is seeking to speed up the creation of firms by setting up venture-capital funds. However, Israeli officials worry that the country is still lagging in its ability to "turn tomato seeds into tomatoes" – to transform start-ups into the sort of giants, like Google and Cisco, that Silicon Valley regularly produces. Such giants, they note, create a greater proportion of high-paying jobs than start-ups. They also worry that Israeli entrepreneurs are taking longer than they used to in turning an idea into an IPO.

One good sign is the emergence of some Israeli companies that are concentrating on providing content for the internet rather than just the plumbing. JVP, a venture-capital company with more than $820 million under management, focuses on developing companies that fuse content with technology. Erel Margalit, the firm's founder, argues that Israel has as much of a comparative advantage in culture as in high-tech: the Jews, he points out, have always excelled in telling stories. Although Jerusalem, where Mr Margalit is based, is synonymous in many people's minds with endless cultural and religious conflict, he argues that it nevertheless stands to benefit from being the meeting-point of three great civilisations.

Going beyond Israel's "Start-Up Nation" model will not be easy. The country's business culture focuses more on dealmaking than on company-building. The army's technological prowess, which provided the know-how behind many a start-up, does not translate as well into providing the internet with content as it did in providing it with plumbing. Israel also has much better links with America and Europe than with the rising powers of Asia.

From strength to strength

There are nevertheless reasons for thinking that Israel's strengths will endure. The government is trying to apply the venture-capital approach that it applied so successfully to start-ups (igniting private-sector creativity rather than picking winners) to late-stage financing. The army is more than a high-tech incubator. It sifts the entire population for talent, giving the most promising techies intensive training in elite units, and inculcates an ethic of self-reliance and problem-solving.

Israel is also good at the sort of technological mash-ups that produce exciting new industries. The inspiration for camera pills (which transmit pictures from inside the human body) came from missiles that can "see" their targets, and the inspiration for heart stents came from drip-irrigation systems. The country has long turned adversity into a source of competitive advantage. For example, it became a world leader in alternative fuel partly because it was surrounded by hostile oil-rich countries.

However, the main obstacle to Israel's long-term economic success has nothing to do with how it creates firms. It lies in its failure to assimilate into its business culture both Arab-Israelis and ultra-orthodox Jews, who will together be about one-third of the population by 2025. Only 39% of ultra-orthodox men and 25% of Arab women are employed. Think-tanks such as the Milken Institute are trying to encourage small businesses in Arab-majority areas such as Galilee and the Negev. Both these economic problems will only be solved by political will: Israel needs to work harder at dealing with its internal Arab problem; and it needs to tell its ultra-orthodox Jews that, however hard they pray, the rest of the country does not owe them a living.

December 2010

Fixing the capitalist machine

Some sensible ideas for reviving America's entrepreneurial spirit

AMERICA HAS BEEN THE WORLD'S most important growth machine since the second world war. In the 1950s and 1960s its GDP grew by 3% a year despite the economy's maturity. In the 1970s it endured stagflation but the Reagan revolution revived the entrepreneurial spirit and the growth rate returned to 3% in the 1990s. The machine was good for the world as well as America – it helped spread the gospel of capitalism and transform the American dream into a global dream.

Today the growth machine is in trouble. It all but exploded in the financial crisis of 2007–08. But even before then it had been juddering. Examine the machine's three most powerful pistons – capital markets, innovation and the knowledge economy – and you discover that they had been malfunctioning for a decade.

The United States once boasted the world's most business-friendly capital markets. But in recent years the boast has rung hollow, as Robert Litan and Carl Schramm point out in their book *Better Capitalism*. Venture capitalists have slashed their spending, dumping more adventurous companies in the process, not least because around 90% of them failed to produce a positive return. The number of initial public offerings is down from an average of 547 a year in the 1990s to 192 since then. This has dramatically cut the supply of new, high-growth companies. Given that companies less than five years old may have provided almost all the 40 million net jobs the American economy added between 1980 and the financial crisis, that is dismal news for the unemployed.

America also used to have one of the most business-friendly immigration policies. Fully 18% of the *Fortune* 500 list as of 2010 were founded by immigrants (among them AT&T, DuPont, eBay, Google, Kraft, Heinz and Procter & Gamble). Include the children of immigrants and the figure is 40%. Immigrants founded a quarter of successful high-tech and engineering companies between 1995 and 2005. They obtain patents at twice the rate of American-born people with the same educational credentials. But America's immigration policies have tightened dramatically over the past decade, a period in which some other rich countries, such as Canada, have continued to woo skilled immigrants, while fabulous new opportunities have opened up in emerging markets like China and India. Why endure America's visa obstacle course when other countries are laying out the red carpet?

Finally, America has long boasted the world's most business-friendly universities. One-fifth of American start-ups are linked to universities, and great institutions like Stanford and MIT spawn businesses by the thousand. But the university-business boom seems to be fading. Federal spending on health-related research increased from $20 billion in 1993 to $30 billion in 2008, for example, but the number of new drugs approved by the Food and Drug Administration fell from a peak of 50 in 1996 to just 15 in 2008. University technology offices, which legally have first dibs at commercialising the faculty's ideas, have evolved into clumsy bureaucracies. The average age of researchers given grants by the National Institutes of Health is 50 and rising.

These problems all bear more heavily on entrepreneurs than established companies. Foreign-born entrepreneurs are finding it harder to gain citizenship. Academics are finding it harder to commercialise their ideas. All sorts of entrepreneurs are finding it harder to obtain seed money and to take their companies public. American capitalism is becoming like its European cousin: established firms with the scale and scope to deal with a growing thicket of regulations are doing well, but new companies are withering on the vine or selling themselves to incumbents.

What can be done to reverse this worrying trend? Messrs Litan and Schramm provide detailed answers. They note that the 2012 JOBS act was a step in the right direction, not least because it suggested that the political elite is beginning to realise the seriousness of the problem. The act exempts new companies, for their first five years, from the onerous Sarbanes-Oxley (SOX) regulations (passed in 2002, in response to a spate of corporate scandals). The act quadruples the number of shareholders that private companies can have (from 499 to 2,000) before they have to go public. It removes barriers to crowdfunding. But Messrs Litan and Schramm also have plenty of suggestions of their own.

Some of their ideas are familiar. They suggest that the government should give green cards to all foreigners who come to America to study science, technology, engineering or maths. Some are more innovative. Exchange-traded investment funds, which have gone from nothing a decade ago to a trillion-dollar industry today, leave promising new companies vulnerable to the fickleness of high-frequency traders: so why not let them exclude themselves from such funds' baskets of shares? SOX is reducing the supply of new companies in the name of protecting investors: so why not let smaller firms opt out of SOX so long as shareholders are duly warned? The authors also argue that university technology offices should lose their monopolies, giving professors more freedom to exploit their innovations.

Will Romney and Obama read it?

These are all admirable ideas. Messrs Litan and Schramm have resisted calling for federal spending on grand projects: they regard the deficit as the most serious long-term threat to American growth. They have also applied themselves to the everyday problems of real-life entrepreneurs instead of drifting into academic abstractions. But it is hard to read such a sensible book in the middle of the presidential-election campaign without a sense of foreboding. With the Republicans intent on forgetting Ronald Reagan's enthusiasm for immigration and the Democrats intent on demonising businesspeople, America's entrepreneurs are more endangered than ever.

September 2012

Rules for fools

The terrible threat of unlicensed interior designers

IN 1941 FRANKLIN ROOSEVELT added two new items to America's ancestral freedoms of speech and worship: freedom from fear and freedom from want. Today's politicians offer a far more generous menu: freedom from unlicensed hair-cutters, freedom from cowboy flower-arrangers and, most important of all, freedom from rogue interior designers. What is the point of enjoying freedom from fear or want, after all, if you cannot enjoy freedom from poorly co-ordinated colour schemes?

In the 1950s, when organisation man ruled, fewer than 5% of American workers needed licences. Today, after three decades of deregulation, the figure is almost 30%. Add to that people who are preparing to obtain a licence or whose jobs involve some form of certification and the share is 38%. Other rich countries impose far fewer fetters than the land of the free. In Britain only 13% of workers need licences (though that has doubled in 12 years).

Some occupations clearly need to be licensed. Nobody wants to unleash amateur doctors and dentists on the public, or untrained tattoo artists for that matter. But, as the *Wall Street Journal* has doggedly pointed out, America's Licence Raj has extended its tentacles into occupations that pose no plausible threat to health or safety – occupations, moreover, that are governed by considerations of taste rather than anything that can be objectively measured by licensing authorities. The list of jobs that require licences in some states already sounds like something from Monty Python – florists, handymen, wrestlers, tour guides, frozen-dessert sellers, firework operatives, second-hand booksellers and, of course, interior designers – but it will become sillier still if ambitious cat-groomers and dog-walkers get their way.

Getting a licence can be time-consuming. Want to become a barber in California? That will require studying the art of cutting and blow-drying for almost a year. Want to work in the wig trade in Texas?

You will need to take 300 hours of classes and pass both written and practical exams. Alabama obliges manicurists to sit through 750 hours of instruction before taking a practical exam. Florida will not let you work as an interior designer unless you complete a four-year university degree and a two-year apprenticeship and pass a two-day examination.

America's Licence Raj crushes would-be entrepreneurs. Consider three people who come from very different states and occupations. Jestina Clayton is an African hair-braider with 23 years of experience. But the Utah Barber, Cosmetologist/Barber, Esthetician, Electrologist and Nail Technician Licensing Board told her that she cannot practise her craft unless she first obtains a licence – which means spending up to $18,000 on 2,000 hours of study, none of it devoted to African hair-braiding.

Justin Brown is an abbot at a Benedictine abbey that supplements its meagre income by making and selling simple wooden coffins. But the Louisiana Board of Embalmers and Funeral Directors has ordered him to "cease and desist". Heaven knows what harm a corpse might suffer from an unlicensed coffin. Barbara Vanderkolk Gardner runs a flourishing interior-design business in New Jersey. But when she tried to expand into Florida, the state's Board of Architecture and Interior Design ordered her to delete all references to "interior design" from her website and stop offering "interior design services" in the Sunshine State.

The cost of all this pettifoggery is huge – unless, that is, you are a member of one of the cartels that pushes for pettifogging rules or an employee of one of the bureaucratic bodies charged with enforcing them. Morris Kleiner of the University of Minnesota calculates that licensing boosts the income of licensees by about 15%. In other words, it has about the same impact on wages as membership of a trade union does. (Trade unionists who are also protected by licences enjoy a 24% boost to their hourly wages.) Mr Kleiner also argues that licensing slows job-creation: by comparing occupations that are regulated in some states but not in others he found that job growth between 1990 and 2000 was 20% higher in unregulated occupations than in regulated ones.

The Institute for Justice, a free-market pressure group, argues that this is only the beginning of the Raj's sins. The patchwork of regulations makes it hard for people to move from state to state. The burden of regulations falls most heavily on ethnic minorities (who are less likely to have educational qualifications) and on women (who might want to return to work after raising their children). States that demand that funeral directors must also qualify as embalmers, for example, have 24% fewer female funeral directors than those that don't.

Uncle Sam will save you from bad feng shui

You might imagine that Americans would be up in arms about all this. After all, the Licence Raj embodies the two things that Americans are supposed to be furious about: the rise of big government and the stalling of America's job-creating machine. You would be wrong. In 2011 Florida's legislature debated a bill to remove licensing requirements from 20 occupations, including hair-braiding, interior design and teaching ballroom-dancing. For a while it looked as if the bill would sail through: Florida has been a centre of tea-party agitation and both chambers have Republican majorities. But the people who care most about this issue – the cartels of incumbents – lobbied the loudest. One predicted that unlicensed designers would use fabrics that might spread disease and cause 88,000 deaths a year. Another suggested, even more alarmingly, that clashing colour schemes might adversely affect "salivation". The bill was defeated. If Republican majorities cannot pluck up the courage to challenge a cartel of interior designers when Florida's unemployment rate is more than 10%, what hope has America? The Licence Raj may be here to stay.

May 2011

Ties that bind

The market for smart people is clogged up by all manner of dubious legal restrictions

THE BUSINESS PRESS is full of heartwarming stories about the "talent wars". It reports that eBay pays its lead technologist twice as much as its chief executive. Apple slipped a high-flyer $8 million to prevent him from jumping ship. Tech firms regularly spend lavishly on start-ups in order to "acqui-hire" their employees. They also compete furiously to provide workers with the best food and the most fashionable yoga instructors.

But the talent wars have a darker side, one that is fought with lawsuits and handcuffs rather than bonuses and California rolls. Firms are increasingly resorting to litigation – some of it extraordinarily unpleasant – to prevent employees from moving to rivals. The result is that the labour market is becoming clogged.

The most popular weapon on this front is the "non-compete" agreement, which prevents employees leaving a firm from working for a rival for a fixed period (usually up to two years but as many as five in Italy) or setting up a competing business. These were once mainly confined to the upper ranks of knowledge-intensive firms. Now they are ubiquitous: about 90% of managerial and technical employees in America have signed them.

Other weapons in the arsenal include "confidential information" and "pre-invention assignment" requirements. Companies can prevent former workers (including those who have not signed non-compete agreements) from moving to a rival on the ground that they are taking trade secrets with them. They can also assert astonishingly wide-ranging rights over their employees' inventions – claiming ownership of ideas that people had been working on for years before they joined the firm or which they came up with in their spare time or even after leaving.

It is easy to see why companies like these weapons. Firms can lose millions of dollars' worth of knowledge and contacts when a senior executive joins a rival. They can lose even more if the executive knows their secret recipe or algorithm. It is equally easy to see why employees hate them. Non-competes prevent people from selling their labour for long periods during which skills atrophy and contacts fade away.

How can the competing claims of employers and employees be reconciled? Judges have tended to put a heavy emphasis on the free-rider problem in dealing with this conundrum. Employers have little incentive to invest in training and innovation if the beneficiaries can move to a rival whenever they feel like it. Restrictions like non-compete clauses ultimately benefit everybody because they increase companies' incentives to invest in human capital without that fear.

In her book *Talent Wants to Be Free*, Orly Lobel, a law professor at the University of San Diego, presents a powerful counterblast to this argument. The drawbacks of the free-rider problem are as nothing compared with the advantages conferred by mobility. The free flow of talent encourages economic efficiency because it allows people to work in jobs and for wages that fit their skills. And no one likes being tied down. It also encourages innovation because it spreads information, extends professional networks and encourages cross-fertilisation.

An obvious example of the virtues of mobility is California: the home of Silicon Valley and Hollywood has been more reluctant than any other state to recognise non-competes and other restrictions on the tide of talent. This might be pure coincidence. But California is part of a more general pattern. American states with weak restrictions have better records of capital investment and innovation than those with strong ones. Freedom of movement is especially valuable for start-ups, which can easily be beaten to death by incumbents wielding a legal stick. Places in the West with lenient restrictions, such as the Scandinavian countries and Israel, tend to be more innovative than countries with tough ones like Germany and France.

That a free market for skilled people benefits the economy as a whole seems to offer cold comfort to firms that open themselves to raiders. But Ms Lobel retorts that the free flow of talent is good for individual companies whether they win or lose a particular battle in the wars. Firms that operate in such open markets for the highly skilled tend to have better-quality human capital. They make more use of performance-related rewards in a bid to recruit and retain stars. Those that lose their best people to rivals can also benefit by learning about their own weaknesses: Schlumberger, an oil-services firm, conducts internal inquiries whenever it loses somebody it wants to keep. Firms can also benefit from a raider's success: Cooley, a big law firm, suffered angst over losing a leading lawyer to a then unknown website. It was forgotten when the ex-employee hired the company to act as eBay's counsel for its $63 million IPO.

America's got talent

Ms Lobel sometimes takes her case too far. Companies surely deserve protection from rivals who try to steal trade secrets by hiring privileged insiders. But her instincts are absolutely correct. Human capital is the most important source of wealth in the modern economy. It is a looming problem that established companies are weaving a web of legal restrictions on the free movement of talent.

Policymakers need to remove these restrictions: they should presume that free trade in human talent is a good thing unless there are obvious attempts to steal corporate secrets. And firms need to stop regarding workers as chattels. McKinsey has done well by treating its ex-employees as alumni to be stroked rather than enemies to be persecuted. Other companies should do likewise. A ball and chain might look like a good idea when confronted by an aggressive competitor. But there is a reason why it is an impediment seldom associated with front-runners.

December 2013

Cronies and capitols

Businesspeople have become too influential in government

IN 1994 MANY ITALIANS voted for Silvio Berlusconi in the hope that he could use his skills as a businessman to revive a sclerotic economy. He had built a property-and-media empire out of thin air. He had reinvigorated one of the country's great football clubs, AC Milan. Surely he would do a better job of running the country than the old guard of corrupt politicians and introverted bureaucrats? Well, *si monumentum requiris, circumspice*. Mr Berlusconi was prime minister of Italy for eight of the ten years between 2001 and 2011. During that time Italy's GDP per head fell by 4%, its debt-to-GDP ratio rose from 109% to 120%, taxes rose from 41.2% of GDP to 43.4%, and its productivity stagnated. Rather than using his business skills to revive the Italian economy, Mr Berlusconi used his political skills to protect his business interests.

The great seducer is an extreme example. And with luck Italy's long Berlusconi-themed nightmare is drawing to a close. But the problem at the heart of Mr Berlusconi's Italy – the commingling of power and business – is a growing worry around the world.

In *Can Capitalism Survive?* (1947) Joseph Schumpeter argued that the answer to that question was probably "no". The great battle of the 20th century was between the state and business. And the state was likely to win because the thinkers and bureaucrats at its service were better at occupying the moral and intellectual high ground. "A genius in the business office may be, and often is, utterly unable outside of it to say boo to a goose – both in the drawing room and on the platform," he said.

Times have changed. Most politicians now believe that businesses are better than bureaucracies at generating growth. Prime ministers and finance ministers flock to Davos not to lay down the law to businesspeople but to court their favours. Businesspeople have learned not just to say boo to a goose but to put a ring through its beak. Today the problem is often the very opposite of the one that

Schumpeter imagined: not the marginalisation of business but its excessive influence.

The emerging world has gone furthest with what might politely be called "public-private partnerships". The state grants franchises to well-connected businesspeople such as Carlos Slim in Mexico or Cyril Ramaphosa in South Africa. Those businesspeople then use their wealth to influence the state. In emerging markets such as China and Russia a group of state-owned enterprises (SOEs) dominate the economy. In "khaki capitalist" countries such as Pakistan and Egypt the army controls businesses that account for big chunks of the economy: their bosses, both as generals and as general managers, enjoy much political clout.

Crony capitalism seems to be getting worse. In China the SOEs call the tune: they suck up capital from the private sector and refuse to pay dividends to SASAC, the government body that nominally oversees them. Many of India's dozens of billionaires made their fortunes in industries such as mining and infrastructure that are prone to rent-seeking, even if the most famous are in relatively politics-free ones such as computing.

This all matters more than it used to. The emerging world may be slowing but it now accounts for more than half of global GDP (using purchasing-power parity) compared with less than a third two decades ago. And SOEs strut the global stage. A quarter of the companies on the latest *Fortune* Global 500 list are from emerging markets, up from 15% in 2010. Of these, 58% are Chinese SOEs. The government has set them a target of getting half their profits from abroad in five years, up from 38% now.

The Anglo-Saxon world looks askance at Mr Berlusconi's mixing of business and politics, and at the French phenomenon of *pantouflage*, in which senior civil servants move on to cushy jobs in business. But its superior attitude is misplaced. In Britain the revolving door is spinning ever more rapidly. Over the past decade 18 former senior ministers and civil servants have taken jobs with the biggest three accountancy firms, whose work includes helping businesses minimise their tax bills and lobby the government. They include Dave Hartnett, until last year the head of the revenue service, now a consultant at Deloitte. The boards of British energy firms are packed with ex-ambassadors and ex-spies.

Rome on the Potomac

In America relations between business and politics are even cosier, and more worrying. Luigi Zingales of the University of Chicago's Booth School of Business left Italy in 1988 because he felt his country was being destroyed by cronyism. But in his book *A Capitalism for the People*, he worries that America is turning Italian. Washington, DC, has taken over from Silicon Valley as the metropolis with the highest income per head. Spending on lobbying has more than doubled in the past 15 years. The *Washington Post*'s new owner, Jeff Bezos, promises that its coverage will not be the servant of his interests – but his company, Amazon, spends millions of dollars a year on lobbying. The Supreme Court's 2010 "Citizens United" decision has given companies carte blanche to spend freely on influencing elections. The Treasury has all but dug an underground passage to Wall Street: four of the past seven treasury secretaries had close ties to investment banks.

Policing the relationship between government and business in a free society is difficult. Businesspeople have every right to lobby governments, and civil servants to take jobs in the private sector. Governments have to find the best people to fill important jobs: there is a limited supply of people who understand the financial system, for example. But governments must also remember that businesses are self-interested actors who will try to rig the system for their own benefit. The sad state of Mr Berlusconi's Italy shows that a government that is too close to businessmen may neither be businesslike nor do much to promote businesses other than their own.

August 2013

The entrepreneurial state

An intriguing book points out the big role governments play in creating innovative businesses

APPLE IS GENERALLY REGARDED as an embodiment of everything that is best about innovative businesses. It was started in a garage. For years it played a cool David to Microsoft's lumbering Goliath. Then it disrupted itself, and the entire entertainment industry, by shifting its focus from computers to mobile devices. But there is something missing from this story, argues Mariana Mazzucato of Sussex University in England, in her book *The Entrepreneurial State*. Steve Jobs was undoubtedly a genius who understood both engineering and design. Apple was undoubtedly a nimble innovator. But Apple's success would have been impossible without the active role of the state, the unacknowledged enabler of today's consumer-electronics revolution.

Consider the technologies that put the smart into Apple's smartphones. The armed forces pioneered the internet, GPS positioning and voice-activated "virtual assistants". They also provided much of the early funding for Silicon Valley. Academic scientists in publicly funded universities and labs developed the touchscreen and the HTML language. An obscure government body even lent Apple $500,000 before it went public. Ms Mazzucato considers it a travesty of justice that a company that owes so much to public investment devotes so much energy to reducing its tax burden by shifting its money offshore and assigning its intellectual property to low-tax jurisdictions such as Ireland.

Likewise, the research that produced Google's search algorithm, the fount of its wealth, was financed by a grant from the National Science Foundation. As for pharmaceutical companies, they are even bigger beneficiaries of state research than internet and electronics firms. America's National Institutes of Health, with an annual budget of more than $30 billion, finances studies that lead to many of the most revolutionary new drugs.

Economists have long recognised that the state has a role in promoting innovation. It can correct market failures by investing directly in public goods such as research, or by using the tax system to nudge businesses towards doing so. But Ms Mazzucato argues that the entrepreneurial state does far more than just make up for the private sector's shortcomings: through the big bets it makes on new technologies, such as aircraft or the internet, it creates and shapes the markets of the future. At its best the state is nothing less than the ultimate Schumpeterian innovator – generating the gales of creative destruction that provide strong tailwinds for private firms like Apple.

Ms Mazzucato says that the most successful entrepreneurial state can be found in the most unlikely place: the United States. Americans have traditionally been divided between Jeffersonians (who think that he governs best who governs least) and Hamiltonians (who favour active government). The secret of the country's success lies, she thinks, in talking like Jeffersonians but acting like Hamiltonians. Whatever their rhetoric, governments have always invested heavily in promoting the spread of existing technologies such as the railways (by giving the rail barons free land) and in seeking potentially lucrative scientific breakthroughs (by financing almost 60% of basic research).

So far, so good. However, Ms Mazzucato omits to acknowledge how often would-be entrepreneurial states end up pouring money down ratholes. The world is littered with imitation Silicon Valleys that produce nothing but debt. Yes, private-sector ventures also frequently fail, but their investors know when to stop: their own money runs out. Governments can keep on throwing taxpayers' money away. It was once fashionable to praise Japan as an entrepreneurial state being guided to world domination by the enlightened thinkers in its mighty industry ministry. Nowadays it is clearer that the ministry has been a dead hand holding back innovation and entrepreneurship.

Ms Mazzucato laments that private businesses are too short-termist. But governments also routinely make investments on the basis of short-run political calculations rather than long-term pay-offs. She worries that anti-statist ideology is reducing the state's ability to make important investments for the future. In fact, the explosion of entitlement spending, which is allocating ever more of the country's income to the old, is doing more to undermine the entrepreneurial state than the Tea Party. She is also too hard on business: putting all those different state-funded technologies together into user-friendly iPads and iPhones required rare genius that deserves rare rewards.

The book offers only hints, rather than a complete answer, to the central practical question in all this: why are some states successful entrepreneurs while others are failures? Successful states are obsessed by competition; they make scientists compete for research grants, and businesses compete for start-up funds – and leave the decisions to experts, rather than politicians or bureaucrats. They also foster networks of innovation that stretch from universities to profit-maximising companies, keeping their own role to a minimum. The Jeffersonian-Hamiltonian paradox is important here: the more governments think in terms of mighty "entrepreneurial states" the less successful they are likely to be.

How not to spend it

Quibbles aside, Ms Mazzucato is right to argue that the state has played a central role in producing game-changing breakthroughs, and that its contribution to the success of technology-based businesses should not be underestimated. She is also right to point out that the "profligate" countries that are suffering the most from the current crisis (such as Greece and Italy) are those that have spent the least on R&D and education. There are many reasons why policymakers must modernise the state and bring entitlements under control. But one of the most important is that a well-run state is a vital part of a successful innovation system.

August 2013

The great mismatch

Skills shortages are getting worse even as youth unemployment reaches record highs

IN PARTS OF EUROPE AND THE MIDDLE EAST more than a quarter of 15- to 24-year-olds do not have a job. In some black spots such as Spain and Egypt the figure is more than a half. Altogether 75 million of the world's young people are unemployed and twice that number are underemployed. This not only represents a huge loss of productive capacity as people in the prime of life are turned into dependants. It is also a potential source of social disruption and a daily source of individual angst. The Japanese have a word for the 700,000 young people who have withdrawn from society into domestic cocoons: *hikikomori.*

Yet at the same time companies complain vigorously that they cannot get hold of the right people. In early 2012 Manpower, an employment-services firm, reported that more than a third of employers worldwide had trouble filling jobs. Shortages are pressing not just in elite areas such as engineering but also in mid-level ones such as office administration. In December McKinsey, a consultancy, reported that only 43% of employers in the nine countries that it has studied in depth (America, Brazil, Britain, Germany, India, Mexico, Morocco, Saudi Arabia and Turkey) think that they can find enough skilled entry-level workers. Middle-sized firms (between 50 and 500 workers) have an average of 13 entry-level jobs empty while large employers have 27.

What is going on? And what can we do about it? McKinsey argues persuasively that a big part of the problem is that educators and employers operate in parallel universes – and that a big part of the solution lies in bringing these two universes together: obliging educators to step into employers' shoes, employers to step into educators', and students to move between the two.

The best way to do this is to revamp vocational education, which outside the German-speaking world has been treated as the ginger stepchild of the education system. Governments have poured money into universities. Universities have competed to sing their own praises. As a result, parents and their offspring have shunned vocational schools: many students surveyed by McKinsey chose to go to academic schools despite thinking that vocational ones would give them more chance of finding work.

But some far-sighted countries, schools and firms are busy reinventing vocational education, McKinsey argues. South Korea has created a network of vocational schools – called "meister" schools, from the German for "master craftsman" – to reduce the country's shortage of machine operators and plumbers. The government pays the students' room and board as well as their tuition. It also refers to them as "young meisters" in order to counteract the country's obsession with academic laurels (South Korea has one of the world's highest university-enrolment rates).

Technical schools are building exact replicas of workplaces in order to make it easier to cross the theoretical-practical divide: the TAFE Challenger Institute of Technology in Perth, Australia, has a fully functioning replica of a gas-processing plant (minus the gas). Talent-starved companies are striking deals with governments to mix practical and academic education: in Egypt Americana Group, a food and restaurant company, has a programme that allows students to spend up to half their time working for Americana (earning wages) and half their time in college.

Policymakers are also enjoying some success in using vocational education to reach underprivileged groups. South Africa's Go for Gold, a partnership between the Western Cape Education Department and the NMC Construction Group, identifies promising schoolchildren for additional instruction and guarantees them a year's paid work experience and a chance at a university scholarship. India's Institute for Literacy Education and Vocational Training sends people to villages to speak to families about the opportunities on offer with blue-chip companies such as Taj Hotels and Larsen & Toubro.

It is easy to be sceptical about these attempts to bridge the gap between education and employment. Academic drift is one of the most powerful forces in educational life: look at the way Britain's technical schools were allowed to wither on the vine and its polytechnics converted into universities.

Nevertheless there are reasons for optimism. For one, technology is greatly reducing the cost of vocational education – which has always been one of the most important reasons for its slow spread. "Serious games" can provide young people with a chance to gain hands-on experience, albeit of the virtual kind, at minimum cost. Miami Dade College, America's largest community college, has introduced a system that sends automatic alerts to faculty advisers whenever one of their charges trips a warning wire, such as falling grades. Colombia's Labour Observatory provides details on the graduation and employment rates of every educational institution in the country.

Master the meister

Second, more and more private-sector institutions are coming up with ideas to improve vocational training. China Vocational Training Holdings specialises in matching students with jobs in the Chinese car industry by keeping masses of data on both students and companies. Mozilla, the creator of the Firefox web browser, has created an "open badges initiative" that allows people to get recognition for programming skills. IL&FS Skills, an Indian training company, gives students a guarantee of a job if they finish its courses.

Better vocational education is hardly a cure-all for the global jobs crisis: millions of young people will be condemned to unemployment so long as demand remains slack and growth sluggish. But it can at least help to deal with an absurd mismatch that has saddled the world not just with a shortage of jobs but a shortage of skills as well.

December 2012

A hospital case

Sweden is leading the world in allowing private companies to run public institutions

SAINT GORAN'S HOSPITAL is one of the glories of the Swedish welfare state. It is also a laboratory for applying business principles to the public sector. The hospital is run by a private company, Capio, which in turn is run by a consortium of private-equity funds, including Nordic Capital and Apax Partners. The doctors and nurses are Capio employees, answerable to a boss and a board. Doctors talk enthusiastically about "the Toyota model of production" and "harnessing innovation" to cut costs.

Welcome to health care in post-ideological Sweden. From the patient's point of view, St Goran's is no different from any other public hospital. Treatment is free, after a nominal charge which is universal in Sweden. St Goran's gets nearly all its money from the state. But behind the scenes it has led a revolution in the relationship between government and business. In the mid-1990s St Goran's was slated for closure. Then, in 1999, Stockholm County Council struck a deal with Capio to take over the day-to-day operation of the hospital. In 2006 Capio was taken over by a group of private-equity firms led by Nordic Capital. Stockholm County Council recently extended Capio's contract until 2021.

St Goran's is now a temple to "lean management" – an idea that was pioneered by Toyota in the 1950s and has since spread from carmaking to services and from Japan to the rest of the world. Britta Wallgren, the hospital's chief executive, says she never heard the term "lean" when she was at medical school (she is an anaesthetist by training). Now she hears it all the time.

The hospital today is organised on the twin lean principles of "flow" and "quality". Doctors and nurses used to keep a professional distance from each other. Now they work (and sit) together in teams. (Goran Ornung, a doctor, likens the teams to workers in Formula One pit stops.) In the old days people concentrated solely on their field of medical expertise. Now they are all responsible for suggesting operational improvements as well.

One innovation involved buying a roll of yellow tape. Staff used to waste precious time looking for defibrillator machines and the like. Then someone suggested marking a spot on the floor with yellow tape and insisting that the machines were always kept there. Other ideas are equally low-tech. Teams use a series of magnetic dots to keep track of each patient's progress and which beds are free. They discharge patients throughout the day rather than in one batch, so that they can easily find a taxi.

St Goran's is the medical equivalent of a budget airline. There are four to six patients to a room. The decor is institutional. Everything is done to "maximise throughput". The aim is to give taxpayers value for money. Hospitals should not be in the hotel business, the argument goes. St Goran's has reduced waiting times by increasing throughput. It has also reduced each patient's likelihood of picking up an infection. However, scrimping on hotel services means that it has to invest in preparing patients for admission and providing support after they are released.

The hospital has helped to change the way Swedes receive health care. Ms Wallgren likens it to a hare that sets the pace of a dog race. The hare can run fast because its staff think of themselves as part of a team, and because managers emphasise collective learning. But St Goran's is also a symptom of a wider change.

Sweden has gone further than any other European country in embracing the purchaser-provider split – that is, in using government money to buy public services from whichever providers, public or private, offer the best combination of price and quality. Private firms provide 20% of public hospital care in Sweden and 30% of public primary care. Both the public and private sectors are obsessed with lean management; they realise that a high-cost country such as Sweden must make the best use of its resources.

St Goran's also acts as a hare for Capio, one of Europe's largest health-care companies, with 11,000 employees across the continent and 2.9 million visits from patients in 2012. Sweden is Capio's biggest market, accounting for 48.2% of its sales (France comes second with 37.6%). The firm performs 10% of all Swedish cataract operations, and much more besides. Capio thinks it can make huge savings in other countries by transferring the lessons it has learned in Sweden. The average length of a hospital stay in Sweden is 4.5 days, compared with 5.2 days in France and 7.5 days in Germany. Sweden has 2.8 hospital beds per 1,000 citizens. France has 6.6; Germany, 8.2. Yet Swedes live slightly longer.

Capitalists under the bed

Spreading efficiency will not be easy, however. Europeans instinctively recoil from private companies making money from health care. British placards protest against modest reforms with pictures of fat cats helping the health minister to disembowel a patient labelled "NHS" (National Health Service). Even in Sweden, the mood has grown more hostile since some private-equity companies were embroiled in scandals at nursing homes.

The public-health business is hardly alluring for investors, either. Cash-strapped European governments are striking hard bargains. Leif Karnstrom, a senior figure at Stockholm County Council, is excited about a new system of "outcome-based health care" that allows him to claim his money back if providers perform poorly. Most people in the private-equity business think there are easier ways to make money than taking over bits of the state.

This is a pity. Private health-care companies have several advantages over public organisations. They have more incentive to make services more efficient, since they typically keep some of the savings. They are better at persuading their employees to adopt new ideas. And they are better at spreading new ideas across borders. Europe should be proud of its public-health services. But if it wants them still to be affordable in the future, it should allow more private companies into the mix.

May 2013

Saving Britain's health service

The NHS needs to learn from innovations in the rest of the world

NO SPECTACLE IS "so ridiculous as the British public in one of its periodical fits of morality", harrumphed Thomas Macaulay, a Victorian historian. Today there is no spectacle so ridiculous as the British public in one of its periodic fits of panic about the National Health Service (NHS). Every decade or so the government tries to reform the NHS – and every decade or so the NHS masses its forces to work the public into a frenzy.

Doctors threaten to strike against "privatisation". Bishops bleat that anxiety stalks the land. The BBC waves blood-stained sheets. And the government eventually backs down. Thus it was with Margaret Thatcher and (more mutedly) with Tony Blair. And thus it is with David Cameron, who came to office promising to reinvent the welfare state but now promises that the NHS of the future "will be much like what we have today".

This is a mind-boggling statement. The internet and the mobile phone are revolutionising social life. New drugs and surgical techniques are revolutionising treatment and prolonging life. Entrepreneurs and innovators are demonstrating that you can use new technology and clever business models to deliver better health care for less money. As Britain ages and its medical bills soar, the NHS must experiment or die.

The NHS was built on the idea that patients are passive recipients of medical wisdom, most of it delivered face-to-face. This is beginning to change: doctors now advise patients to take exercise and eat their vegetables. But it has a long way to go. The private sector has revolutionised productivity by getting customers to do more things for themselves. Rather than waiting for a butcher or baker to serve us, many people now choose their own groceries and scan them themselves at the checkout. This model is now reaching health, too.

Several American organisations encourage people to monitor and manage their own health. The Centre for Connected Health, which works with Harvard Medical School's hospitals, urges patients to wear tiny sensors that generate data about their well-being. This not only allows doctors to call them if something is amiss; computerised "lifestyle coaches" also send them e-mails telling them to modify their behaviour if their indicators grow worse. Kaiser Permanente, a health-care firm, allocates diabetes sufferers a diabetes specialist and then encourages them to get their blood tested at a local pharmacy. The results are analysed and the specialists call their patients if a red flag pops up. The Montefiore Medical Centre in New York has reduced hospital admissions for older patients by more than 30% by using remote monitors which allow doctors to manage them at a distance.

Much of the pressure for a more collaborative approach to health care is coming from the bottom up – from patients themselves and from what David Cameron calls the "big society". Voluntary organisations such as Alcoholics Anonymous have a better record than the NHS at teaching people to look after themselves. People who suffer from rare or debilitating diseases form online groups such as PatientsLikeMe and WeAreUs to swap advice and support each other. There is a growing community of "quantified selfers" who monitor their own bodily functions and hold meetings to discuss their results. This combination of monitoring and self-help holds the key to cost control as well as improved health: about 75% of NHS spending is devoted to 17.5 million people who suffer from long-term problems.

The NHS was also built on the assumption that general hospitals are the flagships of the system. (Mr Cameron promises to defend them.) But across the developing world entrepreneurs are demonstrating that "focused factories", to use the jargon, can use economies of scale and intense specialisation to improve productivity. The Narayana Hrudayalaya Hospital in Bangalore has reduced the cost of heart surgery to $2,000 (60% cheaper than most Indian hospitals). Its 42 surgeons perform an impressive 3,000 operations a year. They become virtuosos in their sub-specialisms. LifeSpring Hospitals, an Indian chain, has used standardised procedures, borrowed from manufacturing, to reduce the cost of delivering a baby to $40, a fifth of the cost at comparable local hospitals. Every year the Aravind Eye

Hospital performs 70% of the number of eye operations performed by the entire NHS for just 1% of the cost.

Entrepreneurs are using new business models to revolutionise routine care as well. Franchising, for example, allows entrepreneurs to piggy-back on other people's infrastructure (particularly retailers) while at the same time fitting in with the rhythms of everyday life. VisionSpring, a social enterprise, provides entrepreneurs in 13 countries with a "business in a bag": all the equipment they need to diagnose and correct long-sightedness. PDA, a Thai social enterprise, distributes condoms and contraceptive advice through a network of restaurants. America's MinuteClinics, which operate in stores, offer health screening and treatment for common ailments under the motto "You're sick, we're quick".

Wanted: a medical Martin Luther

The struggle for NHS reform has not been completely lost. On June 8th 2011 Reform, a think-tank, staged a conference on "disruptive innovation" in health care. NHS veterans repeated the old saw that the NHS is the closest thing Britain has to a national religion. But they also listened excitedly as Indians and Mexicans told stories of innovations back home. And they produced numerous examples of innovations of their own. NHS Direct, a hotline, dishes out medical advice by phone and the internet to 8 million people [the service was decommissioned in March 2014]. Boots and Specsavers, two high-street stores, apply something like the franchise model to the distribution of spectacles. Pointing out flaws in a nation's religion will seldom win you friends. But sometimes it takes a Reformation to save a church.

June 2011

PART 6

The world of workers

The wolves of the web

Booming technology firms are now at the centre of worries about inequality

THE BARONS OF HIGH-TECH like to think of themselves as very different creatures from the barons of Wall Street. They create cool devices that let us carry the world in our pockets. They wear hoodies, not suits. And they owe their success to their native genius rather than to social connections – they are "the crazy ones, the misfits, the rebels, the troublemakers, the round pegs in square holes", in Steve Jobs's famous formulation.

But for many people in San Francisco this is a distinction without a difference. For months protesters blockaded the fleets of private buses that Google and other technology giants use to ferry their employees to and from Silicon Valley 40 miles to the south. They were particularly incensed that the buses pay almost nothing to use public stops, often blocking city buses. Protesters were also angry that an influx of well-paid geeks has pushed up property prices and rents.

This resentment turned a 2014 awards ceremony – the Crunchies, sponsored by a website called TechCrunch – into a festival of tech-bashing. Outside, protesters held their own mock ceremony, the Crappies, with a golden toilet brush for "tax-evader of the year" to Twitter's boss, Dick Costolo (a reference to a legal but controversial tax break it got from City Hall). Inside, John Oliver, the comedian hosting the official awards, gave the assembled billionaires a dressing-down. "You already have almost all the money in the world," he said. "Why do you need awards as well?" He suggested that the next iteration of Martin Scorsese's film, *The Wolf of Wall Street*, should be set on the West Coast with "all the money, all the opulence and about 10% of the sex".

In February 2014 Tom Perkins, a Silicon Valley venture capitalist, compared critics of the tech elite to Nazi stormtroopers on Kristallnacht – thereby handing ammunition to those who accuse that elite, of which he is a member, of being arrogant and out of touch. Nevertheless, much of the criticism is nonsense. San Francisco has more than its fair share of professional protesters – including those who think they have a right to live in one of the world's most desirable places even if they can't rub two pennies together. The much-maligned private buses are providing workers with an energy- and time-efficient alternative to private cars. The much-abused tech money-tree is scattering riches on lower-paid industries too. During the gold rush, Levi Strauss made a fortune by providing the "forty-niners" with jeans. Modern-day equivalents will undoubtedly make fortunes providing geeks with organic food, "dress-pants sweat pants" (a cross between pyjamas and jeans, apparently) and, if one Kickstarter-funded venture pays off, "ten-year hoodies", made to last a decade.

Tech titans have also suffered from backlashes before: Bill Gates was once vilified as a modern robber baron before he transformed himself into the world's greatest philanthropist. Most people outside San Francisco still look on its tech firms with admiration, not disgust. But it would be a mistake to ignore the backlash by the bay entirely. It is being driven by two developments which will eventually reshape attitudes across the world.

The first is the end of tech-exceptionalism. Silicon Valley's elite has always cherished its roots in the counter-culture – in the world of home-brew computer clubs, utopian cyber-gurus and damn-the-establishment hackers. But it also had a conventional side: Hewlett-Packard may have been started in a garage but it soon became a corporate behemoth; tech firms' links to the military establishment were highlighted when Dave Packard became deputy secretary of defence in the Nixon administration. The 2014 protests symbolise a growing recognition that tech is an industry like all others: mostly run by corporate stiffs – square pegs in square holes in Jobs's language – and driven by the need to maximise profits. Sheryl Sandberg, Facebook's chief operating officer, has become a billionaire despite not having founded the company. Apple's success has created huge numbers of manufacturing jobs, almost all in cheaper places than the United States.

Some of the most savage criticisms of the tech industry are inspired by the contrast between its self-image as a haven of hooded nonconformists and the reality of ruthless capitalism. Valleywag, a website, pokes fun at its affection for ostentatiously wacky corporate titles: AOL has a digital prophet, Tumblr has a fashion evangelist and LinkedIn a hacker-in-residence. It also exposes the Valley's addiction to politically correct consumption and frictionless capitalism. Tesla electric cars start at $62,000. Google Glass lets its wearers, "Glassholes", consult the internet as they walk down the street. TaskRabbit, a website, lets geeks contract out domestic chores to the lowest bidder.

The second development is the triumph of the meritocracy. This is not to say that tech is entirely merit-based: women and non-Asian minorities are clearly under-represented. But its logic is nevertheless meritocratic: you can't program a computer or develop an app without a high IQ and a specialised education. So the tech industry is heightening the relationship between IQ, education and reward: young tech geniuses earn many multiples of the wages of the service workers who reply to their ads on TaskRabbit.

Succeed, then secede

Robert Reich, Bill Clinton's labour secretary and now an academic at Berkeley, once complained about the "secession of the successful", as the monied elite moved into gated suburbs. But today's money-gorged young techies want to enjoy the perks of city life. Thus they buy up, occupy and gentrify whole urban districts: they are seceding in plain sight. This inevitably creates tensions as the service class sees a parallel world being constructed before their eyes. San Francisco has a history of anticipating cultural earthquakes, from the hippies of the 1960s to the greenies of the 1980s. The wolves of the world wide web should beware.

February 2014

Hating what you do

Disenchantment with work is growing. What can be done about it?

SUICIDE, PROCLAIMED ALBERT CAMUS in "The Myth of Sisyphus", is the only serious philosophical problem. In France it is also a serious management problem. A spate of attempted and successful suicides at France Telecom – many of them explicitly prompted by troubles at work – sparked a national debate about life in the modern corporation. One man stabbed himself in the middle of a meeting (he survived). A woman leapt from a fourth-floor office window after sending a suicidal e-mail to her father: "I have decided to kill myself tonight ... I can't take the new reorganisation." In all, 24 of the firm's employees took their own lives between early 2008 and late 2009 – and this grisly tally follows similar episodes at other pillars of French industry including Renault, Peugeot and EDF.

There are some parochial reasons for this melancholy trend. France Telecom is making the difficult transition from state monopoly to multinational company. It shed 22,000 jobs between 2006 and 2009, but two-thirds of the remaining workers enjoy civil-service-like job security. This is forcing it to pursue a toxic strategy: teaching old civil servants new tricks while at the same time putting new hires on short-term contracts. Yet the problem is not confined to France. America's Bureau of Labour Statistics calculates that work-related suicides increased by 28% between 2007 and 2008, although the rate is lower than in Europe. And suicide is only the tip of an iceberg of work-related unhappiness.

A survey by the Centre for Work-Life Policy, an American consultancy, found that between June 2007 and December 2008 the proportion of employees who professed loyalty to their employers slumped from 95% to 39%; the number voicing trust in them fell from 79% to 22%. A later survey by DDI, another American consultancy, found that more than half of respondents described their job as "stagnant", meaning that they had nothing interesting to do and little hope of promotion. Half of these "stagnators" planned to look for another job as soon as the economy improved. People are both clinging on to their current jobs, however much they dislike them, and dreaming of moving when the economy improves. This is taking a toll on both short-term productivity and long-term competitiveness: the people most likely to move when things look up are high-flyers who feel that their talents are being ignored.

The most obvious reason for the rise in unhappiness is the recession, which is destroying jobs at a startling rate and spreading anxiety throughout the workforce. But the recession is also highlighting longer-term problems. Unhappiness seems to be particularly common in car companies, which suffer from global overcapacity, and telecoms companies, which are being buffeted by a technological revolution. In a survey of its workers in 2008, France Telecom found that two-thirds of them reported being "stressed out" and a sixth reported being in "distress".

A second source of misery is the drive to improve productivity, which is typically accompanied by an obsession with measuring performance. Giant retailers use "workforce management" software to monitor how many seconds it takes to scan the goods in a grocery cart, and then reward the most diligent workers with prime working hours. The public sector, particularly in Britain, is awash with inspectorates and performance targets. Taylorism, which Charlie Chaplin lampooned so memorably in *Modern Times*, has spread from the industrial to the post-industrial economy. In Japan some firms even monitor whether their employees smile frequently enough at customers.

A more subtle problem lies in the mixed messages that companies send about loyalty and commitment. Many firms – particularly successful ones – demand extraordinary dedication from their employees. (Microsoft, according to an old joke, offers flexitime: "You can work any 18-hour shift that you want.") Some provide perks that are intended to make the office feel like a second home. But companies also reserve the right to trim their workforce at the first sign of trouble. Most employees understand that their firms do not feel much responsibility to protect jobs. But they nevertheless find it wrenching to leave a post that has consumed so much of their lives.

Engineering joy

Can anything be done about this epidemic of unhappiness? There are some people, particularly in Europe, who think that it strengthens the case for expanding workers' rights. But doing so will not end the upheaval wrought by technological innovation in the telecoms sector or overcapacity in the car industry. And the situation in France Telecom was exacerbated by the fact that so many workers were unsackable. The solution to the problem, in so far as there is one, lies in the hands of managers and workers rather than governments.

Companies need to do more than pay lip service to the human side of management. They also need to learn from the well-documented mistakes of others (France Telecom has belatedly hired Technologia, a consultancy which helped Renault with its suicide problem). Bob Sutton of Stanford University argues that companies need to do as much as possible to come clean with workers, even if that means confirming bad news. He also warns that bosses need to be careful about the signals they send: in times of great stress ill thought-out turns of phrase can lead to a frenzy of anxiety and speculation.

As for the workers, the habit of battening down the hatches, which so irritates many companies, may be a sensible response to economic turmoil. In the longer term workers can take comfort from the fact that history may be on their side: in the rich world, low birth rates, an impending surge in retirements and caps on immigration could reduce the number of people of working age by 20–40%. Today's unhappy workers may one day be able to exercise the ultimate revenge, by taking their services elsewhere.

October 2009

Too much information

How to cope with data overload

GOOGLE "INFORMATION OVERLOAD" and you are immediately overloaded with information: more than 7 million hits in 0.05 seconds. Some of this information is interesting: for example, that the phrase "information overload" was popularised by Alvin Toffler in 1970. Some of it is mere noise: obscure companies promoting their services and even more obscure bloggers sounding off. The overall impression is at once overwhelming and confusing.

"Information overload" is one of the biggest irritations in modern life. There are e-mails to answer, virtual friends to pester, YouTube videos to watch and, back in the physical world, meetings to attend, papers to shuffle and spouses to appease. A survey by Reuters once found that two-thirds of managers believe that the data deluge has made their jobs less satisfying or hurt their personal relationships. One-third think that it has damaged their health. Another survey suggests that most managers think most of the information they receive is useless.

Commentators have coined a profusion of phrases to describe the anxiety and anomie caused by too much information: "data asphyxiation" (William van Winkle), "data smog" (David Shenk), "information fatigue syndrome" (David Lewis), "cognitive overload" (Eric Schmidt) and "time famine" (Leslie Perlow). Johann Hari, a British journalist, notes that there is a good reason why "wired" means both "connected to the internet" and "high, frantic, unable to concentrate".

These worries are exaggerated. Stick-in-the-muds have always complained about new technologies: the Victorians fussed that the telegraph meant that "the businessman of the present day must be continually on the jump". And businesspeople have always had to deal with constant pressure and interruptions – hence the word "business". In his classic study of managerial work in 1973 Henry Mintzberg compared managers to jugglers: they keep 50 balls in the air and periodically check on each one before sending it aloft once more.

Yet clearly there is a problem. It is not merely the dizzying increase in the volume of information (the amount of data being stored doubles every 18 months). It is also the combination of omnipresence and fragmentation. Many professionals are welded to their smartphones. They are also constantly bombarded with unrelated bits and pieces – a poke from a friend one moment, the latest Greek financial tragedy the next.

The data fog is thickening at a time when companies are trying to squeeze ever more out of their workers. A survey in America by Spherion Staffing discovered that 53% of workers had been compelled to take on extra tasks since the recession started. This dismal trend may well continue – many companies remain reluctant to hire new people even as business picks up. So there will be little respite from the dense data smog, which some researchers fear may be poisonous.

They raise three big worries. First, information overload can make people feel anxious and powerless: scientists have discovered that multitaskers produce more stress hormones. Second, overload can reduce creativity. Teresa Amabile of Harvard Business School has spent more than a decade studying the work habits of 238 people, collecting a total of 12,000 diary entries between them. She finds that focus and creativity are connected. People are more likely to be creative if they are allowed to focus on something for some time without interruptions. If constantly interrupted or forced to attend meetings, they are less likely to be creative. Third, overload can also make workers less productive. David Meyer, of the University of Michigan, has shown that people who complete certain tasks in parallel take much longer and make many more errors than people who complete the same tasks in sequence.

Curbing the cacophony

What can be done about information overload? One answer is technological: rely on the people who created the fog to invent filters that will clean it up. Xerox promises to restore "information sanity" by developing better filtering and managing devices. Google is trying to improve its online searches by taking into account more personal information. (Some people fret that this will breach their privacy, but it will probably deliver quicker, more accurate searches.) A popular computer program called "Freedom" disconnects you from the web at preset times.

A second answer involves willpower. Ration your intake. Turn off your mobile phone and internet from time to time.

But such ruses are not enough. Smarter filters cannot stop people from obsessively checking their BlackBerrys. Some do so because it makes them feel important; others because they may be addicted to the "dopamine squirt" they get from receiving messages, as Edward Hallowell and John Ratey, two academics, have argued. And self-discipline can be counter-productive if your company doesn't embrace it. Some bosses get shirty if their underlings are unreachable even for a few minutes.

Most companies are better at giving employees access to the information superhighway than at teaching them how to drive. This is starting to change. Management consultants have spotted an opportunity. Derek Dean and Caroline Webb of McKinsey urge businesses to embrace three principles to deal with data overload: find time to focus, filter out noise and forget about work when you can. Business leaders are chipping in. David Novak of Yum! Brands urges people to ask themselves whether what they are doing is constructive or a mere "activity". John Doerr, a venture capitalist, urges people to focus on a narrow range of objectives and filter out everything else. Cristobal Conde of SunGard, an IT firm, preserves "thinking time" in his schedule when he cannot be disturbed. This might sound like common sense. But common sense is rare amid the cacophony of corporate life.

June 2011

Going off the rails

Companies need to keep an eye on their bosses for signs of destructive behaviour

THOSE OF US who still read newspapers over breakfast have had a delicious choice of late: do we start with the story about Bradford's crystal Methodist or the one about Toronto's stuporman? Paul Flowers, the former chairman of Britain's Co-operative Bank and a Methodist minister, allegedly bought cocaine and crystal meth for a "drug-fuelled" orgy. Rob Ford, Toronto's mayor, finally admitted, after months of denials, that he smoked crack cocaine – before adding the comforting proviso that he only did it in "one of my drunken stupors".

What does any of this have to do with Schumpeter's home territory of chief executives? Mr Flowers was no banker: he rose through the co-operative movement's political structures. Mr Ford is an elected politician. But they nevertheless illustrate a problem too often ignored in business, where people are much happier talking about dollars than dolour: how can you tell when a boss is showing signs that he may go off the rails? And what should be done about it?

The corner office is almost a factory for personal problems. Chief executives are under greater pressure to perform at the best of times; how much greater in periods of economic turbulence. Yet at the same time power corrupts. In experiments social scientists have shown, by giving random subjects power over others, that even in small doses it produces overconfidence, insensitivity and an urge to associate with other people with power.

Chief executives' oddities can lead to complete corporate breakdown: it is impossible to read about the implosions at WorldCom or Hollinger or the Royal Bank of Scotland (RBS) without being astonished by the bosses' behaviour. But even in less dysfunctional firms the whims of the man at the top can cause damaging depression or sycophancy below. Chief executives are the nearest things democracies have to sun kings.

An obvious sign of a boss breaking bad is grandiosity. He attributes the company's success wholly to himself, indulges in endless self-promotion or demands ever more extravagant rewards. Jean-Marie Messier, who transformed Vivendi from a staid water utility into a media conglomerate that ran up huge losses, borrowed his nickname – "J6M", which stands for "Jean-Marie Messier Moi-Même-Maître-du-Monde" – for the title of his autobiography. One study shows that chief executives who appear on the covers of business magazines are more likely to make foolish acquisitions. A second sign is over-control. The boss surrounds himself with yes-men and crushes dissent. He tries to control every detail of corporate life rather than building a strong executive team. A third sign is distorted decision-making. The chief conflates personal and corporate assets, is obsessed with buying other companies, or focuses on bizarre details. Mr Messier spent $17.5 million of Vivendi's money on a New York apartment for his personal use. Fred Goodwin, boss of RBS, micromanaged the building of a £350 million ($630 million) head office, called "Fredtown" by his underlings, and found time to redesign the bank's Christmas cards.

A chief executive becomes likelier to succumb to these vanities the longer he stays in the job. He gets used to people fawning over him. He measures himself against other inhabitants of Planet Davos, not those Barack Obama calls "regular folk". Percy Barnevik, the boss of Asea Brown Boveri, an engineering conglomerate, was widely hailed as "Europe's answer to Jack Welch". But the comparison went to his head: he pursued ever more reckless acquisitions and got himself awarded a tax-free pension of $87 million. A boss may think himself so brilliant he refuses to plan for his eventual departure or undermines possible successors. Armand Hammer, of Occidental Petroleum, asked his board to agree to a long-term bonus plan, with a ten-year payout, when in his 90s.

What can companies do to stop the boss behaving oddly – ideally, before he starts? In a study MWM Consulting, a firm of headhunters, argues that boards need to make "behavioural risk" a standard part of their agenda. This might well include taking soundings from senior management. Chairmen also need to start talking to chief executives about the personal side of the job when they are first appointed, and keep talking afterwards.

Remember the Little Bighorn

However, the best answer lies with chief executives themselves, who must recognise that the biggest threat to their success may lie within. They need to cultivate the art of seeing themselves as others see them. Kevin Sharer, the former boss of Amgen, a biotech company, used to get his direct reports to list his strengths and weaknesses annually for the board. He also kept a painting of General Custer in his office as a warning against hubris.

The business world is starting to take these problems seriously. One of the most popular courses at Harvard Business School is Clayton Christensen's course on how businesspeople should guard against an obsession with short-term success. About 40% of the heads of FTSE 100 companies employ "personal coaches". Chief executives last half as long in the job, on average, as they did a decade ago. That may be bad for their nerves, but it makes them less likely to be become marinated in power.

That said, it is foolish to treat a cold as a cancer. Bosses have a right to privacy. In recent years Boeing and Hewlett-Packard have erred in disposing of chief executives after consensual affairs. The border between eccentricity and brilliance can be blurred. Bosses are peculiar anyway: more ambitious and more self-confident than the rest of us. Some of the most creative people in business have been very peculiar indeed: Henry Ford loved conspiracy theories of the blackest hue; Thomas Watson of IBM commissioned company songs in his own honour. The most important business decisions are still, as they have always been, nuanced ones about character and its complexities.

November 2013

The mindfulness business

Western capitalism is looking for inspiration in eastern mysticism

IN HIS 1905 BOOK, *The Protestant Ethic and the Spirit of Capitalism*, Max Weber credited the Protestant ethic with giving rise to capitalism. Now it sometimes seems as if it is the Buddhist ethic that is keeping capitalism going. The Protestants stressed rational calculation and self-restraint. The Buddhists stress the importance of "mindfulness" – taking time out from the hurly-burly of daily activities to relax and meditate. In today's corporate world you are more likely to hear about mindfulness than self-restraint.

Google offers an internal course called "search inside yourself" that has proved so popular that the company has created entry-level versions such as "neural self-hacking" and "managing your energy". The search giant has also built a labyrinth for walking meditation. EBay has meditation rooms equipped with pillows and flowers. Twitter and Facebook are doing all they can to stay ahead in the mindfulness race. Evan Williams, one of Twitter's founders, has introduced regular meditation sessions in his venture the Obvious Corporation, a start-up incubator and investment vehicle.

The fashion is not confined to Silicon Valley: the mindfulness movement can be found in every corner of the corporate world. Rupert Murdoch has a well-developed bullshit detector. But in early 2013 he tweeted about his interest in transcendental meditation (which he said "everyone recommends"). Ray Dalio of Bridgewater Associates and Bill Gross of PIMCO are two of the biggest names in the money-management business, and both are regular meditators. Mr Dalio says it has had more impact on his success than anything else.

What got the mindfulness wagon rolling was the 1960s counter-culture, which injected a shot of bohemianism into the bloodstream of capitalism: witness the rise of companies such as Virgin, Ben & Jerry's and Apple, whose co-founder, Steve Jobs, had visited India on a meditation break as a young man, and who often talked about how Zen had influenced the design of his products. But three things are making the wheels roll ever faster.

The most obvious is omni-connectivity. The constant pinging of electronic devices is driving many people to the end of their tether. Electronic devices not only overload the senses and invade leisure time. They feed on themselves: the more people tweet the more they are rewarded with followers and retweets. Mindfulness provides a good excuse to unplug and chill out – or "disconnect to connect", as mindfulness advocates put it. A second reason is the rat race. The single-minded pursuit of material success has produced an epidemic of corporate scandals and a widespread feeling of angst. Mindfulness emphasises that there is more to success than material prosperity. The third is that selling mindfulness has become a business in its own right.

The movement has a growing, and strikingly eclectic, cohort of gurus. Chade-Meng Tan of Google, who glories in the job title of "jolly good fellow", is the inspiration behind "search inside yourself". Soren Gordhamer, a yoga and meditation instructor, and an enthusiastic tweeter, founded Wisdom 2.0, a popular series of mindfulness conferences. Bill George, a former boss of Medtronic, a medical-equipment company, and a board member at Goldman Sachs, is introducing mindfulness at Harvard Business School in an attempt to develop leaders who are "self-aware and self-compassionate".

Many other business schools are embracing mindfulness. Jeremy Hunter of the Drucker management school at Claremont university teaches it to his students, as does Ben Bryant at Switzerland's IMD. Donde Plowman of the University of Nebraska-Lincoln's business school has even tried to quantify the mindfulness of management schools themselves. The flow of wisdom is not one-way: Keisuke Matsumoto, a Japanese Buddhist monk, took an MBA at the Indian School of Business in Hyderabad and is now applying its lessons to revitalise temples back home.

As for its exploitation as a business, Arianna Huffington runs a mindfulness conference, a "GPS for the soul" app and a mindfulness corner of her *Huffington Post*. Chip Wilson, the boss of lululemon, a seller of yoga gear, has set up a website, whil.com, that urges people to turn off their brains for 60 seconds by visualising a dot. ("Power down, power up, and power forward.")

A walk in the countryside

Does all this mindfulness do any good? There is a body of evidence that suggests that some of its techniques can provide significant psychological and physiological benefits. The Duke University School of Medicine has produced research that shows that, in America, an hour of yoga a week reduces stress levels in employees by a third and cuts health-care costs by an average of $2,000 a year. Cynics might point to the evidence that a walk in the countryside has similar benefits. They might also worry that Aetna, an insurer which wants to sell yoga and other mindfulness techniques as part of its health plans, is sponsoring some of the research that supports them. But it seems not unreasonable to suppose that, in a world of constant stress and distraction, simply sitting still and relaxing for a while might do you some good.

The biggest problem with mindfulness is that it is becoming part of the self-help movement – and hence part of the disease that it is supposed to cure. Gurus talk about "the competitive advantage of meditation". Pupils come to see it as a way to get ahead in life. And the point of the whole exercise is lost. What has parading around in pricey lululemon outfits got to do with the Buddhist ethic of non-attachment to material goods? And what has staring at a computer-generated dot got to do with the ancient art of meditation? Western capitalism seems to be doing rather more to change eastern religion than eastern religion is doing to change Western capitalism.

November 2013

Too many chiefs

Inflation in job titles is approaching Weimar levels

KIM JONG IL, the North Korean dictator, is not normally a trendsetter. But in one area he is clearly leading the pack: job-title inflation. Mr Kim has 1,200 official titles, including, roughly translated, guardian deity of the planet, ever-victorious general, lodestar of the 21st century, supreme commander at the forefront of the struggle against imperialism and the United States, eternal bosom of hot love and greatest man who ever lived.

When it comes to job titles, we live in an age of rampant inflation. Everybody you come across seems to be a chief or president of some variety. Title inflation is producing its own vocabulary: "uptitling" and "title-fluffing". It is also producing technological aids. One website provides a simple formula: just take your job title, mix in a few grand words, such as "global", "interface" and "customer", and hey presto.

The rot starts at the top. Not that long ago companies had just two or three "chief" whatnots. Now they have dozens, collectively called the "c-suite". A few have more than one chief executive officer; CB Richard Ellis, a property-services firm, has four. A growing number have chiefs for almost everything from knowledge to diversity. Southwest Airlines has a chief Twitter officer. Coca-Cola and Marriott have chief blogging officers. Kodak has one of those too, along with a chief listening officer.

Even so, chiefs are relatively rare compared with presidents and their various declensions (vice-, assistant-, etc). Almost everybody in banking from the receptionist upwards is a president of some sort. The number of members of LinkedIn, a professional network, with the title vice-president grew 426% faster than the membership of the site as a whole in 2005–09. The inflation rate for presidents was 312% and for chiefs a mere 275%.

Title-fluffing is as rampant among the indians as among the chiefs. America's International Association of Administrative Professionals – formerly the National Secretaries Association – reports that it has more than 500 job-titles under its umbrella, ranging from front-office co-ordinator to electronic-document specialist. Paper boys are "media distribution officers". Binmen are "recycling officers". Lavatory cleaners are "sanitation consultants". Sandwich-makers at Subway have the phrase "sandwich artist" emblazoned on their lapels. Even the normally linguistically pure French have got in on the act: cleaning ladies are becoming "techniciennes de surface" (surface technicians).

What is going on here? The most immediate explanation is the economic downturn: bosses are doling out ever fancier titles as a substitute for pay raises and bonuses. But there are also structural reasons for the trend. The most basic is the growing complexity of businesses. Many not only have presidents and vice-presidents for this or that product line, but also presidents and vice-presidents for various regions. Put the two together and you have a recipe for ever-longer business cards: vice-president for photocopiers Asia-Pacific, for example.

The cult of flexibility is also inflationary. The fashion for flattening hierarchies has had the paradoxical effect of multiplying meaningless job titles. Workers crave important-sounding titles to give them the illusion of ascending the ranks. Managers who no longer have anyone to manage are fobbed off with inflated titles, much as superannuated politicians are made Chancellor of the Duchy of Lancaster or Lord President of the Council. Everybody, from the executive suite downward, wants to fluff up their résumé as a hedge against being sacked.

Firms also use fancy job titles to signal that they are *au fait* with the latest fashion. The fad for greenery is producing legions of chief sustainability officers and green ambassadors. BP's travails will undoubtedly have the same effect: we can expect a bull market in chief safety officers and chief apology officers.

The American technology sector has been a champion of title inflation. It has created all sorts of newfangled jobs that have to be given names, and it is also full of linguistically challenged geeks who have a taste for "humorous" titles. Steve Jobs called himself "chief know it all". Jerry Yang and David Filo, the founders of Yahoo!, call themselves "chief Yahoos". Thousands of IT types dub themselves things like (chief) scrum master, guru, evangelist or, a particular favourite at the moment, ninja.

But leadership in title inflation, as in so much else, is passing to the developing world, particularly India and China. Both countries have a longstanding obsession with hierarchy (fancy job titles can be the key to getting a bride as well as the admiration of your friends). They also have tight labour markets. The result is an explosion of titles. Companies have taken to creating baffling jobs such as "outbound specialist". They have also taken to staging public celebrations of promotions from, say, assistant deputy director to principal assistant deputy director.

Inflated benefits, understated drawbacks

Does any of this matter? Title inflation clearly does violence to the language. But isn't that par for the course in the corporate world? And isn't it a small price to pay for corporate harmony? The snag is that the familiar problems of monetary inflation apply to job-title inflation as well. The benefits of giving people a fancy new title are usually short-lived. The harm is long-lasting. People become cynical about their monikers (particularly when they are given in lieu of pay rises). Organisations become more Ruritanian. The job market becomes more opaque. How do you work out the going rate for "vision controller of multiplatform and portfolio" (the BBC)? Or a "manager of futuring and innovation-based strategies" (the American Cancer Society)?

And, far from providing people with more security, fancy titles can often make them more expendable. Companies might hesitate before sacking an IT adviser. But what about a chief scrum master? The essence of inflation, after all, is that it devalues everything that it touches.

June 2010

Down with fun

The depressing vogue for having fun at work

ONE OF THE MANY PLEASURES of watching *Mad Men*, a television drama about the advertising industry in the early 1960s, is examining the ways in which office life has changed over the years. One obvious change makes people feel good about themselves: they no longer treat women as second-class citizens. But the other obvious change makes them feel a bit more uneasy: they have lost the art of enjoying themselves at work.

The ad-men in those days enjoyed simple pleasures. They puffed away at their desks. They drank throughout the day. They had affairs with their colleagues. They socialised not in order to bond, but in order to get drunk.

These days many companies are obsessed with fun. Software firms in Silicon Valley have installed rock-climbing walls in their reception areas and put inflatable animals in their offices. Wal-Mart orders its cashiers to smile at all and sundry. The cult of fun has spread like some disgusting haemorrhagic disease. Acclaris, an American IT company, has a "chief fun officer". TD Bank, the American arm of Canada's Toronto Dominion, has a "Wow!" department that dispatches costume-clad teams to "surprise and delight" successful workers. Red Bull, a drinks firm, has installed a slide in its London office.

Fun at work is becoming a business in its own right. Madan Kataria, an Indian who styles himself the "guru of giggling", sells "laughter yoga" to corporate clients. Fun at Work, a British company, offers you "more hilarity than you can handle", including replacing your receptionists with "Ab Fab" lookalikes. Chiswick Park, an office development in London, brands itself with the slogan "enjoy-work", and hosts lunchtime events such as sheep-shearing and geese-herding.

The cult of fun is deepening as well as widening. Google is the acknowledged champion: its offices are blessed with volleyball courts, bicycle paths, a yellow brick road, a model dinosaur, regular games of roller hockey and several professional masseuses. But now two other companies have challenged Google for the jester's crown – Twitter, a microblogging service, and Zappos, an online shoe-shop.

Twitter's website stresses how wacky the company is: workers wear cowboy hats and babble that: "Crazy things happen every day... it's pretty ridiculous." The company has a team of people whose job is to make workers happy: for example, by providing them with cold towels on a hot day. Zappos boasts that creating "fun and a little weirdness" is one of its core values. Tony Hsieh, the boss, shaves his head and spends 10% of his time studying what he calls the "science of happiness". He once joked that Zappos was suing the Walt Disney Company for claiming that it was "the happiest place on earth". The company engages in regular "random acts of kindness": workers form a noisy conga line and single out one of their colleagues for praise. The praisee then has to wear a silly hat for a week.

This cult of fun is driven by three of the most popular management fads of the moment: empowerment, engagement and creativity. Many companies pride themselves on devolving power to frontline workers. But surveys show that only 20% of workers are "fully engaged with their job". Even fewer are creative. Managers hope that "fun" will magically make workers more engaged and creative. But the problem is that as soon as fun becomes part of a corporate strategy it ceases to be fun and becomes its opposite – at best an empty shell and at worst a tiresome imposition.

The most unpleasant thing about the fashion for fun is that it is mixed with a large dose of coercion. Companies such as Zappos don't merely celebrate wackiness. They more or less require it. Compulsory fun is nearly always cringe-making. Twitter calls its office a "Twoffice". Boston Pizza encourages workers to send "golden bananas" to colleagues who are "having fun while being the best". Behind the "fun" façade there often lurks some crude management thinking: a desire to brand the company as better than its rivals, or a plan to boost productivity through team-building. Twitter even boasts that it has "worked hard to create an environment that spawns productivity and happiness".

If it's fun, it needn't be compulsory

While imposing ersatz fun on their employees, companies are battling against the real thing. Many force smokers to huddle outside like furtive criminals. Few allow their employees to drink at lunch time, let alone earlier in the day. A regiment of busybodies – from lawyers to human-resources functionaries – is waging war on office romance, particularly between people of different ranks. Hewlett-Packard, a computer-maker, sacked its successful chief executive, Mark Hurd, after a contractor made vague allegations – later quietly settled – of sexual harassment. (Oracle, a rival, quickly snapped up Mr Hurd.)

The merchants of fake fun have met some resistance. When Wal-Mart tried to impose alien rules on its German staff – such as compulsory smiling and a ban on affairs with co-workers – it touched off a guerrilla war that ended only when the supermarket chain announced it was pulling out of Germany in 2006. But such victories are rare. For most wage slaves forced to pretend they are having fun at work, the only relief is to poke fun at their tormentors. Popular culture provides some inspiration. "You don't have to be mad to work here. In fact we ask you to complete a medical questionnaire to ensure that you are not," deadpans David Brent, the risible boss in *The Office*, a satirical television series. Homer Simpson's employer, a nuclear-power plant, has regular "funny hat days" but lax safety standards. *Mad Men* reminds people of a world they have lost – a world where bosses did not think that "fun" was a management tool and where employees could happily quaff Scotch at noon. Cheers to that.

September 2010

In praise of laziness

Businesspeople would be better off if they did less and thought more

THERE IS A NEVER-ENDING SUPPLY of business gurus telling us how we can, and must, do more. Sheryl Sandberg urges women to "Lean In" if they want to get ahead. John Bernard offers breathless advice on conducting "Business at the Speed of Now". Michael Port tells salesmen how to "Book Yourself Solid". And in case you thought you might be able to grab a few moments to yourself, Keith Ferrazzi warns that you must "Never Eat Alone".

Yet the biggest problem in the business world is not too little but too much – too many distractions and interruptions, too many things done for the sake of form, and altogether too much busy-ness. The Dutch seem to believe that an excess of meetings is the biggest devourer of time: they talk of *vergaderziekte*, "meeting sickness". However, a 2012 study by the McKinsey Global Institute suggests that it is e-mails: it found that highly skilled office workers spend more than a quarter of each working day writing and responding to them.

Which of these banes of modern business life is worse remains open to debate. But what is clear is that office workers are on a treadmill of pointless activity. Managers allow meetings to drag on for hours. Workers generate e-mails because it requires little effort and no thought. An entire management industry exists to spin the treadmill ever faster.

All this "leaning in" is producing an epidemic of overwork, particularly in the United States. Americans now toil for eight-and-a-half hours a week more than they did in 1979. A survey in 2012 by the Centres for Disease Control and Prevention estimated that almost a third of working adults get six hours or less of sleep a night. Another survey by Good Technology, a provider of secure mobile systems for businesses, found that more than 80% of respondents continue to work after leaving the office, 69% cannot go to bed without checking their inbox and 38% routinely check their work e-mails at the dinner table.

This activity is making it harder to focus on real work as opposed to make-work. Teresa Amabile of Harvard Business School, who has been conducting a huge study of work and creativity, reports that workers are generally more creative on low-pressure days than on high-pressure days when they are confronted with a flurry of unpredictable demands. In 2012 Gloria Mark of the University of California, Irvine, and two colleagues deprived 13 people in the IT business of e-mail for five days and studied them intensively. They found that people without it concentrated on tasks for longer and experienced less stress.

It is high time that we tried a different strategy – not "leaning in" but "leaning back". There is a distinguished history of leadership thinking in the lean-back tradition. Lord Melbourne, Queen Victoria's favourite prime minister, extolled the virtues of "masterful inactivity". Herbert Asquith embraced a policy of "wait and see" when he had the job. Ronald Reagan also believed in not overdoing things: "It's true hard work never killed anybody," he said, "but I figure, why take the chance?" This tradition has been buried in a morass of meetings and messages. We need to revive it before we schedule ourselves to death.

The most obvious beneficiaries of leaning back would be creative workers – the very people who are supposed to be at the heart of the modern economy. In the early 1990s Mihaly Csikszentmihalyi, a psychologist, asked 275 creative types if he could interview them for a book he was writing. A third did not bother to reply at all and another third refused to take part. Peter Drucker, a management guru, summed up the mood of the refuseniks: "One of the secrets of productivity is to have a very big waste-paper basket to take care of all invitations such as yours." Creative people's most important resource is their time – particularly big chunks of uninterrupted time – and their biggest enemies are those who try to nibble away at it with e-mails or meetings. Indeed, creative people may be at their most productive when, to the manager's untutored eye, they appear to be doing nothing.

Managers themselves could benefit. Those at the top are best employed thinking about strategy rather than operations – about whether the company is doing the right thing rather than whether it is sticking to its plans. When he was boss of General Electric, Jack Welch used to spend an hour a day in what he called "looking out of the window time". When he was in charge of Microsoft Bill Gates used to take two "think weeks" a year when he would lock himself in an isolated cottage. Jim Collins, of *Good to Great* fame, advises all bosses to keep a "stop doing list". Is there a meeting you can cancel? Or a dinner you can avoid?

Less is more – more or less

Junior managers would do well to follow the same advice. In *Do Nothing*, one of the few business books to grapple with the problem of over-management, Keith Murnighan of Kellogg School of Management argues that the best managers focus their attention on establishing the right rules – recruiting the right people and establishing the right incentives – and then get out of the way. He quotes a story about Eastman Kodak in its glory days. A corporate reorganisation left a small division out in the cold – without a leader or a reporting line to headquarters. The head office only rediscovered the division when it received a note from a customer congratulating the unit on its work.

Doing nothing may be going too far. Managers play an important role in co-ordinating complicated activities and disciplining slackers. And some creative people would never finish anything if they were left to their own devices. But there is certainly a case for doing a lot less – for rationing e-mail, cutting back on meetings and getting rid of a few overzealous bosses. Leaning in has been producing negative returns for some time now. It is time to try the far more radical strategy of leaning back.

August 2013

A guide to skiving

How to thrive at work with the minimum of effort

THE BEST WAY TO UNDERSTAND A SYSTEM is to look at it from the point of view of people who want to subvert it. Sensible bosses try to view their companies through the eyes of corporate raiders. Serious-minded politicians make a point of putting themselves in their opponents' shoes. The same is true of the world of work in general: the best way to understand a company's "human resources" is not to consult the department that bears that ugly name but to study the basic principles of one of the world's most popular, if unrecognised, sciences: skiving.

The first principle of skiving (or shirking, as Americans call it) is always to appear hard at work. This is the ancient jacket-on-the-back-of-the-chair trick: leave a coat permanently on display so that a casual observer – a CEO practising "managing by walking around", for example – will assume that you are the first to arrive and the last to leave. The skill of skiving is subtle: ensure you are somewhere else when the work is being allocated. Successful skivers never visibly shy away from work: confronted with the inevitable they make a point of looking extremely eager. This "theatre of enthusiasm" has fooled almost everyone. Policymakers bemoan the epidemic of overwork. But as Roland Paulsen, of Sweden's Lund University, explains in *Empty Labour*, an example-packed book, innumerable studies suggest that the average worker devotes between one-and-a-half and three hours a day to loafing.

The second principle is that information technology is both the slacker's best friend and his deadliest enemy. The PC is custom-made for the indolent: you can give every impression of being hard at work when in fact you are doing your shopping, booking a holiday or otherwise frolicking in the cyber-waves. And thanks to mobile technology you can now continue to frolic while putting in face time in meetings. There is also a high-tech version of the jacket trick: program your e-mails to send themselves at half past midnight or 5.30am to give your managers the impression that you are a Stakhanovite.

But there is a dark side to IT: one estimate suggests that 27 million employees around the world have their internet use monitored. Dealing with this threat requires vigilance: do everything you can to hide your browsing history. It may also require something that does not come naturally to skivers: political activism. Make a huge fuss about how even the smallest concessions on the principle of absolute data privacy will create a slippery slope to a totalitarian society. Skiving is like liberty: it can flourish only if Big Brother is kept at bay.

The third principle is that you should always try to get a job where there is no clear relation between input and output. The public sector is obviously a skiver's paradise. In 2004 it took two days for anyone to notice that a Finnish tax inspector had died at his desk. In 2009 the Swedish Civil Aviation Administration discovered that some of its employees had spent three-quarters of their working hours watching internet pornography. In 2012 a German civil servant wrote a farewell message to his colleagues, on his retirement, confessing that he hadn't done a stroke of work for the past 14 years. And even if managers can find people who are failing on the "input" side, it is almost impossible to sack them.

Big private-sector organisations can be almost as fertile skiving grounds as public ones. In *The Living Dead* (2005), his memoir of life as an office worker, David Bolchover says that the amount of work he had to do was inversely related to the size of the company that he worked for. He started his career in a small firm where he had to work hard for no title and low pay. He ended up working for a big company where he had a grand title and a fat pay packet but did almost nothing. Mr Bolchover was not a member of the brotherhood: he asked his bosses for more work and, when they failed to oblige, filled his idle hours by writing a management book. But millions of others are perfectly happy to devote their lives to firm-financed leisure.

Hitherto skivers have focused on old-line companies where ageing managers can be bamboozled with the claim that it is quite impossible to build an Excel spreadsheet in anything less than two weeks. But the clever ones are exploring the rich opportunities provided by the new economy. The likes of Google and Facebook make a great fuss about installing the adult equivalent of children's playgrounds – everything from massage rooms to sleep pods and pinball machines – to provide their employees with an opportunity for relaxation between intense bursts of toil. But now that these companies are becoming bloated monopolists there is a perfect opportunity for canny skivers to take advantage of the nap pods without bothering with the frantic work. New-economy companies have even provided a handy way to discover if they are ripe for exploitation: if employees have titles such as "director of visioning" or "vice-chairman of big-data analytics", then you know that it is time to start geekifying your CV.

Cyber-loafing your way to the top

The final principle of skiving is that you should not allow your preference for leisure to limit your ambition. Too many skivers are still bewitched by the old myth that there is a connection between effort and reward. There are inevitably few quantitative studies of skiving. But the ones that exist suggest it is most prevalent at the very top and bottom of the pay scale. A Finnish study in 2010 found that the people who reported the most "empty labour" earned more than €80,000 ($112,000) a year while the runners-up earned less than €20,000. It can be hard to begin your climb up the greasy pole without making some effort: the trick is to be brimming over with clever ideas for other people to execute. But when you become a manager your problems are solved: you can simply delegate all your work to other people while you spend your days attending international conferences or "cultivating relationships with investors".

October 2014

PART 7

Beyond the great disruption

The will to power

Why some people have power over companies and others don't

HENRY KISSINGER was guilty of understatement when he said that power is the ultimate aphrodisiac. In fact, power is the ultimate life-improver *tout court*. Powerful people not only have more friends than the rest of us. They also enjoy better health. Numerous studies demonstrate that low status is more strongly associated with heart disease than physical hazards like obesity and high blood pressure.

The benefits of power have grown dramatically in recent years. CEOs and other C-suite types have seen their salaries surge at a time when the median wage has either stagnated (in the United States) or grown slowly (in Europe). Politicians have learned how to monetise their pull. The Clintons earned $109 million in the eight years after they left the White House. Tony Blair has turned himself into a wealthy man since his retirement from national politics.

But the greasy pole is getting harder to climb and, once you've climbed it, harder to cling on to. Companies have introduced more complicated structures – removing layers, replacing hierarchies with teams and dispersing functions around the world. They have also made life harder for chief executives. In the 1990s it was not unusual to find CEOs who had been in the job for ten or 15 years. In 2000–10 the average tenure of departing CEOs around the world has dropped from 8.1 years to 6.3 years. In the 1990s it was the norm for CEOs to double dip as chairmen (which allowed them to report to themselves). In 2009 less than 12% of incoming CEOs were also given the job of chairman.

So how do you get your hands on power? And how do you keep hold of it once you've got it? Management gurus are surprisingly disappointing on this subject given its overwhelming importance to their clients. Academics and consultants are happier focusing on subjects such as return on investment. Both have an interest in presenting business as a rational enterprise that can be reduced to rules. This leaves the analysis of power to retired businesspeople like

Jack Welch (who strive to present themselves as business geniuses rather than Machiavellis) and practising snake-oil salesmen (who tell you that all you need to do is "unleash the power within" and the CEO's job will be yours).

Jeffrey Pfeffer of Stanford Business School is an exception to this rule. He has been teaching a popular course on "paths to power" for years. Now he has condensed many of his findings into a book that is part academic analysis and part how-to guide, *Power: Why Some People Have It – and Others Don't.*

Mr Pfeffer starts by rubbishing the notion that the world is just – that the best way to win power is to be good at your job. The relationship between rewards and competence is loose at best. Bob Nardelli was a disastrous CEO of Home Depot. But he was paid nearly a quarter of a billion dollars to leave and quickly moved to the top slot at Chrysler, which then went bankrupt. Mr Pfeffer points out that CEOs who presided over three years of poor earnings and led their firms into bankruptcy faced only a 50% chance of losing their jobs (and perfectly successful senior managers are routinely cleaned out when new CEOs take over). There are plenty of things that matter more than competence, such as the ability to project drive and self-confidence.

The best way to increase your chances of reaching the top is to choose the right department to join. The most powerful departments are the ones that have produced the current big-wigs (R&D in Germany, finance in America), and the ones that pay the most. But the trick is to find the department that is on the rise. Robert McNamara and his fellow whizz kids flourished in post-war America because they realised that power was shifting to finance. Zia Yusuf zoomed up the ranks of SAP, a German software company, because he offered something that the engineering-dominated company lacked: expertise in corporate strategy. Men with pay-TV backgrounds have risen in media companies like News Corporation and Time Warner – rightly so, given the importance of cable and satellite TV to those businesses.

Tips for the top

Once you have chosen the right department three things matter more than anything else. The first is the ability to "manage upwards". This means turning yourself into a supplicant: Barack Obama asked about a third of his fellow senators for help when he first arrived in the institution. It also means mastering the art of flattery: Jennifer Chatman, of the University of California, Berkeley, conducted experiments in which she tried to find a point at which flattery became ineffective. It turned out there wasn't one. The second is the ability to network. One of the quickest ways to the top is to turn yourself into a "node" by starting an organisation or forging a link between separate parts of a company. The third, more admirable, quality is loyalty: Booz, a consultancy, calculates that four out of every five CEO appointments go to insiders. Those insiders last almost two years longer in their jobs than outsiders.

And what happens if all this loyalty and networking pays off? How do you keep power once you win it? The old saw about power corrupting has been laboriously confirmed by academic studies of everything from risk-taking to cookie-eating (powerful people are more likely to eat with their mouths open and to scatter crumbs over their faces). The key to keeping power is to understand its corrupting effects. Powerful people need to cultivate a combination of paranoia and humility – paranoia about how much other people want them out and humility about their own replaceability. They also need to know when to quit. People who do not know when to leave an organisation frequently crash and burn. People who jump before they are pushed have a good chance of leaping to yet another aphrodisiacal throne.

September 2010

Of businessmen and ballerinas

Lessons from the Bolshoi brouhaha

THE BASIC FACTS of the case seem clear – and as dramatic as any performance of Prokofiev's *Ivan the Terrible*. Sergei Filin, the Bolshoi ballet's artistic director, arrived home shortly before midnight on January 17th 2013. A masked man emerged from the shadows and flung sulphuric acid in his face. A car-park attendant tried to wash away the acid with snow. But it was too late. Mr Filin's face and eyes had been badly burned.

Making sense of this horrific assault is tricky. One school of thought blames artistic squabbles. The Bolshoi has seen several nasty incidents. Mr Filin's tyres have been slashed and his e-mail hacked. In the past, needles have been inserted into costumes and broken glass into the tips of ballet shoes. A dead cat has been tossed onto the stage in lieu of flowers and an alarm clock set off during a quiet scene. Ballet is not for sissies.

A second school focuses on money and power. Scalpers have made wodges from buying and selling tickets – perhaps with inside help. Bigwigs use their muscle to get their pretty daughters jobs as ballerinas. A lavish renovation of the Bolshoi theatre suffered epic delays and went wildly over-budget.

A third school focuses on sex. The ballet is a hothouse of passion and intrigue. Anastasia Volochkova, a former prima ballerina, once called it a "big brothel". In 2011 Gennady Yanin, a ballet director, resigned when pictures of him engaged in gay sex appeared online. The heterosexual Mr Filin is so good-looking that men and women alike are infatuated with him.

All this is gripping stuff, but what does any of it have to do with business? One answer is that peculiar institutions can tell us a lot about more run-of-the-mill ones. And dysfunction is more common in the business world than you might think. Clayton Christensen, of Harvard Business School, says that he has been struck, at alumni reunions, by how many of his fellow HBS graduates and Rhodes scholars had made a mess of their lives. Jeff Skilling, for example, had gone from making $100 million a year as boss of Enron to a federal prison.

A quick glance around any office suggests that dark passions lurk everywhere. Gossip and back-stabbing are rife. In all companies, bosses wield power, which tends to corrupt. One delightful study shows that giving people power makes them more likely to cheat at games. It also makes them keener to suggest harsh punishments for others who are caught cheating.

All these problems are evergreen. However, three modern trends are making them worse. The first is the enthusiasm for rewarding employees for performance. This is driven by the reasonable insight that paying everyone the same spurs no one to excel. Alas, paying for performance can also have perverse consequences. Banks that pay big bonuses for big profits give traders an incentive to take big risks. Institutions that reward relative performance (ie, did you perform better than your colleagues?) encourage unscrupulous co-workers to sabotage each other. Dancers at the Bolshoi are paid primarily according to the amount of time they spend on stage, so an understudy may not be completely heartbroken if the lead ballerina breaks an ankle.

The second is the economic downturn. Towers Watson, a consultancy, says it has created a class of "trauma organisations" that must take drastic measures to survive. Staff at such companies tend to be pessimistic and cliquish – they huddle together for comfort in the storm. Even in non-traumatised companies, many workers resent having to work harder for stagnant pay. Towers Watson reports that only 44% of British workers have confidence in their leaders.

The third trend is the rise of knowledge-intensive companies that run on "economies of ideas" rather than economies of scale. These companies are all hungry for the best and brightest: for the brilliant pharmacologist who can create a blockbuster drug, for the extraordinary investment banker who can engineer an industry-changing merger or for the razor-sharp accountant who can shave millions off a firm's tax bill.

The need to hire the best means firms have to put up with prima donnas. That has costs. Talent-driven firms can be torn apart by feuds or rendered dysfunctional by egocentric behaviour: clever people are as clever at finding reasons to argue with each other as they are at thinking up new ideas.

Stars can burn you

A creative environment can often be a toxic one. You may have noticed that films about Hollywood always show beautiful people doing ugly things to each other. One assumes that the directors and screenwriters know whereof they speak. Outside Tinseltown, too, some of the most toxic companies have also been some of the most creative. Enron was once revered for revolutionising the energy business. Lehman Brothers was regarded as the smartest of the smart.

Steve Jobs, the founder of Apple, was a genius. He was also "frequently obnoxious, rude, selfish and nasty to other people", according to Walter Isaacson, his biographer. He crushed rivals who stood in his path. He enjoyed humiliating people who were less than A-players. He once stormed into a meeting with suppliers and bellowed that they were "fucking dickless assholes". Joe Nocera, a journalist, commented on his "almost wilful lack of tact". But this very abrasiveness was essential to Apple's success – it kept the company passenger-free and relentlessly focused on producing the next big thing. As the poet John Dryden once put it: "Great wits are sure to madness near allied/And thin partitions do their bounds divide."

February 2013

A tissue of lies

A social psychologist looks at why people lie and cheat and what it means for business

CONTRACT DISPUTES SELDOM produce courtroom drama. But the battle between BSkyB, a broadcaster, and Electronic Data Services (EDS), a software firm, was an exception. Mark Howard, Sky's barrister, cross-examined Joe Galloway, an EDS executive, about his MBA from Concordia College in the US Virgin Islands. Mr Galloway recalled his student days in loving detail, from the college buildings to the hours he had spent sweating over his books. A few days later Mr Howard presented the court with an MBA certificate that his pet schnauzer had earned from the very same diploma mill. The clever schnauzer had even earned a higher mark than the EDS executive.

People have always lied and cheated. And businesspeople may have lied and cheated more than most: in a survey of American graduate students, 56% of those pursuing an MBA admitted to having cheated in the previous year, compared with 47% of other students. Cynics will not be surprised that people in ties sometimes tell lies – remember Enron? Plenty of executives have overstated their educational qualifications: Scott Thompson lost his job as boss of Yahoo! for it.

Lies (and the lying liars who tell them)

However, the punishment for dishonesty is growing harsher. America's 2002 Sarbanes-Oxley Act makes chief executives and chief financial officers criminally liable for misstating financial results. The number of groups that seek to hold companies liable for their misdemeanours, from shareholder activists to NGOs, is multiplying. The internet makes a permanent record of people's peccadilloes (try ungoogling yourself). And more and more people distrust business thanks to scandals and broken promises. Even small acts of dishonesty can cost a firm dearly: the judge cited Mr Gallagher's "astounding ability to be dishonest"; BSkyB was later awarded $320 million in damages.

Yet businesspeople have given little serious thought to managing dishonesty. Managers tend to make two hoary contradictory assumptions. First, that there is a sharp line between good and bad apples, and that a manager's job is to toss out the bad. Second, that everybody cheats if they have the right incentives and the wrong oversight, so managers must ensure that punishment is sure and swift.

A book by Dan Ariely, *The (Honest) Truth about Dishonesty*, may reinvigorate the discussion. Mr Ariely is a social psychologist who has spent years studying cheating. He also teaches at Duke University's Fuqua School of Business. He has no time for the usual, lazy assumptions. He contends that the vast majority of people are prone to cheating. He also thinks they are more willing to cheat on other people's behalf than their own. People routinely struggle with two opposing emotions. They view themselves as honourable. But they also want to enjoy the benefits of a little cheating, especially if it reinforces their belief that they are a bit more intelligent or popular than they really are. They reconcile these two emotions by fudging – adding a few points to a self-administered IQ test, for example, or forgetting to put a few coins in an honesty box.

The amount of fudging that goes on depends on the circumstances. People are more likely to lie or cheat if others are lying or cheating, or if a member of another social group (such as a student wearing a sweatshirt from a rival university) visibly flouts the rules. They are more likely to lie and cheat if they are in a foreign country rather than at home. Or if they are using digital rather than real money. Or even if they are knowingly wearing fake rather than real Gucci sunglasses. They are more likely to lie and cheat if they have been stiffed by the victim of their misbehaviour – companies that keep customers in voicemail hell are frequent victims. And people are more likely to break their own rules if they have spent the day resisting temptation: dieters often slip after a day of self-denial, for example.

Mr Ariely observes that good sales reps understand a lot of this without attending his lectures. Customers like to think well of themselves; but they also like small bribes. The key is to convince them that an inducement is not really a bribe. So drug reps make doctors feel beholden by inviting them to give lectures in golf resorts or by offering to fund their terribly important research. Doctors naturally think their later decisions are taken entirely with their patients' best interests in mind; in fact they may be kidding themselves and cheating their patients. Sales reps also take receptionists out for fancy dinners, since these faithful gatekeepers decide which calls get put through to the boss.

What can be done about dishonesty? Harsh punishments are ineffective, since the cheat must first be caught. The trick is to nudge people to police themselves, by making it harder for them to rationalise their sins. For example, Mr Ariely finds that people are less likely to cheat if they read the Ten Commandments before doing a test, or if they have to sign a declaration of honesty before submitting their tax return. Another technique is to encourage customers to police suppliers: eBay, an online marketplace, hugely reduced cheating by getting buyers to rank sellers.

Let's hope these wheezes work. But human beings have a remarkable talent for getting around rules – including the rules they try to impose upon themselves. And new technologies introduce new opportunities for cheating; just look at the e-mail that slipped through your spam filter. Moreover, the line between succeeding by cheating and succeeding by serving customers is not always clear: the industrial giants of the 19th century were not called "robber barons" for nothing. Great entrepreneurs succeed by breaking the old rules and pursuing crazy visions. Great salesmen invariably stretch the truth. Mr Ariely and his students will have no shortage of material for follow-up books.

June 2012

The status seekers

Consumers are finding new ways to flaunt their status

KARL MARX began *Das Kapital* by noting that the wealth of capitalist societies presents itself as "an immense accumulation of commodities". He didn't know the half of it. These days, supermarkets stock tens of thousands of different products. Established brands breed new variations without cease. The problem for companies is working out which of these products will become a hit and which will gather dust on a shelf. To help them, an entire industry of consumer-watchers has appeared.

These are the people who lurk in supermarkets to see which washing-up liquid you put in your basket, or ask you to fill out a five-page questionnaire in return for a chance to win an upgrade from cattle class. The market for consumer-watchers is as crowded and competitive as any other. Established giants such as Nielsen and Mintel strain to fight off upstarts and niche players such as William Higham of Next Big Thing and Faith Popcorn.

Consumer-watchers of all sizes have several things in common. They constantly coin annoying neologisms, which they would doubtless call "annoyologisms". Ms Popcorn chirps about "manity" (male vanity) and "brailing the culture" (spotting trends). They hype passing fads as seismic shifts. And their propensity to be spectacularly wrong seems not to damage their business at all. Mark Penn, Hillary Clinton's campaign manager, argued that the American presidential election of 2008 would be driven by micro-trends (eg, the voting preferences of left-handed vegans) when it was clearly driven by a couple of macro-trends (hope and change).

One of the trendiest trend-watchers is called trendwatching.com. A consultancy based in London and Amsterdam, it is fashionably "networked" and "global". Five full-time employees pore over acres of data sent in by 700 trend-watchers in more than 120 countries. Trendwatching.com is as irritating as any of its competitors: its reports are littered with references to "nowism" (instant gratification), "maturialism" (consumer sophistication) and "tryvertising" (offering free samples). But the company has also produced a fascinating argument, illustrated with thousands of examples, about the changing ways in which consumers seek to flaunt their status.

Consumption is partly about pleasure: chocolate tastes good, silk feels soft and so on. But it is also about showing off, and what is deemed bragworthy has changed dramatically over time. In the 1950s it was about "keeping up with the Joneses" – amassing as much new stuff as your neighbours. Today everyone in the rich world has a washing machine, so people increasingly seek to advertise their hipness or virtue instead.

Rather than buying their clothes from predictable European fashion houses, they trawl the world for exotic designs from Brazilian *favelas* or South African townships. They customise their purchases to express their personalities. Bike by Me, a Swedish firm, allows you to choose the colour of every part of your bicycle. Trikoton, a German fashion house, allows you to buy clothes that reflect the sound of your voice (a computer turns your speech patterns into knitting patterns).

Possessions are plentiful; time is scarce. So there is cachet in being able to boast about the places you have been to and the things you have done. Savvy companies increasingly offer experiences as a way of hooking customers. For example, Tiger Beer gives loyal drinkers access to concerts and gigs. Dunhill, a luxury firm, promotes 1930s-style exotic travel, including hunting with eagles in Mongolia.

Many people want to make it clear that they are deeply, deeply concerned about the world's problems, so a growing number of goods are designed to convey this message. Toyota's Prius hybrid car is not only green; it is also instantly recognisable as such. Bed Stu makes shoes that look as if they are covered with oil from the Gulf oil spill. Mango Radios are hand-crafted in an Indonesian village using sustainable materials. And so on.

Another effective marketing tool is to help customers learn new skills. Kraft's Triscuit crackers division has distributed 4 million cards containing basil and dill seeds, along with guides to gardening. Sheraton's Nha Trang hotel in Vietnam has opened a purpose-built cooking school for guests. Seattle's Sorrento hotel has sponsored a night school where guests can gather of an evening to discuss the latest hit book.

Today's status-conscious consumers have a weapon that their predecessors were denied – the internet. Connectedness is now a crucial social signifier. (Social Printshop, an American website, lets you create a high-resolution print of your Facebook friends and hang it on your wall, to show how popular you are.) The internet helps you demonstrate your virtue by buying products from the farthest corners of the earth (if you are a fair-trade enthusiast) or from just round the corner (if you are a locavore). Or both, presumably, if you are both. It also helps you make friends with other people whose interests match yours, a fact companies have been quick to exploit. Edelman, a PR firm, finds that 82% of Generation Y have joined brand-sponsored online communities.

The customer is always righteous

In the long run, other trends may shape markets more. The rich world is rapidly ageing. People over 50 will account for two-thirds of all growth in consumer spending in France over the next two decades. Emerging markets are starting to look like America in the 1950s: people are obsessed with acquiring their first fridges and cars. The recession is forcing Western consumers to pay more attention to prices than they used to. But people, like peacocks, will never tire of displaying to friends and potential mates just how wonderful they are. Firms whose offerings scream "status" will never want for customers.

December 2010

When stars go cuckoo

What John Galliano's fall tells us about the perils of relying on creative geniuses

ON FEBRUARY 24TH 2011 John Galliano, Christian Dior's star designer, launched an anti-Semitic rant in a Paris bar, Le Perle – or so it is alleged. Mr Galliano denied the offence and there were no independent witnesses. But a few days later a video surfaced of Mr Galliano engaged in similar behaviour. "I love Hitler," he told an unidentified group. "Your mothers, your forefathers, would all be fucking gassed." Christian Dior first suspended him and then, as outrage over the video grew, sacked him.

Mr Galliano shared the headlines with another exploding star, Charlie Sheen. While holidaying with a couple of girlfriends – one of whom is a professional porn star – Mr Sheen decided to tell a radio show what he thinks of his producer, Chuck Lorre: a "charlatan" and a "turd" (he denied any anti-Semitic intent in referring to Mr Lorre by the Hebrew version of his name, Chaim). CBS and Warner Brothers pulled the plug on Mr Sheen's hit television comedy, *Two and a Half Men*, for which he was being paid a reported $1.2 million an episode.

These two incidents have inevitably been compared to an even bigger explosion. For years Mel Gibson was one of the most feted stars in Hollywood – the sexiest man alive according to *People* magazine and the hottest celebrity in the world according to *Forbes*. But Hollywood's love affair with Mr Gibson ended abruptly on the Pacific Coast Highway in 2006. Mr Gibson told a traffic cop that "the Jews are responsible for all the wars in the world" before asking "are you a Jew?" He also added a bit of sexism to his racism by calling a female police officer "sugar tits".

Why do people who live such enviable lives – being paid millions to do what they love – act so outrageously? Drink and drugs clearly play an important part. The video of Mr Galliano's rant suggests that he was sozzled. Mr Sheen has been in and out of rehab. Mr Gibson had an open bottle of tequila next to him on the seat of his car. Alexander McQueen, another British maverick who made it big in the Parisian fashion world before committing suicide, also had a long history of drink and drug problems. This is par for the course in the creative industries: the two best places for young people on the make in Hollywood to meet the players are bars and Alcoholics Anonymous meetings.

But celebrity can be an even more powerful drug than cocaine. It encourages people to push the limits: the more scandalous they are the more they attract the attention of the paparazzi. Mr Galliano produced ever more outrageous fashions as his fame grew. In 2000 he dressed his models like tramps – *le look clochard* – with newsprint dresses and dangling pots and pans. He probably counted the fact that protesters surrounded Dior's offices as a publicity triumph. Celebrity also makes people think they are fireproof: their fans love them come what may. Mr Sheen seems to have revelled in his bad-boy image. But there is clearly a line that you cross at your peril: insulting your boss in Mr Sheen's case or endorsing the Holocaust in Mr Galliano's.

How should creative companies deal with stars' bizarre behaviour? Sometimes the sins are so egregious that they have no choice but to drop them. Christian Dior congratulated itself on taking a stand on Mr Galliano. But in fact it was a simple commercial decision. Mr Galliano is undoubtedly a talented designer who sprinkled Dior's once dowdy fashion house with pixie-dust. But he was nevertheless a small part of the empire: Mr Galliano's couture accounted for only 4% of Dior's €21 billion ($29 billion) in sales in 2010. Mr Galliano also alienated some of Dior's other big names: Natalie Portman, an Oscar-winning (and Jewish) actress who advertises a Dior perfume, made it clear that she would not be associated with Mr Galliano in any way.

But in most cases they are much more lenient. Creative industries are driven by their stars. They also feed on the buzz that bad behaviour generates. Warner and CBS forgave Mr Sheen a succession of misdemeanours – including assault on his third wife – because he was the star of one of its most successful shows: without him there would be no *Two and a Half Men*. Mr Sheen's fatal error was to pit his brand against his producer's: Mr Lorre is credited with almost single-handedly reviving the traditional "four-camera sitcom" – a comedy that is cheap to make (Mr Sheen's enormous salary aside) and repeats well.

The growing risk of sticking with the talent

The business reason for sticking with "the talent" is that there is a long list of stars who have revived their careers after egregious gaffes. Eric Clapton survived a racist rant that he delivered in Birmingham in 1976. The Beatles suffered no long-term damage from John Lennon's declaration that they were "bigger than Jesus". Mr Gibson may be on the way back: a 2011 profile in *Vanity Fair*, "The Rude Warrior", was full of affectionate quotes from the likes of Whoopi Goldberg and Jodie Foster. Mr Sheen is not going without a fight: a permanent guest on the chat shows since his "meltdown" he became one of the most popular new arrivals on Twitter. Who wants to ditch an asset like this?

But new technology may be changing this calculation, both by making it easier to catch stars who act like idiots and by making it harder for companies to rehabilitate them: Mr Galliano's anti-Semitic rant will live for ever on YouTube.

Furthermore, great creative machines like Hollywood and the fashion industry have another reason to abandon assets who become liabilities: there is always more talent to replace them. No sooner had Mr Galliano imploded than the fashion industry began debating whether Riccardo Tisci of Givenchy, or Alber Elbaz of Lanvin, or Hedi Slimane, a former Dior man, would make the best successor (in fact the eventual winner was Raf Simons). Mr Lorre no doubt can find other actors to speak his lines. Charles de Gaulle once said that the graveyards are full of indispensable men. The same can be said of the bars of Los Angeles and Paris.

March 2011

No rush

In praise of procrastination

THERE IS NOTHING LIKE A DEADLINE to focus the mind. This columnist finds that, whenever his editor starts yapping, his mind focuses on the following subjects. (1) His toenails. Surely they need to be cut? (2) Walter Russell Mead. What is the bearded sage saying about East Timor in his blog? (3) His dogs. They seem desperate for a walk. (4) His inbox. It would be rude not to reply to that graduate student from the University of Tomsk.

Life is getting trickier for timewasters. Businesses that depend on just-in-time delivery cannot tolerate lateness. Stockmarkets trade millions of shares every minute. Twenty-four-hour news channels bombard us with information. Blogs and tweets provide a blizzard of instant comment. The situation is so dire that a quarter of Americans eat fast food every day.

Employers are getting better at squeezing out time-wasting. ODesk, an American firm that links employers with freelances over the internet, boasts that its software gives buyers an "unprecedented ability" to monitor the people they hire. In 2011 the Tokyo Stock Exchange shortened its lunch break from a leisurely 90 minutes to a miserable 60. High-tech companies such as Google and Hewlett-Packard used to pride themselves on giving their employees time to pursue their own projects. Now they are either cutting back on "tinkering time" or policing it more carefully. And employees are policing themselves: digital tools such as RescueTime allow you to ration your access to the internet or to incoming e-mail.

Compensation is becoming more short-term. The proportion of Americans who are paid by the hour has been rising since the 1970s. Today 59% of Americans (including professionals such as lawyers) are paid by the hour.

But is it wise to be so obsessed with speed? High-speed trading can lead to market meltdowns, as almost happened on May 6th 2010, unless automatic breaks are installed. And is taking one's time so bad?

Regulators are always warning people not to buy things in the heat of the moment. Procrastinators have a built-in cooling-off period. Businesses are forever saying that they need more creativity. Dithering can help. Ernest Hemingway told a fan who asked him how to write a novel that the first thing to do was to clean the fridge. Steven Johnson, a writer on innovation, argues that some of the best new products are "slow hunches". Nestlé's idea of selling coffee in small pods went nowhere for three decades; now it is worth billions.

These thoughts have been inspired by two (slowly savoured) works of management theory: an obscure article in the *Academy of Management Journal* by Brian Gunia of Johns Hopkins University; and a popular book, *Wait: The Art and Science of Delay*, by Frank Partnoy of University of San Diego. Mr Gunia and his three co-authors demonstrated, in a series of experiments, that slowing down makes us more ethical. When confronted with a clear choice between right and wrong, people are five times more likely to do the right thing if they have time to think about it than if they are forced to make a snap decision. Organisations with a "fast pulse" (such as banks) are more likely to suffer from ethical problems than those that move more slowly. (The LIBOR scandal that engulfed Barclays in Britain in 2012 supports this idea.) The authors suggest that companies should make greater use of "cooling-off periods" or introduce several levels of approval for important decisions.

Mr Partnoy argues that too many people fail to recognise what good public speakers and comedians all understand: that success depends on knowing when to delay, and for how long. The important thing is not to do things first but to do them right. And doing them right often involves taking a bit more time.

It's Just Lunch, a dating agency for professionals, prevents customers from judging each other on first impressions by not allowing them to post their photos on its website. Warren Buffett, the world's most successful investor, holds stocks for the long term rather than churning them. He writes that: "lethargy bordering on sloth remains the cornerstone of our investment style." Fabius Maximus, a Roman general nicknamed "The Delayer", wore Hannibal's invading army down by avoiding pitched battles.

Make haste slowly

Delay even works in fields where time might seem to be of the essence. Doctors and pilots can profit from following a checklist, even when doing things they have done many times before. A list slows them down and makes them more methodical, as Atul Gawande describes in *The Checklist Manifesto*. The best sportsmen wait until the last split second before hitting the ball.

Mr Partnoy argues that people need to learn how to manage delay just as they learn how to manage everything else. Sometimes putting things off makes sense: the silliest impositions on our time occasionally have the decency to self-combust. Still, the rules of sensible time-management apply to procrastinators as much as everyone else. Don't delay tackling problems that will grow worse if ignored, such as your credit-card bill. And create a to-do list to fool yourself into doing your second-most-important job while procrastinating over the most important one.

This sounds too clever by half. But Mr Partnoy is right to warn against business's growing obsession with speed for its own sake. And he is right to skewer the notion, always popular among managers, that time can be sliced up into segments of equal worth. The secret of modern brain work is that it requires a combination of fast and slow. Brain workers dither for ages but then are struck by a flash of insight or a burst of creativity. Remove all deadlines and you are left with dithering. Become too obsessed with deadlines and you are left with the intellectual equivalent of fast food – and toenails that need cutting.

July 2012

Sticking together

Advice on managing partnerships, courtesy of Keith Richards and Michael Eisner

FEW PEOPLE WILL READ Keith Richards's book, *Life*, for its insights on business. There are far more exciting things to learn about. Where did Mr Richards first have sex with Anita Pallenberg? (In the back of his Bentley, somewhere between Barcelona and Valencia, apparently.) What are his reflections on the mayhem at the Altamont concert? ("If it hadn't been for the murder, we'd have thought it a very smooth gig.") How did he survive all those years of self-medication? (He took the finest heroin and cocaine, and avoided "Mexican shoe-scrapings".)

But *Life* does nevertheless throw light on one of the most intriguing problems in business – how to keep a creative partnership alive. The music business "is one of the sleaziest businesses there is", Mr Richards argues, only one step above gangsterism. Most partnerships, from Lennon and McCartney on down, are destroyed by a lethal cocktail of ego, greed and lust. But, for all their ups and downs, Keith Richards and Mick Jagger have been in business together for half a century.

Most business pundits have little interesting to say about partnerships. Journalists focus on solo superheroes – all those mighty chief executives and mould-breaking entrepreneurs. Management gurus fixate on the next big trend in such areas as innovation or business models. But there are signs that the subject is starting to get the attention it deserves. Michael Eisner, a former boss of Disney, devoted a book to it, *Working Together: Why Great Partnerships Succeed.*

A striking number of businesses were created by partners, despite all the fuss made over lone geniuses. Where would Goldman have been without Sachs? Or Hewlett without Packard? Arthur Blank and Bernie Marcus – known as BernieArthur to their colleagues – revolutionised the retail business when they founded The Home Depot. Bill Gates worked with a succession of partners while he was at Microsoft – most notably Paul Allen and then Steve Ballmer – and now runs his foundation with his wife, Melinda. ("I've never done anything solo", he told Mr Eisner, "except take tests".) Warren Buffett has worked with Charlie Munger, his sidekick, confidant and best friend, since before the Rolling Stones were formed.

It must be said that successful partnerships are rather rarer than failed ones: business people tend to be alpha types, and money and fame can destroy even the solidest friendships. Disney thrived when Mr Eisner was running it jointly with Frank Wells. But when Mr Wells died and Mr Eisner tried to replace him with Michael Ovitz the result was a disaster: the rows prompted key people to leave, and Mr Ovitz himself quit after 14 months, with a sizeable pay-off.

Dysfunctional partnerships seem to be particularly common in high-tech industries. Although Google's Larry Page and Sergey Brin remain so close that they share an office, Facebook and Twitter have both been plagued by feuds between founders: Twitter's Evan Williams failed to get on with Jack Dorsey; and Mark Zuckerberg has a testy relationship with Facebook's other surviving founder, Dustin Moskovitz.

There are few iron rules on why some partnerships succeed where most fail. Messrs Buffett and Munger seem to get along effortlessly, as if joined by a chemical bond. Mr Gates, however, has had to work at his partnerships: after leaving the chief executive's chair at Microsoft he almost drove Mr Ballmer to distraction and the two had to make peace over dinner in 2001. But Mr Eisner argues that there are some general principles that increase the chances of success. Partners need to be able to trust each other absolutely. Mr Eisner notes that many successful partners split the profits down the middle regardless of their contribution to particular projects. Partners also need to possess a delicate balance between similarities and differences. A striking number of successful partners combine similar backgrounds with very different attitudes to fame. Messrs Buffett and Munger are Midwesterners who grew up a few miles from each other. But Mr Buffett adores the limelight whereas Mr Munger prefers the shadows.

Not fading away

Mr Richards echoes many of these arguments. He also has some good advice on how to repair your partnership after it has been torn apart by money and fame. Messrs Jagger and Richards enjoyed the solidest partnership in the music industry: "Glimmer Twins", as they called themselves, who had fallen in love with American blues as teenagers in London. Mr Richards laid down the riffs and Mr Jagger provided the vocal pyrotechnics. But time took its toll. Mr Richards's decision to give up heroin destroyed the delicate division of labour in which Mr Jagger took care of the details while Mr Richards took the drugs. Mr Jagger started to refer to the Stones as "his" band. He even performed the group's songs on solo tours. A formal break-up looked likely.

But in 1989 the two decided to solve their problems in the same businesslike way as Messrs Gates and Ballmer. They met on neutral turf – Barbados – and thrashed out their differences. Three things helped them to succeed where so many other bands have split: their "under-rooted friendship", as Mr Richards puts it, forged in London in the 1960s; their recognition that they were much better together than apart (who remembers any of their solo work?); and their mutual love of money.

There are clearly still tensions between the two: Mr Richards takes a perverse delight in mocking Sir Mick's "tiny todger", for example. But after 50 years as partners Mick and Keith still recognise that "I pull things out of him; he pulls things out of me." At a time when the French are griping about raising the retirement age to 62 these doughty senior citizens are contemplating yet another world tour.

November 2010

Philosopher kings

Business leaders would benefit from studying great writers

IT IS HARD TO RISE TO THE TOP in business without doing an outward-bound course. You spend a precious weekend in sweaty activity – kayaking, climbing, abseiling and the like. You endure lectures on testing character and building trust. And then you scarper home as fast as you can. These strange rituals may produce a few war stories to be told over a drink. But in general they do nothing more than enrich the companies that arrange them.

It is time to replace this rite of managerial passage with something much more powerful: inward-bound courses. Rather than grappling with nature, business leaders would grapple with big ideas. Rather than proving their leadership abilities by leading people across a ravine, they would do so by leading them across an intellectual chasm. The format would be simple. A handful of future leaders would gather in an isolated hotel and devote themselves to studying great books. They would be deprived of electronic distractions. During the day a tutor would ensure their noses stay in their tomes; in the evening the inward-bounders would be encouraged to relate what they had read to their lives.

It is easy to poke fun at the idea of forcing high-flying executives to read the classics. One could play amusing games thinking up titles that might pique their interest: "Thus Spake McKinsey", or "Accenture Shrugged", perhaps. Or pairing books with personality types: *Apologia Pro Vita Sua* for a budding Donald Trump and *Crime and Punishment* for a budding Conrad Black. Or imagining what Nietzschean corporate social responsibility would look like. Or Kierkegaardian supply-chain management.

Then there are practical questions. Surely high-flyers are decision-makers rather than cogitators? And surely they do not have time to spend on idle thought? However, a surprising number of American CEOs studied philosophy at university. Reid Hoffman, one of the founders of LinkedIn, was a philosophy postgraduate at Oxford

University and briefly contemplated becoming an academic before choosing the life of a billionaire instead. Anyway, executives clearly have enough time on their hands to attend gabfests such as Davos, where they do little more than recycle corporate clichés about "stakeholders" and "sustainability". Surely they have enough time for real thinkers.

Inward-bound courses would do wonders for "thought leadership". There are good reasons why the business world is so preoccupied by that notion at the moment: the only way to prevent your products from being commoditised or your markets from being disrupted is to think further ahead than your competitors. But companies that pose as thought leaders are often "thought laggards": risk analysts who recycle yesterday's newspapers, and management consultants who champion yesterday's successes just as they are about to go out of business.

The only way to become a real thought leader is to ignore all this noise and listen to a few great thinkers. You will learn far more about leadership from reading Thucydides's hymn to Pericles than you will from a thousand leadership experts. You will learn far more about doing business in China from reading Confucius than by listening to "culture consultants". Peter Drucker remained top dog among management gurus for 50 years not because he attended more conferences but because he marinated his mind in great books: for example, he wrote about business alliances with reference to marriage alliances in Jane Austen.

Inward-bound courses would do something even more important than this: they would provide high-flyers with both an anchor and a refuge. High-flyers risk becoming so obsessed with material success that they ignore their families or break the law. Philosophy-based courses would help executives overcome their obsession with status symbols. It is difficult to measure your worth in terms of how many toys you accumulate when you have immersed yourself in Plato. Distracted bosses would also benefit from leaving aside all those e-mails, tweets and LinkedIn updates to focus on a few things that truly matter.

Looking for answers

The business world has been groping towards inward-bound courses for years. Many successful CEOs have made a point of preserving time for reflection: Bill Gates, when running Microsoft, used to retreat to an isolated cottage for a week and meditate on a big subject; and Jack Welch set aside an hour a day for undistracted thinking at GE. Clay Christensen of Harvard Business School was so shocked at how many of his contemporaries ended up divorced or in prison that he devised a course called "How will you measure your life?". It became one of HBS's most popular courses and provided the basis of a successful book.

"Mindfulness" is all the rage in some big corporations, which have hired coaches to teach the mix of relaxation and meditation techniques. Big ideas are becoming as much of a status marker in high-tech hubs as cars and houses are in the oil belt. Peter Thiel, a Silicon Valley investor, holds conferences of leading thinkers to try to improve the world. David Brendel, a philosopher and psychiatrist, offers personal counselling to bosses and recently penned a blog for *Harvard Business Review* on how philosophy makes you a better leader. Damon Horowitz, who interrupted a career in technology to get a PhD in philosophy, has two jobs at Google: director of engineering and in-house philosopher. "The thought leaders in our industry are not the ones who plodded dully, step by step, up the career ladder," he says, they are "the ones who took chances and developed unique perspectives."

Inward-bound courses would offer significant improvements on all this. Mindfulness helps people to relax but empties their minds. "Ideas retreats" feature the regular circus of intellectual celebrities. Sessions on the couch with corporate philosophers isolate managers from their colleagues. Inward-bound courses offer the prospect of filling the mind while forming bonds with fellow-strivers. They are an idea whose time has come.

October 2014

Index

PublicAffairs is a publishing house founded in 1997. It is a tribute to the standards, values, and flair of three persons who have served as mentors to countless reporters, writers, editors, and book people of all kinds, including me.

I. F. STONE, proprietor of *I. F. Stone's Weekly*, combined a commitment to the First Amendment with entrepreneurial zeal and reporting skill and became one of the great independent journalists in American history. At the age of eighty, Izzy published *The Trial of Socrates*, which was a national bestseller. He wrote the book after he taught himself ancient Greek.

BENJAMIN C. BRADLEE was for nearly thirty years the charismatic editorial leader of *The Washington Post*. It was Ben who gave the *Post* the range and courage to pursue such historic issues as Watergate. He supported his reporters with a tenacity that made them fearless and it is no accident that so many became authors of influential, best-selling books.

ROBERT L. BERNSTEIN, the chief executive of Random House for more than a quarter century, guided one of the nation's premier publishing houses. Bob was personally responsible for many books of political dissent and argument that challenged tyranny around the globe. He is also the founder and longtime chair of Human Rights Watch, one of the most respected human rights organizations in the world.

· · ·

For fifty years, the banner of Public Affairs Press was carried by its owner Morris B. Schnapper, who published Gandhi, Nasser, Toynbee, Truman, and about 1,500 other authors. In 1983, Schnapper was described by *The Washington Post* as "a redoubtable gadfly." His legacy will endure in the books to come.

Peter Osnos, *Founder and Editor-at-Large*